Against Architecture:
The Writings of Georges Bataille

Denis Hollier

translated by Betsy Wing

An OCTOBER Book

The MIT Press
Cambridge, Massachusetts
London, England

French edition published in 1974 under the title *La Prise de la Concorde*, © 1974 Editions Gallimard, Paris.

This book was set in Baskerville
by Graphic Composition Inc., Athens, Georgia,
and printed and bound in the
United States of America.

Library of Congress Cataloging-in-Publication Data

Hollier, Denis.
    [Prise de la Concorde.   English]
    Against architecture : the writings of Georges Bataille / Denis
Hollier ; translated by Betsy Wing.
        p.   cm.
    Translation of: La prise de la Concorde.
    "An October book."
    Bibliography: p.
    ISBN 0-262-08186-5
    1. Bataille, Georges, 1897–1962—Criticism and interpretation.
    2. Bataille, Georges, 1897–1962—Knowledge—Architecture.
    3. Architecture and literature.   I. Title.
    PQ2603.A695Z713   1989
    848'.91209—dc20   89-32117
                                                                         CIP

For Michel Leiris
who is at the origin of this book

Contents

Contents

Introduction: Bloody Sundays

There is something anachronistic in associating Bataille, a writer who died even before people started to talk about structuralism, with poststructuralism. The connection, however, is justified if one recalls how insistently throughout the sixties etymology was called upon to make a connection—via the Latin verb *struere*, construct—between structuralist inspiration and architecture. The student uprising of May 1968 has often been described as a revolt against the structuralist establishment. There is a desire to loosen the symbolic authority of architectures in poststructuralism, and in retrospect it is possible to see Bataille as the precursor of this critical view of architecture.

A short article published in *Documents* in 1929 served as my point of departure in writing *La Prise de la Concorde* in 1972. In those two pages Bataille denounces architecture as a prison warden—its complicity with authoritarian hierarchies. Architecture is society's authorized superego; there is no architecture that is not the Commendatore's. There have been endless arguments over whether the origin of architecture was the house, the temple, or the tomb, etc. For Bataille it was the prison. "Architecture," says Bataille, "is the expression of every society's very being. . . . [But] only the ideal being of society, the one that issues orders and interdictions with authority, is expressed in architectural compositions in the strict sense of the word. . . . Thus great monuments rise up like levees, opposing the logic of majesty and authority to any confusion: Church and State in the form of cathedrals and palaces speak to the multitudes, or silence them. It is obvious that monuments inspire social good behavior in societies and often even real fear. The storming of the Bastille is symbolic of this state of affairs: it is hard to explain this mass movement other than through the people's animosity (animus) against the monuments that are its real masters."[1]

Foucault's book on prisons, *Surveiller et punir*, also sets out to be a critique of architecture, one that also originates in an analysis of incarcerating institutions. Just as, in *Histoire de la folie*, he put on architecture the responsibility first of the invention and then of the production of madness, in *Surveiller et punir* he describes the invention of criminality through techniques of spatial planning. Nonetheless, the conceptions of architecture implied by these two critiques (to say nothing of their style) are considerably different. Bataille's prison derives from an ostentatious, spectacular architecture, an architecture to be seen; whereas Foucault's prison is the embodiment of an architecture that sees, observes, and spies, a vigilant architecture. Bataille's architecture—convex, frontal, extrovert—an architecture that is externally imposing, shares practically no element with that of Foucault, with its insinuating concavity that surrounds, frames, contains, and confines for therapeutic or disciplinary ends. Both are equally effective, but one works because it draws attention to itself and the other because it does not. One represses (imposes silence); the other expresses (makes one talk). The gap between them is similar to the one at the beginning of *Surveiller et punir* that separates the public executions of the Ancien Regime from disciplinary institutions of modern societies. When Bataille thinks in terms of authoritarian representations, Foucault thinks in terms of spatial planning, institutionalization, and the technology of power. Bentham's panopticon, the central emblem of his book, thus supports Foucault's conception of an "architecture that would be operative in the transformation of individuals":[2] it is not just a simple container, but a place that shapes matter, that has a performative action on whatever inhabits it, that works on its occupant.

Is prison then the generic name designating all architectural production? Is architecture in a position to reply to poststructuralist accusations that reveal and denounce a prison in every monument or building? Is it possible to conceive of an architecture that would not inspire, as in Bataille, social good behavior, or would not produce, as in Foucault's disciplinary factory, madness or criminality in individuals? Architectural devices, according to Foucault, produce subjects; they individualize personal identities. But why would they not work

in reverse, leading against the grain to some space before the consti-
tution of the subject, before the institutionalization of subjectivity? An
architecture that, instead of localizing madness, would open up a
space anterior to the division between madness and reason; rather
than performing the subject, it would perform spacing: a space from
before the subject, from before meaning; the asubjective, asemantic
space of an unedifying architecture, an architecture that would not
allow space for the time needed to become a subject.

A current important project for public spaces in Paris has been
presented in terms of just such an architecture, an architecture that
Derrida has described as "spaced out" (or "spacy").[3] Bataille's 1929
article interpreted the storming of the Bastille as the revolt of the
mob against the monuments. The Parc de la Villette would realize a
paradoxical storming of architecture—by itself. A Bastille in no way
different from its own storming. "Architecture against itself," Bernard Tschumi, the park's architect, labels it: architecture against architecture.[4] As if a donjuanesque architecture would escape finally
from the stiff, punitive order of the Commendatore. It would enter
into games and begin to dance. "The program can challenge the very
ideology it implied." Such a project calls upon a loss of meaning, to
give it a dionysiac dimension: it explicitly takes issue with what
Tschumi describes as an essential premise of architecture, "the idea
of a meaning immanent in architectural structures"; the park, a post-
modern "assault on meaning," claims as its main purpose to "dismantle meaning."

—Would Dedalus be happy at losing the meaning of the labyrinth
he constructed? What is hiding under this uncanny park that somehow claims to be the official park of the Uncanny? Or really, what
would a labyrinth be without a minotaur: a labyrinth without blood?
And, since this is all taking place in real space, in a real city, since this
performative loosening of space takes place in a precise spot on the
map of Paris, namely La Villette, I am going to take a short detour to
the butcher's.

The greatest motive for Bataille's aggressivity toward architecture
is its anthropomorphism. The article "Architecture" describes it as an
essential stage in the process of hominization, as a sort of mirror stage
that might be called in a parody of Lacan's title "the architecture stage
as formative function of the We, man's social imago." In this sense,
even though he seems to denounce the repression exercised over

man by architecture, Bataille is really intervening against the cata-
chresis requiring that man only take form with architecture, that the
human form as such, the formation of man, be embedded in architecture. If the prison is the generic form of architecture this is primarily because man's own form is his first prison. In other words, it
is not possible simply to oppose the prison to the free man. Nessus's
lion skin stuck to the skin of Hercules. In the same manner, man's
revolt against prison is a rebellion against his own form, against the
human figure. And this is precisely what, in Bataille's view, the mythical figure of Acephalus was intended to show: the only way for man
to escape the architectural chain gang is to escape his form, to lose
his head. This self-storming of one's own form requires, in fact, an
infinitely more underhanded strategy than one of simple destruction
or escape. The image of Acephalus, thus, should be seen as a figure
of dissemblance, the negative imago of an antimonumental madness
involved in the dismemberment of "meaning." The painter André
Masson drew this figure and Bataille wrote an aphorism to go with it:
"Man will escape his head as a convict escapes his prison." [5]

"Architecture" is not the only entry Bataille wrote for the *Documents*
dictionary. Two other contributions, the article "Abattoir" (Slaughterhouse) and the article "Musée," shed some light on the relations between architecture and the unthinking expenditure of *dépense*.

The entry "Abattoir" is accompanied by Elie Lotar's crude photographs of La Villette. *Documents* specialized in this sort of illustrations,
ones resolutely turning their back on surrealism's erotic aestheticiz-
ing. They remind today's reader that, in fact, not too long ago, there
was some bloody meat at the very spot where today architecture is
turning against itself. Which is what Bataille's article was precisely
about.

Whereas the killing of the Minotaur is usually presented as a
humanizing exploit by means of which a hero frees the city from
whatever is archaic and monstrous, bringing society out of the labyrinthine age, for Bataille the sacrifice functions in an opposite manner: striking a blow at the organic imago, it opens the labyrinth up
again. With his grandiose humor, Bataille—relying on Marcel Mauss's
theory of sacrifice as a basis—gives the slaughterhouses of La Villette
a religious dimension. But what we have is a deserted, unconscious
religion: no one ever attends the sacrifices. "The slaughterhouse re-
lates to religion in the sense that temples of times past . . . had two

purposes, serving simultaneously for prayers and for slaughter. . . . Nowadays the slaughterhouse is cursed and quarantined like a boat with cholera aboard. . . . The victims of this curse are neither the butchers nor the animals, but those fine folk who have reached the point of not being able to stand their own unseemliness, an unseemliness corresponding in fact to a pathological need for cleanliness."[6]

"Abattoir" describes, therefore, a movement of sacred horror, of religious repulsion before the killing of an animal. The second article, "Musée," describes the opposite movement. Attraction follows repulsion. Those who took refuge in their own unconscious unseemliness when faced with the sacrificial butchering, those who opposed their own proper ugliness to the expropriating ugliness of butchering, those who could not bear the image of decomposition reflected to them by the slaughterhouses go to museums to compose themselves again. They flee the unredeeming ugliness of slaughterhouses for the beauty of museums. Bataille writes: "On Sundays at five o'clock, at the exit to the Louvre, it is interesting to admire the stream of visitors visibly animated by the desire to be similar in every way to the heavenly visions still delighting their eyes."[7] "A museum is like the lungs of a great city: the crowd floods into the museum every Sunday like blood and it leaves purified and fresh."

Slaughterhouses, along with the museum, make up a system in which the ambivalence defining the sacred nucleus is at work: the slaughterhouses are the negative pole, the generator of repulsion, the centrifuge (they are placed farther and farther away from the center of the city). Museums, the pole of attraction, are centripetal. But within the heart of one the other is hidden. At the heart of beauty lies a murder, a sacrifice, a killing (no beauty without blood). Bataille reminds us that the Louvre is turned into a museum by the Convention when the function of royalty has been put to an end. The museum is what the Terror invented to replace the king, to replace the irreplaceable. "The origin of the modern museum," he comments, "would thus be linked to the development of the guillotine."

The main thing about this system, as it is transcribed into cadastral hieroglyphics, is not, however, the conjunction of these two poles but the space between them. One does not exist without the other, but it does not exist with the other either. The following remarks will be dedicated to analyzing several ideological problems and problems of city planning connected to this gap, connected to the fact that, although slaughterhouses and museums remain two distinct institutions, museums have a strange way of following in the footsteps of slaughterhouses, like their shadow, as if some strange destiny condemned museums to rise up on the site of abandoned slaughterhouses. *Wo es war . . . soll Museum werden.*

This cultural appropriation, this redressing of the repugnant, can be interpreted in the light of Bataille's theory of *dépense*. This is primarily a theory of the need for loss rather than a theory of loss strictly speaking. It responds to the need to believe that there is a pure loss, that there is a difference between consuming and consummating, that there is lost time and there are waste lands, unproductive expenditures, things one never gets over, sins that cannot be redeemed, garbage that cannot be recycled. The slaughterhouse and the museum (religion and art), from this point of view, are two sorts of enclave within the economic continuum; the sacrificial nature of the first, and the fact that it is on Sunday that one visits museums, connect both to a sabbatical or Sunday rhythm, that is, to how one spends time on the seventh day. (What should one do when work is forbidden?) But one of the ways of spending it is clean and the other one dirty: one attracts and the other repels. The question thus is one of knowing whether a theory of *dépense* can work without the difference between high and low, between dirty and clean; whether a theory of *dépense* is not, first of all, a theory of the difference between two expenditures, a proper, clean one and an improper, dirty one. That is, the difference, when all is said and done, between slaughterhouses and museums. And it is precisely this difference that gets lost with the conversion of slaughterhouse into museum, a conversion that lays money on the hypothesis that an integral appropriation of expenditure is possible—as if it were possible to spend and be spent without getting dirty, as if *dépense* could be thoroughly presentable, spending energy without polluting, shamelessly, nothing repugnant about it, right at home in a public space, with everybody looking.

Put a little differently, how is the project at La Villette any different from the numerous programs thought up by nineteenth-century philanthropy to appropriate and discipline proletarian expenditure, to acknowledge but also to reabsorb nonwork time, particularly Sundays and holidays among the working and dangerous classes? How is it any different from the attempts from all sides—Catholic and socialist—to put workers into their Sunday best, to train and organize them and make them presentable when they are not actually working, to make presentable the expense of those with nothing to spend: the offal from mechanisms of appropriation who are refused access to property as well as to what is clean and proper. To circumvent a threatening privatization of vacations.

But, perhaps, this is the place to leave Bataille and the latest great cultural projects in Paris.

In 1867, Emile Zola, a young journalist, dedicated one of his articles to the upcoming inauguration of a public space. The piece is entitled "The Squares." It begins: "The gates to the new Parmentier square, built on the site of the former Popincourt slaughterhouse, will soon be opened to the public." Then come two pages of sarcasm directed at the absurdity of urban landscaping, where lawns try to recall nature for consumptive city dwellers. "It looks like a bit of nature that did something wrong and was put in prison."[8] A square is not a museum, but it too is a place for soft expenditure, it is an enclave through whose gates Parisian workers escape the implacable law of labor: they take the air (regenerate their lungs just as do the museum visitors observed by Bataille). For lack of an animal they kill time.

Today's cultural reconversion of slaughterhouses, the transformation of a harsh expenditure into a soft one, is, therefore, not an absolutely novel phenomenon. This event is programmed in the logic of the modernization of urban space. It has not changed since Haussmann: the Popincourt slaughterhouses, like all slaughterhouses in the various districts of Paris, in the Second Empire were swept along in the concentration of the city's alimentary track that culminated with the simultaneous creation of the central markets of Les Halles and the slaughterhouses of La Villette. The small neighborhood slaughterhouses were recycled into green spaces, urban parks, just as the central slaughterhouses of La Villette are being recycled, a century later, into a park of science and industry. Thanks to this conversion a nice, clean expenditure takes the place of a dirty one and the visitor takes over for the worker. Doing in the slaughterhouses makes room for educational parks, spaces where workers on holiday see demonstrated the meaning of their work. At the park of science and industry they celebrate Labor Day by looking at their work.

Despite his sarcastic remarks about squares, a mere detail in Hauss-mann's overall plan, Zola is vigorously in favor of the modernization of Paris. Naturalism as he conceived of it was first of all the celebra-tion—aesthetic if not moral—of the Paris created by the Second Em-pire, with its stations, its department stores, its exhibition halls, and especially its great boulevards. And the first real naturalist manifesto, Zola's 1872 novel *Le Ventre de Paris*, is primarily an anti-*Notre-Dame de Paris* directed against the romantics like Hugo who yearned after the unhealthiness of the old Paris. Claude Lantier sees in the superb side-walks and the tall houses of the Haussmannian city the harbinger of a new art. Once the Second Empire falls, Zola's admiration for the Seine prefect's city planning is unreserved. He approves of straight-ening things out in the name of an aesthetic of cleanliness: straight avenues are essential against stagnant humors. Blood is aerated in large arteries. In the modern city, the capital of the world of work, everyone is busy. Everything found there has its function, a physio-logical justification. For Zola who has always identified laziness with waste, the modern city's beauty comes from its being a space in which whatever has no use has no place. And it is precisely this shiftlessness, this spatial uselessness that makes him condemn the interruption of the active urban fabric by squares. There is nothing as beautiful as a city at work, but also a city is only beautiful when it is at work: Zola is allergic to the squares because the city takes its rest there, or, more precisely, because these idleness preserves are urban. Not that Zola is opposed to stopping work (workers have a right to recreation), but he is opposed to this happening in the city. If one is not working one should leave. Expenditure is uplifted by means of the centripetal mo-tion that carries it out into the islands and undergrowth *extra muros*.

The two chapters in T. J. Clark's *The Painting of Modern Life* that are devoted to how Parisians used to spend their spare time correspond to the two headings Zola used for such spending: go out on the town, or go out of town, to the bar at the Folies-Bergère or to the outskirts of Paris, urban or suburban pleasures, internal or external. Clark analyzes the Impressionists' reaction to the merging of these two brands, when the suburbs become urban under the double pressure of both leisure and industrialization. The evolution of Monet's gar-dens, which Clark interprets as a nostalgic return to a sort of *hortus conclusus*, would thus be evidence of the painter's quasi-denial of this transformation of the landscape, a way of protecting oneself against the denaturation of the suburbs by intensifying nature at home, by a sort of inclusion, a confinement of the exterior.[9]

Zola, too, reinforces the line between city and country at the very moment that it was beginning to erode. His landscapes, as well as the Impressionists', deny this contamination: his country outings take place in suburbs that are more pastoral than any of his country places. His resistance, however, unlike that of the Impressionists, does not stem from the urbanization of the outskirts of Paris but from what is happening in Paris itself. It is rooted in the need to sort expenses, to separate good spending, which is rural, and bad spending, which is urban, and results from the need to reserve some exteriority into which the urban fabric will be able to spill, pouring out its idleness: workers must not be allowed to rest in the city.

Clark mentions the famous editorial that Zola published in *La Tribune* of October 18, 1868, on his return from a Sunday spent on the island of Saint-Ouen.[10] In some ways it constitutes a counterpart to the article against the squares. Zola returns with a portrait of an impeccable workerly holiday, blameless and unsullied, spending and consuming. "I stayed until evening in the midst of the people in their Sunday best. Not many cardigans, lots of workshirts: a gay and open crowd of workers, young girls in cloth hats showing their bare fingers covered with needle-pricks, men wearing cotton whose rough hands still bore the imprint of tools. The joy in this crowd was a healthy one; I did not hear a single quarrel, I did not see a single drunk. . . . It was the gaiety of good children, sincere bursts of laughter, pleasures with no shame attached." And he goes on into the famous hymn to the joys of workers: "The joy of the people is a good and beautiful thing. I like to hear the wretched of this world laughing, those who eat their hard bread and sleep in attics. When poor people are having fun poverty vanishes from the earth."[11] Next to the sight of a city at work, there is no more beautiful spectacle for Zola than discharged laborers spending their sabbath, workers relaxing, their after-work release. Real pleasures cannot be bought: reserved for those who have no possessions, these are clean treats that do not pollute; they can be had for nothing extra and are consumed without leaving waste. Zola did not see any drunks at Saint-Ouen, or hear any quarrels. Everything can be taken away from the poor and they will still have free joys, the first of which is spending their own energy. The park at Saint-Ouen is the scene of a secular miracle. Those who have nothing still have themselves to spend.

The contrast between this out-of-town fair and the city squares is emphasized by two fantasies that act as foils to the idyll. Each has as its object those ways of spending Sunday that are unhealthy precisely because they are urban. The first takes place in the Bois de Boulogne, another urban park, that is to say, another mistake—on a larger scale than the squares—by Haussmannian city planning as far as leisure is concerned: that is where all the idle of the capital parade on Sunday, all the little deadbeats and prostitutes. "The workers," says Zola, "must stay away from these too clean groves . . . they could easily become seriously angry and question why they earn so little when these rascals steal so much."[12] The second phobic description is set in "the cramped, muddy sections" of the inner suburbs, the Parisian faubourgs such as Mouffetard, where the workers wallow. "When Sunday comes around, not knowing where to go to breathe a bit of clean air, they settle down at back tables in the cabarets; it is fatally downhill from there, work requires recreation and when there is no money, when the horizon goes nowhere, one takes whatever pleasure is at hand." *L'Assommoir*, we recall, the novel of alcoholism, is precisely the only one of Zola's Parisian novels that has no country outing, no Sunday out of doors. Class opposition is secondary in this geography of leisure; it is just as unhealthy for the privileged people in the Bois de Boulogne as for the wretched inhabitants of Mouffetard not to get out of the city on Sunday.

In this article T. J. Clark sees the expression of Zola's opposition to Haussmann's politics of popular leisure. And Zola, in fact, clearly states: "I know that Haussmann does not like popular festivities." But this politics of leisure has two sides to it. It has a negative aspect, the prohibition of the fairs that traditionally were held in communes annexed by the Second Empire. It also has a positive aspect: the opening up of leisure spaces inside the city, such as the squares and the Bois de Boulogne. And if Haussmann, according to Zola, does not like popular festivities, Zola himself only likes them from a distance: this city dweller does not want them to be urban. The institutionalization of idleness *intra muros* awakes old anxieties in him. One of his first stories, "Celle qui m'aime," was set in one of those urban carnivals of the faubourgs before Haussmann forbade them. With its background of alcohol and prostitution, with its nocturnal setting, there is nothing in it to evoke the hygienic fresh air of the proletariat at Saint-Ouen. The narrator feels uncomfortable, worried, and anxious from being in contact with the people idle in their Sunday best. "I have never been in a large crowd of people without feeling a vague uneasiness."[13] The intense agoraphobia of Zola, the bourgeois, provides a great deal of the energy in his campaign to provide leisure spaces for the proletariat outside the city. "Open up the horizon, call the people outside the walls, give them outdoor celebrations and you will see them bit by bit leave the cabaret benches behind for carpets of green grass." But, in many ways, the Pied Piper of Hamlin who musically rid the town of rats is the model for this call to clear out: the centrifugal movement of the purification of spending is also an expulsion, a protection against its expansiveness. Expenditure is only clean from a distance, it is only clean at large. Zola, who is myopic, always thought it was inappropriate to get too close to it. And perhaps this is because in every act of spending he sensed the threat of an undisciplined, uncontrollable energy, because there is a nonresolvable ambivalence in expenditure and in nonwork, because there is no expenditure, whether in the country or in the city, that does not end up threatening to turn into something dirty.

For in Zola's work itself the idealized country setting of Saint-Ouen, for example, is no absolute guarantee against the dangers of improper expenditure. The article in *La Tribune* is not the first account by him of an October Sunday on the suburban island. Several months before addressing his proletarian pastorale to Haussmann, he had used the same setting as a backdrop for a far more sinister episode. Chapter 11 of *Thérèse Raquin* is an account of a sunny October Sunday in this Impressionist landscape. There, in the midst of the healthy rejoicing of the people who are spending the day, Laurent, one of the numerous failed painters in Zola, murders the husband of his mistress. Stain in Paradise. Blood, meat, sacrifice, and slaughterhouse, all leave their mark at the heart of this recreational space. *Thérèse Raquin* was published in December 1867. But by October 1868 any trace of crime had disappeared. Less than a year after *Thérèse Raquin* Zola describes the worker's Sundays as paradise. Where is the blood? Camille's blood has disappeared without a trace in this portrait of clean spending.

One can connect this amnesty, this erasure of a murder by a holiday, to another scene in Zola that figures more than forty years later, in 1901, in one of his last novels, the socialist gospel entitled *Travail* (Work). This symphonic poem, more symbolist than realist, describes the triumph of social justice in an industrial world that has finally recognized that work is the source of all happiness, all beauty, everything good, all wealth, all of existence. "There is nothing that can stand still in idleness."[14] Being is being at work, in labor. As in Fourier's socialism every passion performs a task, has a social purpose. In this socialist city where no passion is outlawed, only one crime remains, only one sin, one single unnatural vice: idleness. So the figures of the Ancien Regime, where the idle had pride of place, one after another will disappear. The final episode of this elimination of parasites is the collapse of the church, the temple of an immobile god, the only useless space remaining in this beehive, which falls down on Father Marle holding services before empty pews. No one destroys it: it falls down by itself, wrecked by disaffection, swept off by the energy of unstoppable life cutting a swath through whatever opposes its path. "And nothing remained in the bright sunlight but a huge pile of rubble, in which even Father Marle's body could not be found, his flesh apparently eaten by the dust of the flattened altar which also drank his blood. . . . And later, when the debris had been cleared away, a garden was put there with beautiful trees and shady paths through fragrant lawns. . . . After a happy working day roses in full bloom sprung from every bush. And, in this delightful garden where the dust of a religion of poverty and death was sleeping, now human happiness grew, the exuberant flowering of life."[15] The next chapter tells about the celebration of labor that takes place on June 21, the summer solstice; on the seventh day the industrious people stop, look back to contemplate their work, and find it good.

The anti-Catholicism in Zola's last novels depends on good taste for much of its argument. Zola, after having disgusted an entire generation of readers, suddenly plays the disgusted role in the presence of the ticky-tacky religiosity of the iconography surrounding fin-de-siècle neo-Catholicism, a flayed Christ and his martyrs showing off their saintly bruises: "What a butcher's stall," he writes in *Paris*, "with guts, muscles, blood."[16] Zola, like Bataille, in fact, comes to associate religion and slaughterhouses. But, whereas Bataille condemns a religion that refuses to accept its kinship with butchering, Zola condemns a religion that puts it on display. In this sense, his replacement of the church by a public park prefigures the replacement of the slaughter-houses of La Villette with a park of science and industry. The vocabulary used by Zola in describing the death of Father Marle emphasizes this homology. It is a vocabulary combining the registers of communion and butchering: the dust of the altar, he says, ate his body and drank his blood. But where did they go? There is nothing left of them. Just as the crime committed by Laurent at Saint-Ouen is sublimated after *Thérèse Raquin* into the hymn to the people's spending Sunday in trickless treats, the body of Father Marle disappears, in turn, into an uncanny holocaust, a pure consumption with no remains, no trace, a total sacrifice, bloody but with a blood that does not stain, that leaves no memory. Bloody Sunday, bloodless Sunday.

What is architecture? According to Adolf Loos: "When walking through a wood, you find a rise in the ground, six foot long and three foot wide, heaped up in a rough pyramid shape, then you turn serious, and something inside you says: someone lies buried here. *That is architecture.*" In this definition architecture is recognized first by the affect it produces, an affect that has nothing in common with those one seeks out on playgrounds or in Luna Parks: you turn serious, hearing the telltale notes of a sort of *Et in Arcadia ego* that makes one think something invisible is present, or rather that one perceives an absence, evoking someone not living here, or rather someone here, not living. As if there were a house not made to be lived in, nobody's house, a house for nobody. Architecture, for Loos, begins with a dwelling that lacks an address.

On Zola's playground, however, nobody turns serious. And this is all the more astonishing because Luc, the builder of the socialist town in *Travail*, is an architect by profession.[17] But utopia ignores waste, waste lands, anything absent. No cemetery appears on the urban inventory. A religion is dead, but no one is in mourning. This death has not been followed by melancholic identification. So the festivities in full swing are beating time on a ground that no archaeologist has probed to see if it sounded a little hollow in spots.

Here the difference between Zola's Sundays and Bataille's becomes clear. The title *La Prise de la Concorde* referred to the importance of a Parisian square, the Place de la Concorde, and to the hold it had on Bataille's imagination. In many respects this place is comparable, in its origins and history, to the park where the Crêcherie church stood. Both were laid out where some major form of the system of the irreplaceable collapsed: where the Terror guillotined the king and where the last mass was said. But they are different. On its fairgrounds, Zola's "city of concord and peace" celebrates the Sunday of life. No emptiness remains. But there is no loss. Nothing is lacking after lack and nothing have been eliminated. There is nothing that would make you notice that nothing is missing. Lack is abolished and leaves no mementos. There is no madman to disturb the secular harmony with Nietzsche's message that God is dead. Bataille's Place de la Concorde, on the contrary, is the place where loss is incarnate—embodied in a man who identifies himself by his lack. The headless man, Acephalus, rises up where the guillotine let in the freezing gales of empty space.

For the first half of the nineteenth century, this esplanade was a source of uneasiness for developers and city planners. Should it be made into a place of memory and expiation or one of laughter and forgetting? How should one walk, with what sort of tread, where blood—including the king's—had run? Taking advantage of this indecision fairs and festivals temporarily set themselves up on this quasi-wasteland. But even a monarchist like Chateaubriand would see nothing wrong in this merry turnaround. "When they go to dance on the Champs-Élysées, when they shoot off firecrackers on the place sprinkled with the blood of the Just, they will have to remember the Martyr-King's scaffold."[18] Victor Hugo is less optimistic. He does not believe in festive commemorations: the people forget when they have fun. A poem in *Les Rayons et les ombres* depicts him, the only pensive one, in the midst of a public celebration taking place on the Place de la Concorde.[19] This is not the festival conscious of its sacrificial origins that Chateaubriand had in mind, it is closer to Zola's celebration: no one remembers. No one in the crowd thinks about what is absent, no one thinks of the dead on whose blood they are dancing. But whereas Zola looks kindly on this thoughtlessness, Hugo turns serious. He misses lack, and the task of his poem is, precisely, to reintroduce a false note—lack, loss, blood—into the popular plenitude.

Bataille's Place de la Concorde, in contrast to Chateaubriand's and Hugo's, is not the site of spring festivals. Louis XVI was executed in January and Carnival is a winter celebration. This conjunction interested Bataille enough so that, when he was involved in the College of Sociology, he had a project for a book on the carnival origins of democracy. [20] However, Bataille's carnival has not much in common with the one Bakhtin was celebrating almost simultaneously in his 1940 book on Rabelais. "Carnival," according to a recent book on Bakhtin, "is not time wasted but time filled with profound and rich experience."[21] There is no *Et in Arcadia ego* to be heard, but this is above all because there is no one to say "I" anymore in Bakhtin's carnival, because the first person has disappeared, a joyful purge has swept subjects away in the great anonymous, or dialogic, sewer: the grammar of the irreplaceable has been excluded from the festivities. Bataille's carnival, on the contrary, is the moment in which the I lives its loss, lives itself as loss. This is not a time of plenitude, it is, on the contrary, the time when time's emptiness is experienced. This is not innocence rediscovered, but bottomless guilt. If carnival is a "gap" in the fabric of society, if it is a celebration of the "gaps and holes" in both the individual and the social body, does one celebrate these holes by filling them in, by plugging them up?—Can the celebration of a gap as gap result in plenitude? Bataille's Acephalus does not merely represent a grotesque celebration of upside downs and bottoms up, but the more abysmal image of a topless bottom. The concept of heterology, a neologism invented by Bataille, does not simply indicate a warm, euphoric relationship to otherness. Otherness, in other words, is not simply a matter of pleasure and enjoyment. There is no carnival without loss. No Luna Park without a slaughterhouse.

Against Architecture

The Hegelian Edifice

Death, if that is what we wish to call this unreality, is the most terrible thing of all and sustaining death's work is what demands the greatest strength. Impotent beauty detests conceptualization, because it requires beauty to do this thing it is incapable of doing. Now, the life of the spirit is not life that cringes at death and saves itself from destruction, but life that can bear death and is preserved in it.

Hegel, Preface to *Phenomenology*

A Simple Beginning

Only that which is simple constitutes a beginning.

Hegel, *Science of Logic*, Book I

The simple beginning is something so insignificant in itself, so far as its content goes, that for philosophical thinking it must appear as entirely accidental.

Hegel, *Aesthetics*

We shall begin with architecture. "Architecture confronts us as the beginning of art, a beginning grounded in the essential nature of art itself." [1]

Not that we have any intention of building a system like Hegel, constructing an aesthetic, or classifying the fine arts. There is nothing constructively edifying about our project. It is, instead, an attempt to bring closer whatever wrecks projects as well as edifices. Rather than outline a structure, we hope to follow and bring into play a crack that frustrates plans and shatters monuments.

We shall begin with architecture: beginning with the beginning—
archè. But this beginning will not inevitably control the consequences
it opens up. No value is to be accorded *archè* simply because of its
inaugural value. *Archè* has no advance control over some *telos* that in
retrospect will make any trace of the arbitrary, of contingency, or of
accident disappear from itself.

We shall, therefore, begin as Hegel begins his *Aesthetics*, with symbolic art and its privileged form—architecture. Beginning, then, like
Hegel, but at the same time, simply because we begin *like* him, not
beginning as Hegel did. Beginning like him, but for other reasons.
No longer in order to rediscover in architecture the *archè* of the arts
that follow or accompany it, the *archè* of artistic activity, of aesthetic
activity in general present to itself under the mode of immediacy and
simplicity; but to loosen this *archè* from its resolution, dismantling
this beginning by turning it into a mere beginning, which is never
more than the semblance of an inauguration. Like Hegel, but
metaphorically.

The Hegelian Edifice

Between 1818 and 1829 Hegel developed the aesthetics course edited
and published by his students after his death in 1835. The course
does not exactly begin with architecture: the first part is a general
introduction to aesthetics, the second is devoted to the idea of beauty.
But it attributes the beginning of art—which is the object of aesthetics—to architecture. It does this twice: when it lists the three aesthetic
moments (symbolic, classical, and romantic), then when it lists the five
particular arts (architecture, sculpture, painting, music, and poetry).
Each art form passes through each of the three moments (architecture, painting, etc. are each by turn and each in its own way symbolic
first, then classical, before becoming romantic), with the result that,
properly speaking, the beginning of art is constituted by symbolic architecture, which is architecture in its purest form and in its most
appropriate moment; for Hegel has defined it as the symbolic art par
excellence. "If therefore in the series of particular arts architecture is
treated first, this must not merely mean that it is presented as the art
offering itself for treatment first on the strength of its being so determined by the nature of art; on the contrary, it must equally clearly be
seen to be the art coming first in the existence of art in the world." [2]

History and concept, chronology and logic, fact and law all thus
concur, if Hegel is to be believed, in acknowledging architecture's inaugural value for aesthetics as a whole. However, in the pages devoted to this, it is striking that, instead of a serenely confident
description of his object, we find the anxiety of someone attempting
to grasp an object that is elusive. This anxiety is even more legible
when, because it is a posthumous text reconstructed by course notes
taken at different times, possible vaguenesses of articulation between
one sentence and another, between one paragraph and another, have
not been reworked. Hegel's discourse on the beginnings of art is awk-
ward therefore, and the difficulty experienced in its development is
nowhere more apparent than in the first pages of the section devoted
to architecture, those dealing with "Independent Architecture." This
is the title of the chapter in which architecture is described at the
purest moment of its status as symbolic art, giving it the right to an
inaugural position.

Hegel has some difficulty reconciling the requirements of law and
the factual evidence. Simple beginnings do not have the simplicity
that would permit them to be made into origins. The origin is still
lacking at the beginning. And Hegel will apply himself more to the
correction of this lack than to the description of architecture. In fact,
as a result of the logic of *Aufhebung* (in which each moment
supersedes—that is, simultaneously does away with and preserves—
its antecedents), his entire construction, the entire edifice of his *Aesthetics,* depends on it. This logic rules in particular the succession of
the arts, each one confirming in turn a victory over the materiality of
the preceding art. From sculpture to the last art, poetry, which will in
turn also be superseded, supersession permits an exit from the realm
of art and will constitute aesthetics itself (discourse on art) as a moment of philosophical reflection. Thus poetry and art are superseded
by "the prose of thought," in which the spirit, says Hegel, is immediately in touch with itself with no need for a detour into the exteriority
of signifying materiality: the concept does not really need words and
letters to make itself known. The best example of this prose is, in fact,
Hegelian discourse itself. The *Aesthetics,* a part of this system, constitutes a superseding of art, setting art up by this very fact as something
dead, something from the past. "Art transcends itself and becomes
prose."[3] As the first moment of absolute spirit (see the third section
of the third part of the *Encyclopedia*), art gives way first to revealed

religion and then to philosophy. "In the hierarchy of means serving to express the absolute, religion and culture stemming from reason occupy the highest level, far superior to that of art."[4]

Art is dead. With his *Aesthetics,* Hegel constructs its tomb. Art, which began with the construction of tombs, also ends with a tomb. The pages on architecture, thus, would be a sort of redoubling of aesthetics as a whole and, by extension, of the entire system in which this aesthetics lies. In both cases a certain relationship to death is translated into constructive practices. Architecture is something appearing in the place of death, to point out its presence and to cover it up: the victory of death and the victory over death. This allows it to be simultaneously the first of the arts—in its empirical, limited form as a stone edifice—and their tomb—in this major and sublimated form: the Hegelian edifice. The *Aufhebung* insures the return of the *archè* and its liberation in the *telos.* But this final fusion is only possible if the *archè* indeed has the simplicity allowing it to reappear completely in each succession of its supersessions. To accomplish this there must be something to *support* the identity that Hegel's discourse requires between origins and beginnings, law and fact. But—to say the least— one must admit that this identity is not immediately apparent.

The Tower of Babel

In fact, the beginnings of architecture—or at least what we know of these beginnings as passed on to us through tradition—are far from corresponding to what the concept of art would have them be. The beginnings: "turning to the earliest beginnings of architecture, the first things that can be accepted as its commencement are a hut as a human dwelling and a temple as an enclosure for the god and his community. Impossible to go any further."[5] Impossible to go back in time any further than the hut and the temple. And also futile to go any further, because with the hut and the temple we are, in any case, *not yet* in the area of art; we are still short of its origins. Beginnings come before origins. At least for anyone who sticks to the traditional facts. Hegel will not do this, but will himself produce the origin of architecture, going to great lengths through a critique of this tradition to fix a beginning that would be, literally, original; that is, a beginning whose attributes are the simplicity and immediacy implied by any inaugural or first position. Whereas, on the contrary, both house and temple are constituted according to a complex structure of mediation. In fact: "In the case of a house and a temple and other buildings the essential feature which interests us here is that such erections are mere *means,* presupposing a purpose external to them. A hut and the house of god presuppose inhabitants, men, images of the gods, etc. and have been constructed for them."[6]

Two themes overlap in this critique of the beginnings of architecture: first, the hut and the temple are means; second, they are the means to ends external to art, to nonaesthetic ends to which whatever beauty they may possess will always remain subservient. The apparently simple distinction between these two themes will, however, be constantly put in question throughout Hegel's exposition.

Art is a pertinent concept only for whatever has as its end the manifestation of the idea of beauty; and the fact that house or temple presuppose other ends, that they are first of all the products of a nonartistic purpose, condemns them to remain external to art as well. For the moment the possible difference between the requirements of material existence (such as building oneself a shelter against cold, rain, etc.) to which house construction is subjected, and the requirements of the religion manifesting itself through its temples, is unimportant. Hegel fixes on the externality of the end, in order to exclude from art any construction subjected as a means to such an end.

But the second reproach made to the traditional version of the beginnings of art, going back to the first, throws the economy of his argument off balance, because he no longer brings in the positioning of the end (extra- or intra-aesthetic) but takes into consideration only the status as means. Any means, in fact, is means to an end from which it is separate, which is external to it not simply for accidental reasons varying according to the nature of the end, but by virtue of a necessity intrinsically bound up with the status of means. In other words, externality here is no longer a function of a topography of ends; it is thus no longer merely externality to art, but rather unspecified externality itself, which slips in between means and end, and as a result is precluded from any originating position. On the one hand, therefore, insofar as they are subjected to extra-aesthetic purposes, hut and temple are extraneous to art; on the other hand, as means, they are excluded from any moment of origin. Mediacy can only and must always be derivative: "We cannot go back to this division for origins, for in its nature the origin is something immediate and simple, not a relativity and essential connection like this. Instead we must look for some point beyond this division."[7]

Descriptive serenity gives way to a normative tension marked by the decision of law to subject fact to itself, but which marks, just as easily, the inadequacy of law and fact. This inadequacy can be perceived, for example, in the notion of "falling short" inherent in the division between means and ends brought to light by the analysis of hut and temple. One wonders how this "falling short" goes with the already stated impossibility of "going beyond"—going back further than the cave and the temple. "Falling short" has a logical value. It designates a moment logically anterior to this division, whereas chronologically this regression is first of all impossible, but above all useless, because with the hut and the temple we are *not yet* in the area of art. This indecision must be read as the symptom of a decision: one to place architecture at the origin of art, a decision that by its very abruptness will perhaps tell us as much about architecture as anything Hegel says.

Architecture must be the origin of art, even if everything would tend to exclude it from the domain of art. For it is hard to conceive of a building exempt from utilitarian space, one whose only purpose is aesthetic. In these pages there are other signs of this decision, underlining to what extent it is bound up with an almost fetishistic attachment to the values connoted by the term "architecture."

Hence, unable to find in architectural production any building corresponding both to the concept of the work of art and to that of an original moment, Hegel is obliged to borrow a model from sculpture: "we will have to look around for buildings which stand there independently in themselves, as it were like works of sculpture, and which carry their meaning in themselves and not in some external aim and need."[8]

Let us be content to note that the problematic of meaning has taken the place here of that of mediacy. At the very least it is remarkable to see that all the properties Hegel demands of architecture (with no success in discovering them there) are presented to him without difficulty by sculpture—from which he does not demand them. What is more: sculpture will serve as the controlling model in the search for a building true to the concept of art. This paradoxical situation will soon lead Hegel to define, contrary to any proper hierarchy, architecture, the first of the arts, as a type of the second, sculpture:

independent architecture can be called, he says, "an inorganic sculpture."[9]

The house and temple are hollow. It is *inside* their walls that come to dwell inhabitants, men or images of gods, constituting the intended purpose of the construction—the purpose Hegel judges to be external, *outside* them. Into this hollow, into this emptiness inside the first constructions, therefore, some exteriority penetrates that forbids them access to architecture; this lack of simplicity rules them out as the origins of art. The true beginnings sought by Hegel will have to be faultlessly exempt from this original lack; they will have to stop up this hole and fill this void. They will have to be full—which, we note in passing, excludes caves and cavities, etc., just as well as houses or temples—they will have to be unoccupied by this flaw: this dehiscence inside which the exteriority of purpose could dwell; this innermost cleavage constituted by the exteriority of end and means. Not only must their aim be in themselves, but their purpose must not break their homogeneity, the immediacy of their self-presence. This, according to Hegel, is what independent architecture as inorganic sculpture must do.

In order for the origin to regain its threatened simplicity and for architecture to regain its value as *archè*, as fundamental, Hegel sets out in search of edifices that are neither houses nor temples, that have no purpose outside of art and are not undermined by the negativity of mediation. He finds them in Mesopotamia:

"What is the sacred?" asks Goethe. And he immediately replies: "What links souls together." Starting from this definition, one may say that the sacred as the aim of this union, and this union itself, constitute the first content of independent architecture. The most familiar example of this is in the legend of the Tower of Babel. In the distant valleys of the Euphrates, people constructed an enormous architectural work; all mankind worked on it in common, and this community was at the same time both the aim and the content of the work.[10]

We would have to know more than we do about the composition of the text of the *Aesthetics* to draw any certain conclusions from this, but it is not beside the point to note that in "The Symbolic Form of Art" there was no mention of the Tower of Babel or any similar sort of building. On the other hand, in the chapter "Symbolism Proper" there is a discussion of Egyptian pyramids, whose exemplary status this tower will replace in "Architecture.' The tower appears at the beginning of the chapter "Independent or Symbolic Architecture" where it precedes (we shall see later what gives it the right to do so) the pyramids, which now are no longer anything more than one form of the "Transition from Independent to Classical Architecture." Undeniably, the pyramid has become less exemplary from one part of the *Aesthetics* to another. The example of the symbol that, in accordance with symbolic structure, must be the symbol of the symbol as well, is no longer the pyramid but the Tower of Babel.

This tower would be, therefore, the work of the symbolic art par excellence; independent architecture or architecture proper; the moment that will be followed by "Architectural Works Wavering between Architecture and Sculpture," such as phallic columns, obelisks, etc., then by the "Transition from Independent Architecture to Classical Architecture," with Indian and Egyptian subterranean buildings, housing for the dead such as pyramids, utilitarian architecture, etc. The origin of architecture, its original status as symbol, is found with the Tower of Babel.

The Symbol

"The symbol is *prima facie* a *sign*." But it is not just any sign. An ordinary sign has a "sensuous form" that does not represent itself but represents on the contrary something other than the sensuous form it is: its "content." This *content* is thus, by virtue of the very structure of the sign, *exterior* to the sensuous form expressing it: it has no "proper affinity whatever" with it; "the connection which meaning and its expression have with one another is only a purely arbitrary linkage."[11]

No doubt the symbol, for Hegel, is first and foremost a sign, but a very specific sign since it is defined by the absence of the property that has just been used to characterize the sign. The externality of the sensuous form and the ideal content expressed by it, the arbitrary connection between meaning and its expression, are not to be found there. The sensuous form of the symbol, its materiality, as such, is already charged with a meaning that is truly *its own* meaning since it is one for which it has a natural inclination, not one that is decided. Its meaning is (this time literally) *contained* in its form and warranted by it. The symbol is a sensuous form that represents itself. There is no discontinuity or externality separating form from content. Meaningful form in itself; meaning itself. "Taken in this wider sense, the symbol is no purely arbitrary sign, but a sign which in its externality comprises in itself at the same time the content of the idea which it brings into appearance." [12]

The exteriority of form and content in the sign is described by Hegel in terms he will return to for describing nonaesthetic architecture (that which remains subordinated to the external purpose of habitation). It is, therefore, not by chance that in both cases this exteriority is transcended by a symbolic status. Such a way of transcending them situates both the problematic of sign to thing and of means to end, of meaning and of teleology, in the same perspective. Just as the symbol represents itself and has its meaning in itself, symbolic architecture would refer only to itself, would express only itself, would say only what it is.

In reality, all is not so neat in Hegel's text. And traces of the decision bound up with the requirements of the system are to be found here also. The title of the chapter containing the Tower of Babel can be translated as "Architectural Works Intended to Be Used as a Meeting Place for Peoples," a title that, at this point in the Hegelian development, poses several problems. These problems can be reduced to two categories:

1. What connection is there between the fact that the tower is "intended to be used as a meeting place" for the peoples who built it and its being—according to Hegel—the very example of independent architecture, thus functioning symbolically? How is this intention immediately present? How is it immediately represented in the materiality of the tower? In what sense does such an intention derive from the aesthetic realm and consequently authorize architecture to be counted among the arts?

This question arises especially because in the chapter in which Hegel describes what corresponds, as it were, to the superlative state of symbolness, the most symbolic—that is, the purest, the least contaminated—form of symbolic art itself, it is not symbolism but rather human community that comes up. The word "symbolic" is scarcely used. It does not figure in the title, and in the text itself it only appears three times: twice apropos the symbolism of the "number *seven*" found in the architecture of the temple of Baal and of the city of Ecbatana, and another time, *in extremis*, apropos the Tower of Babel. Here it is to justify the tower's connection to the realm of symbolism—

that is, to explain an articulation that is at first sight very surprising between the fact that the tower is intended to be used as a meeting place and the conclusion concerning its symbolic nature deduced from this fact. And in this cursory mention the symbol is to lose the difference that served to define it, distinguishing it from the sign: "Such a building is symbolic at the same time since the bond, which it is, it can only hint at; this is because in its form and shape it is only in an external way that it can express the sacred, the absolute unifier of men." [13]

The symbol, thus, is now defined by the externality of form in relation to what it expresses. Whereas Hegel had just described this externality as the distinguishing characteristic of the nonsymbolic sign. The distinction between symbol and sign is shown in these pages to be as fundamental as it is shaky. Virtually absent from the place where one would most expect its effects, the place where it seems such a distinction should be fully operative, when it does put in a brief appearance the purpose is to erase the difference that had allowed one to produce this very distinction. The concept of the symbol was supposed to lessen the externality of the signifier and signified, and at the very spot where this reduction carries the most urgency, Hegel reintroduces externality and does so by means of the symbol itself.

2. This same wavering concerning externality exists not between content and the form expressing it, but between the end and its means. The Tower of Babel is intended to be used as a meeting place; its intention, its final cause is to be what "links souls together," in other words, according to Goethe, the "sacred." Now we recall that the temple was excluded from independent architecture and stripped of any pretension to set itself up as the origin of architecture precisely for the reason that, being dependent on a religious purpose, it did not belong in the realm of art. Hegel now, however, attributes religious purpose especially to buildings of the same sort as the Tower of Babel without even bringing up the slightest consideration of the idea of beauty: "The primary purpose behind such explicitly independent buildings is only the erection of something which is a unifying point for a nation or nations, a place where they assemble. Yet along with this there is the subordinate aim of making obvious, by the mode of configuration, what does in general unify men: the religious ideas of peoples." [14]

Hegel's newly discovered origin, which he substitutes for the temple (guilty of subordination to a religious purpose) follows no less, however, the dictates of this same religious purpose. That the main factor in the definition of the tower is not this religious purpose, which it was for the temple, but the fact that it is used as a meeting place, in no way changes the indecisiveness about what is accomplished by this retreat, since Hegel had already defined the temple itself as "an enclosure for the god and his community,"[15] that is, as a meeting place for peoples.

Just as, shortly before, the sign and the symbol were sometimes distinct and sometimes identical, religion and what unites peoples are now, depending on the context, compared or contrasted as being external or internal to the realm of art. In both instances it is unclear what is gained. It was supposed to allow a (re)uniting with the *archè* that continues to be elusive. What we can read in this system of self-denying contradictory gestures that merely succeed in baring the arbitrariness of a desire, and in this determination *not to place the pyramid at the origins of art,* is something like the presence of a fantasy that would come, literally, to fulfill the origins. The pyramids were still hollow, like the house or the temple; they were inhabited by a dead being or by Death. Towers, on the other hand, are full: "In the middle of this sanctuary, we are told by Herodotus who had seen this colossal structure, there was a tower of solid masonry (not hollow inside but solid, a πύργος στερεός)."[16] The Tower of Babel has come to fill up the hole in the pyramid, a flaw that would have risked ruining this tomb of death that the Hegelian structure in its entirety is meant to be.

The Architectural Metaphor

Notre-Dame de Rheims

This may have seemed a forced beginning. But at least one must admit it was in both senses of the word. Forced because, at first glance, it was not about Bataille, and there is no evidence that he claimed to be an architectural theoretician or that academic discussions about aesthetics were ever interesting to him. As for Hegel, Bataille knew only those texts of his that Kojève discussed, essentially two or three passages from *Phenomenology*, but he never seems to have spent any time on *Aesthetics*. (Otherwise, he would have been sensitive to how anti-Hegelian the subtitle of his study on Lascaux was, dating "the birth of art" not from the first constructions, but from the first painted images, and what is more ones painted on the walls of underground crevices, that is, totally independent of architecture.) Forced upon us also, however—perforce, necessary—because Bataille did begin with architecture.

The title of his first published text was *Notre-Dame de Rheims*. It is a meditation, according to the most religious definition of the form and spirit of this term, on the cathedral. Bataille never mentioned its existence. It was only known through an allusion in an obituary by the librarian André Masson, who had been in his class at l'École des Chartes. There is absolutely no doubt that it was written before 1920, the year in which Bataille broke with Catholicism. It would seem to date from the summer of 1918: one may sense the end of the war in "anguished awaiting of the Te Deum." If we set aside the dissertation *L'Ordre de chevalerie* published in 1922 as his thesis at l'École des Chartes, his unsigned 1926 note on medieval "Fatrasies" that ap-

peared in *La Révolution surréaliste,* and the notes and articles on numismatics written between 1926 and 1929 for *Aréthuse,* ten years of a
silence that is broken only for professional reasons separate *Notre-
Dame de Rheims* from Bataille's first writings: *Histoire de l'oeil, L'Anus
solaire,* the text "L'Amérique disparue," and the first articles in *Documents* (the first two of which—"Le Cheval académique" and "L'Apocalypse de Saint-Sever"—moreover, both in subject matter and the
second in its form as well, are directly related to his practice as a
librarian).

Ten years of silence, at the end of which this text will be buried in
silence. But it is possible, now that the six pages of *Notre-Dame de
Rheims* have been found again, to force open this silence. As a beginning. And to read in this silence the rupture through which Bataille's
writing was produced. All of Bataille's writing would be aimed at the
destruction of this cathedral; to reduce it to silence he would write
against this text. Not, in a fetishistic fixation with some sort of original
sin, against this text alone, against these six pages that in retrospect
are so incongruous, but against the veiled ideological necessity controlling it, against a far vaster and more secret cathedral in which it is
thoroughly trapped and which somehow prevents it having been
written, which makes writing only possible *afterward* and against this
text, against the oppressive architecture of constructive values.

Notre-Dame de Rheims[1]
by Georges Bataille

To some youths of Haute-Auvergne

You have heard tell of Rheims, the great city on the plains of Champagne. It
had an ancient history: Clovis the barbarian, baptised by Saint Remi, gave a
pious renown to the good Christian city, and there the kings of France were
crowned. In Joan of Arc's time it was a city with a secure bourgeoisie inside
its walls, and the white cathedral in first youth watched like a shepherd over
its bleating flock down on a thousand pointed rooftops, the hodgepodge of
humble, familiar joys. And when the blessed Joan of Arc entered through the
slightly twisty roads (as they are still in old crannies of the city), all the good
folk of France were there: mothers showing their children the young Saint
who was such a warrior and the king: joyful men who ran as they shouted
"Noel."

Now the Saint never forgot the good welcome; she said she would have liked to go to her eternal rest next to her good people of Rheims, who were so Christian and so devout. And when she—who lived in the sunlit garden of her own voices—rode off again on new missions, she must often have fondly recalled this memory of the coronation: the people exultant with pious joy and hope, the cathedral white and immense as victory, and the whole city open like the ornate portals of Notre-Dame to anyone coming in the name of the Lord.

I too, when I was living in the old city, saw this, this vision as lovely as our dreams of paradise. There was much too much noise then in the new streets, too much noise and garish light—but always the cathedral was there and always her existence was a triumph of stone. The two towers rose straight into the sky like long-stemmed lilies and the image of friendly crowds slipped under the portals into the company of saints gesturing for eternity in hieratic robes, where their faces showed a joy that stone never smiled. And in the central portal Our Virgin Lady beneath her high crown was so regal and so maternal that all the company of the faithful could not help becoming joyous as children, like brothers, and all the stone was bathed in maternal and divine goodness.

And I think that for one to live one has to have seen this light glowing. There is too much pain and gloom among us and everything looms larger under the shadow of death. Joan of Arc, so full of voices and hopes, went to prison and to the stake: we ourselves will have our days of sorrow and the day of our death lurks in wait for us like a thief. We too thirst after consolation. It is true that the light of God shines for us all, but we stray off into our daily wretchedness which is like the ashes in a cold room, like a November fog. Now one day when I was pitifully bemoaning these woes, a friend told me not to forget the cathedral in Rheims and suddenly I saw it again, so large in my memory that it seemed to me projected outside of myself into a light that was ever new. I saw it as the highest, most marvelous consolation left among us by God, and I thought that as long as it lasted, even if in ruins, we would still have a mother for whom to die. That is the vision that consoled the blessed Joan of Arc in her cell throughout her long ordeal; for in the darkest hours the bells of Rheims still trembled for her in the triumphant light for which she yearned with a desire greater than any man or any misery. And Joan of Arc's vision, still so thrilling to myself four years later, is the light I offer up to your desires, the vision of Notre-Dame de Rheims bathed in sunlight.

Only today, mutilated, she rises in desolation.

I saw almost the last days of her splendor, in the fever of August 1914. I saw her naves full of soldiers who came to prepare themselves to die well. The faithful crowded in, aquiver with prayer or anguish. In the morning there was silence as the cardinal most fervently offered a mass for France; it was like being on the eve of a martyrdom, because we expected something too great. Because of their anguish he had wanted to come and pray with his people, and, lit by the sparkling glow of stained-glass windows, he seemed to exist in the peace of a final day, as if he were haloed, already beyond humanity, come to bless us.

This abrupt vision—the cardinal then left for Rome to attend the conclave—was like a final flicker of peace in Rheims. Soon fear was in the city. Convoys of people in flight driven ahead of the invasion in distress as dire as human wretchedness; carts crammed with furniture and families perched on top came one after the other, and along the roads there were burdened, pathetic people, letting all their destitution show like those for whom all hope is lost. There were women going mad because they had lost their children in the flight. And a huge, miserable fear invaded Rheims. There was fighting in the Ardennes and our side fled; carts where the wounded lay bleeding in the straw unloaded the horror of nearby battle throughout the city. And, in the sudden heat of the moment, this became for some an exodus and for others the invasion by the German army, as inexorable as war.

I did not see this first denouement, nor that of the victory that came later: that time one of our detachments flung itself down on the city, exhausted but energized by the glory of a whole country weeping with joy. And yet misfortune persisted in Rheims.

And on September 19 shells tore through, killing children, women, and old people; fire crackled and raged from street to street; houses collapsed; people died, crushed by the rubble, burned alive. Then the Germans set the cathedral on fire.

There is no more painful turmoil and confusion than when a city burns. And one's heart rebels in far too violent agony at the sight of such a senseless spectacle. What is revealed then, in the red glow of flames and in the acrid smoke, is the symbol of war as crazy and brutal as fire and as dark as the smoke dimming the sky. The luminous balance of life is broken, because there is no one whose eyes are not burned by the light of the intense flames and whose flesh is not wounded by this bloody cruelty. So everyone who saw the cathedral burn was so weighed down with anguish that the vision they had was of a wound scarring the whole world, desperately tearing apart all that used to make our life and our happiness.

When, therefore, I returned to this city where in reality, in the shadow of the cathedral, I was born again to the life and happiness God gives us, all I found were signs of death and desolation. I had hoped, despite her wounds, to see in the cathedral once again a reflection of past glories and rejoicing. Now the cathedral was as majestic in her chipped or scorched lace of stone, but with closed doors and shattered bells she had ceased to give life; the statues of saints and of the Virgin, whose simple joy had formerly wrapped me in marvelous consolation, had disappeared under a pile of sand bags that protected them against further destruction. And I thought that corpses themselves did not mirror death more than did a shattered church as vastly empty in its magnificence as Notre-Dame de Rheims. Truth to tell a skeleton's rictus grimaced from the cracks torn in the formerly living stone, like on a human face.

The cathedral kept just enough semblance of life to sadden one, regretting the former glory and consolation she provided then as Mother of the Lord; for she had truly been Mother of Christ, Mary herself, whose charity lived among us, and the grief at seeing her broken-down frame and leprous facade was all the sadder for this. In the November mist the cathedral seemed a ghostly vessel, a wandering derelict, masts broken, crewless, on an empty sea: she turned every life-providing hope to ice.

Did we then have to despair and resign ourselves to seeing the world in agony and everything most wanted on earth, everything so marvelously desired, die? Was all our life's blood going to spill through the gaping wounds of numberless corpses slumping in eternal silence? That day the cannon, muffled as death, never stopped shaking the ground, and its answer was pitiless.

But there is one light stronger than death: France. And France was not about to want the enemy to reenter Rheims at whose gates the German divisions impotently and bloodily exhausted themselves. Dismantled, empty, disfigured, the cathedral is still part of France. Despair is not reflected in her ruins and the only suffering is in the anguished awaiting of the Te Deum, which will exalt a glorious liberation and renewal.

One should not seek among her stones something belonging to the past and to death. In her awful silence flickers a light that transfigures her vision; it is the flickering light of hope. Of course, she is stretched out like a corpse in the midst of plains that are a vast cemetery—without peace. But I realized that within her there was a great shout of resurrection. She is too sublime, too lofty in her frenzied soaring to give death's filth a hold on her, and she cries out to all the surrounding dead that it is in light that they are buried. She calls them to the eternal triumph contained in her sorrow. And it is not in vain that former centuries raised such a hope in God. The light I described for you is not dulled but transfigured by sorrow and anguish.

You are the ones from whom she awaits renewal, for she is none other than a direct manifestation of Our Lady; and she shows you the light along the way leading to Christ. Others work for liberation in tortures such that they cannot be written except with bleeding hands, and truly Christ alone was able to write them with his blood. You must be worthy of those who suffer thus for you. You have to devote yourself to praying Jesus on the cross for them so that he will teach them what blood is worth. Above all, it is for you to take, in happy peacetime, the way they have opened for you.

Remember that the world has suffered because it believed it saw the light extinguished that keeps God, alive and in peace, on earth. It will only shine again in your youthful desires. Peace is not a weary, heavy sleep after the storm: it is awakening to life and to all its beauty, to goodness, for you will love with new ardor. You will love our Lord because he has loved you so much he gave his blood for you so that your hope would not falter in suffering. And you will love one another, because mankind has suffered too much for having forgotten how to love each other.

Then you will imitate your ancient fathers towering above you from the past. They built cathedrals under God's heaven in order to open a luminous way for those who come in the name of the Lord toward the One who lived among us. And you will build the holy Church in your heart so that the light that leads to God will always shine within you. You will be glad sons of Notre-Dame and never will I see a youth more splendid.

The dread of castration erected itself a monument by creating this substitute.

Sigmund Freud, "Fetishism."

"You have heard tell of Rheims, the great city on the plains of Champagne." This then would be Bataille's first published sentence. The piece is dedicated "to some youths of Haute-Auvergne."

These two opening geographical references are worth some attention. Though they have biographical value (Bataille was born in Auvergne and studied at the lycée in Reims), the way they function here overshadows simultaneously spatial externality and biographical contingency: the cathedral is only a diaphanous, ethereal symbol traversed by impulses of religious fervor; Auvergne is only the locus of hopes for a patriotic and Christian renaissance. The cathedral is not the object of a description, but of a "vision." The entire text functions in this mode, which is regressive; it is dominated by the maternal image, one restoring continuity and reducing externality.

Continuity is even part of the style of this text. Or rather, it is a text (doubtless the only one Bataille wrote) that multiplies stylistic effects, style being precisely, as Barthes once defined it, this sort of homogeneous varnish spread uniformly on a text to mask its discontinuities— to mask, that is, the work of writing. The lyrical tone, the pseudo-medieval vocabulary, each in turn adds a binding agent of effusion and spirituality; while the syntax, after every punctuation, starts in again on the great uninterrupted flood of meditation. For example, just on the first page there are two sentences beginning with the conjunction "and," a coordinating conjunction whose anaphora revives the continuity of discourse interrupted by punctuation: "And when the blessed Joan of Arc . . . ," "And when she . . . rode off again . . ."All the paragraphs of the text also are introduced by an explicit articulation with what went before: "Now the Saint . . . ," "I too . . . ," "And I think . . . ," "Only today . . . ," etc.

This stylistic continuity reflects the demands of the message. In fact, the sense of the text is almost solely a denial of any break, the erasing of wounds and the elimination of an evil consisting precisely in discontinuity and wrenching division. This is clearly apparent in its schoolishly Hegelian three-part progression. (Bataille had not yet been exposed to Hegelian thought, and it is likely that only such an ignorance permitted him to write a text with a Hegelian dialectical schema.) First a thesis: the cathedral, symbol of continuity, of good, of youth, and of faith; second an antithesis: the war, connected to contemporary materialism, destroyer of the cathedral, etc.; third a synthesis in the form of an exhortation addressed to the youth of Haute-Auvergne: the negation of the negation of the cathedral that was war, it reestablishes continuity of the faith: "And you will build the holy Church in your heart so that the light that leads to God will always shine within you."

The cathedral is the symbol of this continuity, embodying it in a mystical radiance bringing together all the history and geography of France to turn it into a sort of vast and glorious resurrected body, a maternal body in glory—intact, removed from time and death because it is sustained by an immortal heart. All around her the cathedral multiplies positive attributes: goodness (just in the same first page "good" appears four times: "the good Christian city," "the good folk of France," "the good welcome," "her good people of Rheims"); whiteness and youth (the cathedral is "white," "in first youth," or "white and immense"); safety (at her feet, Reims "was a city with a secure bourgeoisie within its walls," etc.). The unity of these descriptions is dominated by maternal presence, not just because the cathedral is, like any house, a symbol of prenatal place, not just because it is *dedicated* to Notre-Dame, but because it itself *is* Notre-Dame, the real mother of God ("she had truly been mother of Christ");[2] the monarchy of the mother. The Virgin on the portal is described as "regal and maternal." If Bataille insists that "there the kings of France were crowned," it is above all as a mark that royalty itself is given only by the mother. The king, God, Christ only put in brief appearances in this hymn to the feminine (to Notre-Dame, to Joan of Arc, to the Virgin, to the Church, to France, etc.).

Then came the war. "I saw almost the last days of her splendor in the fever of August 1914." Bataille gave another account of this episode in August 1914, another version written during another war, the second: "November 6, 1915, in a bombed city, four or five kilometers from the German lines, my father died, abandoned. My mother and I abandoned him during the German advance, in August 1914."[3] In this new version Bataille does not say one word about the cathedral. Just as in the first he did not speak of his father. *Notre-Dame de Rheims*, dominated by every feminine and maternal value, goes so far in reducing the name of the father to silence that it silences its own gesture of obliteration, or something more or less directly the most obvious result of that gesture: the actual death of the father. This obliteration, the blind point of the text, is produced by the conjunction of a number of motives that can be divided between two poles, religion and war.

1. Religion: in *Le Petit*, Bataille brings it up apropos these same events. "My father, irreligious, died refusing to see a priest. At puberty I myself was irreligious (my mother indifferent). But in August 1914 I went to see a priest and until 1920 rarely went a week without confessing my sins! In 1920 I switched again, stopped believing in anything except my luck."[4] It was thus in August 1914 (on the one hand, the time war was declared, but also on the other, the time he was preparing to follow his mother, to abandon his irreligious father to the luck of the front) that he converted. Conversion is the first component of this murder of the father that is both carried out and silenced in *Notre-Dame de Rheims*. Silenced, although one sentence, one word nonetheless does point to it: Bataille says that it is in the shadow of the cathedral that he was "born again to the life and happiness God gives us." This new birth that comes from turning to the bosom of our Holy Mother the Church, no matter how trite the metaphor, is a clear statement of how committed he was to paternal filiation. In August 1914 Bataille was about to be seventeen.

2. War: it is, in French, a synonym of the name of the father: Bataille. This name will be deleted in another way by the erotic texts that appear under a pseudonym (Lord Auch, Louis Trente, Pierre Angélique). But in *Notre-Dame de Rheims* the denial works on the signified: this text is a message of peace. But war here is not merely a synonym of the name of the father, it is also the result of a paternal attribute: impiety, irreligiousness. It is because France no longer has a strong enough faith, because religion is no longer alive there, that war was able to break out and the cathedral was wounded.[5] "Remember that the world has suffered because it believed it saw the light extinguished that keeps God, alive and in peace, on earth."

At seventeen Bataille, abandoning his father, left with his mother.

Was his older brother (whose given name, Martial, was warlike as well) with them? Did he remain in Reims? It never comes up. But we should mention that this brother would be extremely shocked when, nearly fifty years later, he learned how Bataille portrayed his father in *Histoire de l'oeil*.[6]

Bataille abandons his father for peace, religion, the cathedral. And he goes with his mother. In this context the father's figure makes its appearance cut in two, split by the action of the maternal image: if, on the one hand, there is a royal father (who possesses royalty only, however, because a woman took him under her wing—Joan of Arc had to force Charles VII to have himself crowned king at Reims), on the other hand there is an obscene, lecherous, irreligious father, described for example in the "Reminiscences" in *Histoire de l'oeil*, the one escaping the maternal order. Contrasting Charles VII, who needed a woman to be brought to the crown, one might evoke here Gilles de Rais, another among the military men surrounding Joan of Arc, one soon to be tried for sexual murders that will give rise to the legendary Bluebeard and to whom Bataille's last book was going to be devoted. Law on the one hand, crime on the other, but the law is that of a domesticated father, captured by the mother. The king, the good father, is immortalized by the mother. The entire ideological system organized around the cathedral rests on this castration of the father.

Of the two versions given by Bataille concerning the events of the summer of 1914, versions separated by a critical period between wars (*Notre-Dame* probably dates from the summer of 1918; *Le Petit*, published in 1943, dates, no doubt, from 1942), the second can be seen as a denouncement of the first, unmasking the silence it concealed. We might say it puts in writing the traumatic series of events buried under the style of the other. Specifically, this writing now puts war at play explicitly and, through war's synonymic connotations, reestablishes the connection that identifies the forbidden father. ("Today, I know I am 'blind' beyond measure, the man 'abandoned' on earth like my father at N.")[7] He does not go back on the father's death, but now joins to it an aggression perpetrated against the maternal body, the womb of churches, cathedrals, and monuments.

In some ways all of Bataille's work will be a rewriting of this initial text, a reworking intended to dismantle such a beginning and draw out its silences. But once again, not because of a paralyzed guilt; rather because this text itself is the almost anonymous (and for this reason negligible) result of the vast ideological system symbolized and maintained by architecture. In order to loosen the structure that is hierarchical and at the same time creates hierarchy, Bataille will introduce the play of writing. Writing in this sense would be a profoundly antiarchitectural gesture, a nonconstructive gesture, one that, on the contrary, undermines and destroys everything whose existence depends on edifying pretensions.

It is a question of reopening a hole, remarking a hollow, a cave once more. The very holes that works of architecture plugged up. To show—after the narcissistic erection of the maternal cathedral—a hole at its summit, at the highest point of the temple roof, the pinnacle.

Pinnacle (French, *pinacle*): the name given to the cupola of the temple in Jerusalem. The highest point of this cupola was a hole (to recall the ascension of Christ commemorated by the temple). Derives from *pinna*, whereas pineal (the slit in crenelations) derives from *pinea* (pine cone). For Bataille, the pineal eye will mark the hole at the top.

On Bataille

> *Bataille: abattage d'humain bétail. (Battle: slaughter of human cattle.)*
>
> Michel Leiris, *Glossaire: j'y serre mes gloses*

So. Is this to be a study on Bataille? or over him? or above him?

Writing on is the epitome of a discourse in control, calmly assured of its position. It is deployed with complete assurance in a realm over which it has taken possession, one it has inventoried after first closing it off, to make sure it is absolutely safe. This discourse runs no risk at all: it is not uneasy about the future, it steadily expands. One chooses an object and relies on it. Writing *on* is not clearing paths or opening routes by using a pen, for example to take on the homogeneous, undifferentiated surface of a blank page. Rather, one might say it is like being a tourist, miraculously able to go anywhere you decide to go along established tracks. Writing *on* is almost always overseeing one's property, going around as the master who controls "his" subject, simultaneously sealing it off and deliberately skirting around it.

We will again encounter the "Icarian" gesture providing the energy for discourse *on*; Bataille, in "La 'Vieille taupe' et le préfixe *sur*" (The Old Mole and the Prefix *over*), demonstrated the illusoriness of the security upon which it bases its assurance.[8] But first one must wonder how the use of this form of discourse can be pertinent or what results it might have when it bears on Bataille.

It is always tempting to arrest a form. Form is discourse's temptation. It is in taking form that discourse is developed and then becomes fixed and acknowledged. In some ways Bataille did not do this: he was able to save the violence of desire from the temptation of form. We propose to read Bataille here starting from this refusal, a refusal that produces the heterogeneity, in contrast to the continuity pursued by discourse as its ideal, that will be indicated by the term *writing*. However, it is not a question of reducing everything to this refusal, nor of making writing the locus of a new totality. It is not a question of giving writing the privileges that belonged to discourse. Writing does not acknowledge any privilege, hence also does not acknowledge privilege for itself. It has to be defined as that which maintains lack, or rather as that which produces a hole where totality becomes incomplete. The term *writing* is used here to mark the appearance in discourse form of that incompletion that form used to reject, the indestructible but always repressed bond of desire and of "its" dissatisfaction. Perhaps Bataille's work gets its greatest strength in this refusal of the temptation of form. This refusal is the interdiction making it impossible in advance for his works ever to be "complete," impossible for his books to be only books and impossible for death to shut his words up.[9] The transgression is transgression of form.

This transgression is never an object of knowledge or recognition. But to speak *on* something imposes a form on it—because of a specific requirement of this type of discourse, one specific to discourse as such—from that moment on, it becomes an object of knowledge. Form is the temptation of discourse to arrest itself, to fix on itself, to finish itself off by producing and appropriating its own end. Bataille's writing is antidiscursive (endlessly deforms and disguises itself, endlessly rids itself of form): "I think the way a girl takes off her dress."[10] The writing responds with perhaps unequaled rigor and readiness to the desire to let death (which is not of the order of the word, does not speak and does not finish anything, is the equivalent of completing nothing) have the "last word." The urgency of this desire demanded that such writing never be anticipated except in the "form" of incompletion. "Actually," he wrote in 1961, a year before his death, in the preface to the reedition of *Le Coupable* (Guilty), "the language I use could only come to an end with my death."[11] The death that, elsewhere, he called in some sense an imposture.

"Writing is never more than a game played with an ungraspable reality."[12] Writing *on* is laboriously doing everything possible to grasp this reality. Writing *on* Bataille is thus intensifying death's imposture, first by not recognizing it, that is by taking it seriously (as if death, something that does not allow of being considered an event, could put an end to the play of writing), then by profiting from it.

Every one of Bataille's statements heralds the repetition that will erase it. From the moment of its formulation every statement is shaken by its disappearance. Nowhere does writing meet with the opportunity to conform itself. Never does it provide thought with a place to collect itself, for example, into a thesis that would be permanently shielded from its destructive productivity. Instead of completion, obliteration.

To write *on* Bataille is to consider this incompletion as a regrettable accident, but one that can be remedied. Discourse *on* is a discourse of truth, making truth dependent upon completion. Writing *on* Bataille would be, thus, proposing to do what he himself did not manage to do, taking the authority of his death to complete his work. Collecting the theses and themes whose proliferation he was unable to conclude. Laying them out according to a plan showing how they go together, whereas Bataille himself was lost in them. Proposing an idea, therefore, while dominating from the full height of a masterful discourse, that would allow one to answer a question like "What about Bataille?" Giving him the form of an idea. Turning what used to be the name of a subject into the signifier of a concept.

Transgression does not belong to the same space as the idea, except as something that subverts it. That is why transgression is a matter not for theory but for practice. Writing is one of the modes of this practice, not the only one, but nevertheless not just any mode. If writing *on* is formalizing, this operation cancels transgression by reducing (or elevating) it to the level of concepts. As if Bataille never *wrote*. To write *on* Bataille is thus to betray him. At the same time to miss him. To write *on* Bataille is not to *write* on Bataille.

Bataille himself wrote *Sur Nietzsche* (On Nietzsche).[13] That is the title of one of his books. But in actual fact this book is no more a book than it is "*on* Nietzsche." It hardly corresponds to what one expects from the title, to the demands of this form. This inadequacy, one both formal and theoretical as far as the rules of knowledge are concerned, does not, however, constitute an imperfection that Bataille (because he lacked sufficient university training or perhaps was driven by some pathological identification) could not have corrected. On the contrary: down to the most incongruous elements (like the presence in this book on Nietzsche of the most autobiographical of journals occupying three quarters of the volume), it corresponds to the strategy Bataille worked out for a relationship with Nietzsche.[14] To not betray Nietzsche one must not *respect* him. To make him an object of knowledge or even of fervor is first to make him an object, stifling a desire within a tomb. "But let's leave Nietzsche be." Nietzsche himself called for this, in *The Gay Science*. This "gay science"—closer to not-knowing than to knowledge. Let's leave Bataille be.

Besides, Bataille is dead now. Death interrupted his discourse, laid down his cards and showed his hand. This is our authorization to write *on* and almost above him. To write *on* is to bury a dead person and to build a (scholarly) tomb. Yet the dead person is not out of the game. Play continues with his hand spread out on the table. The dummy. Without death there would be no room for play. Death does not stop the sense of the discourse. It is perhaps to soon to write *on* Bataille. But it will always be too soon to do so. Too soon ever to think the game is over. Write on!

Meaning exists only at risk. It is never fixed, never arrested. There are no guarantees. Meaning is uninsured. Not covered. Science and philosophy (models of discourse *on*) would like to fix and accumulate meaning in a closed language where clearly defined terms are enumerated hierarchically according to finite, calculable connections with no lateral linkage. They invest meaning in the lexicon, which as a result is allotted to control by the concept. In contrast, the meaning put in play by Bataille's writing does not hoard but rather expends itself. There is no meaning except through sacrifice—which is meaningless. This is where his writing transgresses any formalism: by refusing to subject wordplay to meaning, and, on the contrary, setting it off again by constantly deranging syntax.

A word's meaning always refers back to some other word: the word "table" to the word "furniture," the word "mandolin" to "guitar," and so forth. This movement, which no dictionary, no language can claim to escape, is however limited as far as possible by scientific languages, which are considered "well constructed" precisely to the extent that they limit this circulation to the minimal number of elements—whose play they are able to circumscribe by this economy, stabilizing the cross references. On the contrary, in what might be called Bataille's tongue, words do indeed refer to other words (as in any language) but to words that *are not where they belong*, words out of place because in the meantime they moved. Which would condemn any lexicographical inventory of Bataille's language to be nonsense. There is no dictionary of Bataille's language because this tongue is produced as a transgression of lexical stability. Such a dictionary would be incomplete by definition. There is no possible dictionary for a language whose violent syntax undoes the meaning of all words. Whereas the formal discourses, science or philosophy, because they want to *retain* meaning, are condemned (which is Bataille's reproach) to be totally meaningless, the paradoxical project of such a dictionary would consist not in endowing words with one or more meanings but in expending them unthinkingly.

"Painters," said Matisse, "need no dictionary." This in contrast to architects whose production is encoded in a language so technical that it requires specialized dictionaries.

For literature, joining modern painting in its critique of architecture—a critique that put painting in the forefront of cultural revolutionary practices for more than half a century—would mean by implication to work against dictionary and grammar, the tools of the academy that cut language off from history. To write against the word, against the sentence. To rediscover the glossopoetic energy that makes writing something that works on language (on a language in progress), the glossopoetic energy whose trace European literatures, between Rabelais and Joyce, have virtually obliterated.

In his thesis Marx recalled Epicurus's claim that he was an enemy of grammar. Around the thirties, writers indeed make more and more grammatical errors, they invent words that belong to no dictionary. No one understands them any more. Portmanteau words, glossolalia, badly constructed sentences, no more punctuation: the Tower of Babel. And in this context several mock dictionaries appear.

1. The first is *Glossaire: j'y serre mes gloses* by Michel Leiris (appearing first in April 1925 in *La Révolution surréaliste*). A dictionary is com-

pletely bound up with a representational and communicational conception of language: it stabilizes the meaning of words so that thoughts can be transmissible from one subject to another. From this function derives the rhetorical form that defines dictionary as a literary genre: articles (one for each word) succeed each other in alphabetical order, in each instance setting the word to be defined next to its definition, linking as in an equation a word and its meaning. Leiris's *Glossaire* looks like it respects this typographic model.

But that is just how it looks. The one rule governing this *Glossaire* is a determination to make the bar separating the word and its definition, the signifier and the signified, porous; to make the signifier constantly overflow onto the signified so that what appears in the place appointed for meaning remains completely stuck in the materiality of the word to be defined. In place of a definition one finds only an echo of the signifier, its sustained vibration overflowing and expanding. This is what the very title states and performs exemplarily, picking up where the article in which dictionary defines itself leaves off: *Glossaire* (Glossary): *j'y serre* (that's where I put away) *mes gloses* (my gloss). A mock dictionary, the *Glossaire* unsticks language from its function as communication and representation by emphasizing the materiality where it must be canceled. The dictionary becomes for the first time a poetic genre. "Some monstrous aberration makes men believe that language was born to facilitate their mutual relations." Thus Leiris introduced the glosses published in *La Révolution surréaliste*.[15] A note by Artaud followed: "Yes, from now on language has only one use—as a means for madness, for elimination of thought, for rupture, as folly's maze, not a DICTIONARY where certain pedants in the neighborhood of the Seine channel their intellectual strictures."[16]

2. Chronologically the second of these fake dictionaries, these antidictionaries, is the "Dictionnaire critique," which would appear regularly starting with *Documents,* no. 2, and which was compiled by contributors to this review. This time there is another style of subversion of lexical order; no longer rejecting (as in Leiris's *Glossaire*) the fundamental distribution of language between signifier and signified, but discerning behind the meaning, and sometimes independent of the meaning, what "job" words do. Bataille uses the term "besogne" (job, work with a notion of drudgery) in the article "Informe," where he clarifies the project governing this dictionary. The job: lexical units

wrested from the symbolic code, joined to extralinguistic practices, charged with a libidinal intensity referring not to a process of representation or communication, but to a productivity in which the word functions as a center of energy, a productivity in which the word is not defined by what it means (its "sense") but by what it does, by the effects it induces (its "job"). See also Carl Einstein's statement in the article "Rossignol" of the "Dictionnaire critique" (*Documents*, no. 2, May 1929): "Words are used as personal ornaments. Words, in general, are fossilized things that provoke automatic reactions in us. . . . What is called the soul is, for the most part, a museum of signs devoid of meaning."

3. Finally, in 1938, Breton and Eluard published the *Dictionnaire abrégé du surréalisme*. Here the subversion of the dictionary is far more feeble (doubtless, the presence of numerous proper names among the articles collected in this autocelebration implicated it from the beginning). Besides, there is no mention of any such project of subversion; the authors content themselves with proposing unexpected associations between the word and its definition. The word "God," for example, is followed by Breton's definition "God is a pig" (taken from *Le Surréalisme et la peinture*): "Someone recently suggested to me that God be defined 'as a tree' and I, once again, saw the caterpillar and did not see the tree. Without knowing it I was going between the tree's roots as if I were on a road somewhere near Ceylon. Besides one does not describe a tree, one does not describe what is formless. All one describes is a pig. God, whom one does not describe, is a pig." [17]

Bataille gives some explanation of what the "Dictionnaire critique" of *Documents* was supposed to be, the nature of the project, in one of the fourteen articles he participated in writing—the article "Informe" (Formless), which here is given the job generally granted to the article "Dictionary" itself. In the *Documents* dictionary, this self-reflection does not take place at the place assigned to it by the lexicographical code: this is the first transgression of the discourse where it is produced. The second transgression is the valorization of formlessness— something every dictionary aims at repressing. The meaning (that a dictionary fixes) is identified with the concept, with the idea: *eidos* = form. Because this reduplication occurs in the article "Informe" (Formless), the dictionary, rather than being closed back on itself, opens up to expansive expenditure of sense, to infinite incompletion.

FORMLESS.—A dictionary would start from the moment in which it no longer provides the meaning of words but their job. *Formless* is thus not merely an adjective with such and such a meaning but a term for lowering status with its implied requirement that everything have a form. Whatever it (*formless*) designates lacks entitlement in every sense and is crushed on the spot, like a spider or an earthworm. For academics to be content, the universe would have to assume a form. All of philosophy has no other goal: it is a matter of fitting what is there into a formal coat, a mathematical overcoat. On the other hand to assert that the universe resembles nothing else and is only *formless* comes down to stating that the universe is something like a spider or spit.[18]

The distinction between words' *meaning* and their *job* makes language into a place of specific productivity. In language and in every connection to it some practice is at stake. To privilege meaning at the expense of work is to believe that this practice can be put into parentheses. The French word *besogne,* with its overtones of drudgery, has a contemptuous ring. The *job* is not the *usage.* Usage doubtless introduces a certain historicity of language because it refers to linguistic practices in current use at the present time and in the present society. But a lexicographical attitude is content with making a report concerning these historical data. Usage only functions in a space still dominated by the category of meaning—formulable meaning. What Bataille calls job is of a different order, a tonal one. It indicates all those processes of repulsion or seduction aroused by the word independent of its meaning. For example, the job of the word "formless" is presented in the reactions of disgust accompanying its utterance: a word not merely pronounced but spat out, flung in someone's face. By the same token, in Bataille's articles written for *Documents,* the word *bas* (low) will never be reducible to its meaning. It will always have a job that is different from the gist of the sentence containing it, where it will clash and sound off-key. Hence the word is the locus of an event, an explosion of affective potential, not a means for the expression of meaning. To write, here, is to organize around the word the void allowing the charge of its fissile energy to shatter the accumulation of meaning. If the meaning of words comes to light in a syntax obeying grammatical dictates, the job is simultaneously that which drives and is revealed by the syntax of insubordination.

And so everything must have its form. Dictionaries see to it. They exclude the formless as unnamable. In this lexicographical imperative it is not just the vocabulary that is in question. The same goes for

the universe. Just like Noah calling the roll of creation to fill up his
arc. No species was going to survive the flood, hence reproduce, that
did not answer to a name. The nameless is excluded from reproduction, which is above all the transmission of a name. But Bataille's writing relentlessly stages the perverse linguistic desire to make what is
unnamable appear within language itself—the desire to make a certain nakedness forbidding any guarantee to the codes' reproduction
reappear under the "mathematical overcoat": "I think the way a girl
takes off her dress."

Through the intermediary of this article "Formless," Bataille's language opens up onto an incomplete universe with which his interrupted dictionary communicates through this very wound, through
this flaw in form that prevents it from folding back on itself.

For reasons that have nothing to do with the alphabet (an article
"Abattoir" [Slaughterhouse] would be written later), this "Dictionnaire critique" began with "Architecture."

Architectural Metaphors

Books are not made like children but like pyramids.
Flaubert to Feydeau, 1858.

The "jobs" taken on by the word "architecture" certainly have more
import than its meaning. When architecture is discussed it is never
simply a question of architecture; the metaphors cropping up as a
result of these jobs are almost inseparable from the proper meaning
of the term. The proper meaning itself remains somehow indeterminate, which is all the more surprising since it is associated with jobs
that are strikingly clear and urgent. Architecture refers to whatever
there is in an edifice that cannot be reduced to building, whatever
allows a construction to escape from purely utilitarian concerns,
whatever is aesthetic about it. Now this sort of artistic supplement
that, by its addition to a simple building, constitutes architecture,
finds itself caught from the beginning in a process of semantic expansion that forces what is called architecture to be only the general locus
or framework of representation, its ground. Architecture represents
a religion that it brings alive, a political power that it manifests, an
event that it commemorates, etc. Architecture, before any other qual-
ifications, is identical to the space of representation; it always repre-

sents something other than itself from the moment that it becomes distinguished from mere building.

This encroachment by an irreducibly metaphorical situation, with architecture defined as the representation of something else, extends to language, where architectural metaphors are very common. There is the facade, generally concealing some sordid reality; there is the secret, hidden architecture itself that one discovers in seemingly the freest works of art, in living beings, indeed in the universe itself where one acknowledges the creator's unified plan; pillars are not all literally pillars of the church; keystones prevent systems (whether political, philosophical, or scientific) from collapsing; to say nothing of foundations, etc., etc. These metaphors seem too inevitable for us to see them as sought-after literary effects. Their cliché nature and their anónymity are, however, an indication that they are not innocent, but rather surreptitiously accomplishing some ideological task for which they are the instruments. Never mind if the proper meaning of architecture remains subject to discussion. What is essential is that it always do its job. No metaphor is innocent; and the less it is contrived the less it is innocent. Its self-evidence is the ground floor where thought can safely walk in its sleep.

Hubert Damisch has shown that Viollet-le-Duc's *Dictionnaire de l'architecture française* followed a structuralist analytical method (one since developed by Saussure and the linguists) before the term was invented.[19] This homology is not purely coincidental. Instead of seeing the architect's discourse as a preformation of the linguist's, the homology requires in fact that linguistic analysis be thought of as dominated by the importation of an architectural vocabulary. The term "structure" itself is not the least of the evidence. That it is used today to describe practically all organizations and all systems shows just how far the domination extends.

(In memoriam. The metaphor here will be borrowed from Jacques Lacan in his praise for an "edifice": the theoretical work of Ernest Jones, to contrast it with the pragmatism reigning in what he calls the professional psychoanalytic "building." "This edifice is appealing to us. For, metaphoric though this may be, it is perfectly constructed to remind us of what distinguished architecture from building: that is, a logical power organizing architecture beyond anything the building supports in terms of possible use. Moreover no building, unless reduced to a shack, can do without this order allying it with discourse. This logic coexists harmoniously with efficacy only when dominating it, and in the art of construction their discord is not just a possibility.")[20]

There is consequently no way to describe a system without resorting to the vocabulary of architecture. When structure defines the general form of legibility, nothing becomes legible unless it is submitted to the architectural grid. Architecture under these conditions is the archistructure, the system of systems. The keystone of systematicity in general, it organizes the concord of languages and guarantees universal legibility. The temple of meaning, it dominates and totalizes signifying productions, forcing them all to come down to the same thing, to confirm its noologic system. Architecture is a compulsory loan burdening all of ideology, mortgaging all its differences from the outset.

It is as if, by allowing themselves to be named metaphorically by a vocabulary borrowed from architecture, the various fields of ideological production uncovered a unitary vocation. This metaphor provides the system's form in every area where it appears. Which results in the repression of anything resembling play, exteriority, or alterity. The system tends to be monodic: it has only one voice, the other voice is not heard there. There is a sort of gigantic internal monologue that it organizes. Otherness is excluded; it has no other place than outside. In an exterior which, reduced to silence, has no voice in the matter.

(Félibien counts Noah's ark as a work of architecture and suggests the tight connection between this art and religion. "This people," he writes, speaking of the Jewish people, "held architecture in special esteem, no doubt because this art has some divine element, and because God not only is called in the Scripture the sovereign architect of the Universe, but because he was willing himself to teach Noah how the Ark should be built.")[21]

The great architect is, by metaphor, God, or to use the rationalist litotes, the Supreme Being. Starting with the activity of the architect conceiving his work as its analogon, ideology gives hints of what the final word will be, the word on which its entire meaning hangs. But the impact of the analogy is not limited to cause, it is equally valid for effect. The image of the world itself is caught in the architectural analogy. But this analogy programs architecture in advance in a religious and theological perspective, imposing a cosmic function on it. The world is legible only if one starts with the temple's dome, and God is the great architect only because the temple the architect has constructed celebrates the divine work. Such a metaphor only functions on the basis of the architect's commitment to the economy of faith. In other words, it is faith that makes the architect. Cosmic symbolism is not self-evident and the homology between temple and cosmos is not a given but a requirement, a must with which the architect must comply. But faith is what upholds the resemblance.

Let's not forget this shattering of the economy of mimesis that defines the ideology function of architecture: it does not produce copies, but models. It produces itself as model. It does not imitate an order but constitutes it: whether the order of the world or of society.

In Quatremère de Quincy's *Dictionnaire d'architecture* the autoproduction of architecture produces a similar breakaway beyond mimesis. The structure of mimesis is called into question there by "accomplished" architecture, which has no existing model anywhere for itself and which thus must itself produce what it is to imitate. In fact Quatremère says: If architecture begins by imitating itself, by mechanically reproducing its own origins (as it still does for mere buildings—sheds, houses, etc.); and if then it imitates the human body, doubtless not as sculpture (which only deals with external forms) does, but by studying and drawing on its knowledge of the proportions and the organization that make up its beauty, whose relationships it will reproduce in its edifices; in its most accomplished stage architecture "imitates" nature itself, it "reproduces" the harmonious system of cosmic laws:

It is no longer from wooden frames or huts that it will obtain its origins, nor from the human body whose proportions it will use to regulate its relationships; it is nature itself, in its abstract essence, that it takes for its model. It is nature's order par excellence that becomes its archetype and its genius. . . . It is thus that this art, seemingly more materially dependent than others, in this last respect was able to become more ideal than they, that is, more fitted to exercise the intelligent side of our soul. Nature, in fact, beneath its material exterior, provides only intellectual analogies and relationships for it to reproduce. This art imitates its model less in material than in abstract qualities. It does not follow it but goes alongside. It does not make things it sees, but watches how they are made. It is not interested in the results but in the cause producing them.

As nature's emulator, its efforts are bent to the study of nature's means and to reproducing its results on a smaller scale. Thus, whereas other arts of delineation have created models that they imitate, architecture must create its own, without being able to seize upon it anywhere in reality.[22]

Architecture, consequently, has no "created" model; it must create this. It follows an archetype, but one that does not exist independent of itself. Far more importantly, it must itself produce this archetype. Which is how the unity of plan between architecture and nature is guaranteed. By constituting itself as a microcosm, architecture delineates the world and projects the shadow of the great architect behind it. Without architecture the world would remain illegible. Nature is the archetype of architecture only insofar as architecture is the archetype of nature. It is less that architecture is cosmic than that the cosmos itself is architectured.

(Taine in *Philosophie de l'art* defines architecture as the production of a harmonious whole whose example is not found in nature: "In every art there must be a whole made up of connected parts modified by the artist so as to manifest some character; but it is not necessary in every art that this whole correspond to real objects; it is enough for it to exist. Hence, if it is possible to encounter wholes made of connected parts that are not imitative of real objects, there will be arts that do not have imitation as their point of departure. This does happen, and thus architecture and music are born. In fact, apart from the connections, proportions, organic and moral dependencies copied by the three imitative arts, there are mathematical relationships worked out by the other two that imitate nothing.")[23]

Vitruvius begins his book (in some ways the bible of architecture) with this definition: "Architecture is a science that must be accompanied by a great diversity of studies and knowledge, by means of which it judges all the works of the other arts." Omniscience is the architect's greatest virtue. It is the quality permitting him, whether he is "great" or of lesser stature, according to Boullée, to "make himself the one who implements nature,"[24] which is what distinguishes his art from the simple art of building, which concerns merely the execution of a plan: first it must be conceived. Conception as a precondition implies recourse to all branches of knowledge, so as to judge, for example, the appropriateness of the mathematical proportions of the edifice to its purpose, as well as its geographical surroundings or its insertion into communal life, etc. All branches of knowledge converge thus in architecture, which for this reason occupies a position that can be very exactly defined as *encyclopedic*. And, if we are to believe Perrault, in his edition of Vitruvius, this would even be the word's etymological sense: "Architecture is of all the sciences the one to which the Greeks gave a name signifying superiority and stewardship over the others."

The primacy of architecture is assured by its unifying function. It constitutes the unity of the sciences, no matter if following a theological or mathematical inspiration: it sets unity as the required vocation. Locus of peace, *Place de la Concorde*.

(Alberti, in *Della tranquillità dell'animo* [1442], recommends that, to flee anxiety and pain, one devote oneself to mathematics or to architectural revery: "Sometimes I have designed and built finely proportioned buildings in my mind, arranging their orders and numerous columns with cornices and panels. And I have occupied myself with constructions of this kind until overcome by sleep." [25] Architecture restores peace to the soul.)

Architecture represents this silent, homologous, gravitational mass that absorbs every meaningful production. The monument and the pyramid are where they are to cover up a place, to fill in a void: the one left by death. Death must not appear, it must not take place: let tombs cover it up and take its place. Death comes with time as the unknown borne by the future. It is the other of everything known; it threatens the meaning of discourses. Death is hence irreducibly heterogeneous to homologies; it is not assimilable. The death wish, whose action Freud recognized whenever a return to the inanimate could be noted, whenever difference was denied, wears the elusive face of this expanding homology that causes the place of the Other to be imported into the Same. One plays dead so that death will not come. So nothing will happen and time will not take place.

Summa Theologica

> *The book of stone, so solid and so durable, would give way to the book of paper, even more solid and more durable.*
>
> Victor Hugo, *Notre-Dame de Paris*

The Middle Ages are, for Bataille, a heavily charged field of reference. For reasons pertaining to his professional specialization: he was educated as a medievalist. But before his entrance at the École des Chartes he had already written the hymn to the glory of *Notre-Dame de Rheims*. The Middle Ages, in Bataille's system of historical references, occupies the position of greatest taboo. First, it is the period of uncontested, victorious Christianity. It will not depart from this function even though it will embody opposite values over the years. The Middle Ages of *Notre-Dame de Rheims* is white, luminous, pious, and monarchical, that of *La Tragédie de Gilles de Rais* will be nocturnal and feudal. There is the Middle Ages of cathedrals and that of fortified castles, that of religion and that of war, etc. The locus of the strongest taboo is the place also of the most astounding crimes.

Gothic cathedrals of the thirteenth century unquestionably have been the clearest historical illustration of the system of architectural metaphor. This system is found in every other period but never to the extent that is true with cathedrals. Architecture itself, perhaps, never fulfilled its metaphoric potential to such a degree anywhere else. Gothic cathedrals are linked to a vast movement of political and intellectual restructuring by means of which the monarchy relies on the cities in order to weaken the feudal system. After the splintering that resulted from the disintegration of the Carolingian empire (one of whose effects had been the withdrawal into the cloisters of all that remained of religious and intellectual life), the twelfth century saw the beginnings of a centralizing movement. One of the most active centers would be the cathedral schools—later transformed into universities. This centralization took place at the level of then-forming nations, but also at the level of Christianity. The role played by France, and by Paris in particular, sets them at the head of this movement.

Knowledge and its transmission are entirely in the hands of the clergy. The Church also has close control over the abundant artistic production as its most important silent partner. Painter and sculptor are nothing more than those who merely execute very detailed projects laid out by ecclesiastical authorities, who decide which characters are to be represented, their positions and attributes, and the dimensions and general order that must govern the composition. As for architecture, its orthodoxy was even more obvious, because more often than not the abbots themselves took charge of carrying out construction projects. Only with the erection of cathedrals does the corps of architects come into being as an independent profession, but this independence is not accompanied by any ideological autonomy. Cathedrals constituted a point too strategically important in the network with which the Church maintained its control over society for there to be really any question of such autonomy. They were, in effect, schools and corresponded in their very project to a pedagogical program: they were to be simultaneously the place where knowledge was embodied and where it was transmitted, the place where the ideological capital amassed by theological culture was to be reproduced. Between the knowledge and the edifice that was supposed to collect it— accommodate it—there was no room for play at all.

The studies Émile Mâle devoted to French medieval art establish in a particularly striking way, at least in its iconographic material (the subjects represented, the arrangement adopted), the extent to which this vigilant supervision exercised by the Church over the production of works of art was, nonetheless, not taken as an arbitrary yoke hindering the freedom of inspiration. Such authority was acknowledged, instead, by this very inspiration that was inseparable from religious fervor. Discursive knowledge, illuminated by the scriptures, provides a reflection of the world, and art provides a reflection of discursive knowledge. From that point on, the cathedral can be defined simultaneously as a microcosm and an encyclopedia, at the center of a society that is closed back on itself through this series of secular cross references. "The thirteenth century is the century of Encyclopedias. In no other period were so many Surveys, Mirrors, or Pictures of the World published. . . . Now, while the Doctors were constructing the intellectual cathedral that was to shelter all of Christianity, our stone cathedrals, which were like the visible image of the other, were being erected. The Middle Ages put all of its convictions into them. They were in their own way Surveys, Mirrors, and Pictures of the World."[26]

Émile Mâle's work was essential in the elaboration of the Proustian aesthetic and in the genesis of *A la recherche du temps perdu*, as important as Ruskin's with which—much more modestly and in a form Proust found to be more French—it has many affinities.[27] Proust borrowed from Mâle the material for an article he published in *Le Figaro* (in 1904) against the Briand law project for separating church and state.[28] As a result of the break between the French government and the Vatican, this project was to lead to closing numerous churches. Churches that are closed die. Faith built them and faith alone can make them live. Their beauty cannot be separated from the religious unanimity of the crowds they welcome. Without the spectacle of living faith and of the liturgy giving it order, this beauty disappears. Just as for the Bataille who wrote *Notre-Dame de Rheims*, it is less war than anticlericalism and atheism that threaten the churches. Proust: "It is better to devastate a church than to close it down." [29] The Proustian aesthetic, at least at its beginning, is caught up in this religious perspective: art is only what we have left of religion. And if literature remains (a sign of the times) the only substitute for religion to which we are still receptive, it must, at least, work to revive through celebration those products of a more vigorous faith—the cathedrals.

A la recherche also begins with architecture—and even with a church that, if not a cathedral, is nonetheless magnified by the capital letter with which Proust honors it: "The Church!" [30] which is the maternal, familiar, familial church ("our Church")[31] at Combray. This church around which the opening of *A la recherche* unfurls is set forth in its almost inaugural position as the model for the work of art in general, but also as the model of the work set in motion by its evocation. Proust explicitly defines his project in a letter in which he refers to the structure of the cathedral. "When you talk about cathedrals to me," he writes his correspondent, "I cannot help being moved by the intuition allowing you to guess something I have never told anyone and that I write now for the first time: that I wanted to give each section of my book the title: portal, apse, windows, etc.; just to respond in advance to the stupid criticism when people say I lack construction in books whose only merit, I could prove, lies in the interdependence of the least of their parts." [32] The lost time is also the time of former faith, the time of childhood or of the Middle Ages. Art is a way to regain the assurance of immortality, formerly guaranteed sufficiently by religion. The Proustian project in many ways will be belied in its very realization. There are holes in the enclosure of his text; the text itself repudiates such closure. And Bataille will be most sensitive to this failure in Proust.[33] Still, on the whole, Proust's work will lend itself to a formal reading that confirms its project.

Many readers have expressed their surprise that no trace is to be found in *A la recherche* of the death of a mother for whom, in the first volumes, the narrator demonstrated the strongest attachment. Let us just suggest in passing, and in a sense metaphorically, that this mother had already taken on the shape of the hidden cathedral that is espoused by Proust's work. Metaphor, according to a famous Proustian phrase, removes sensations from temporal contingencies. The church at Combray is the metaphor of the work of art because it is removed from evolution. For anyone knowing how to read it by the light of faith, it appears as already outside of time, or rather as a being that would find a further basis in time whereas whatever makes up the everyday world is simply on the road to ruin. It occupies, says Proust, "a four-dimensional space—the fourth being Time—spreading its nave out through the centuries, from bay to bay, from chapel to chapel, it seemed to conquer and to cover not merely a few meters but successive epochs from which it emerged victorious."[34] It is this fourth dimension that constitutes the church as a metaphor and makes it escape the metonymic pollution of the profane milieu with which its three others put it in contact.[35] Like the ark built by Noah to allow God's creation to escape the flood, the nave of the church, the church as vessel, victoriously traverses the flow of time. Metaphorical erection is simultaneously architectural. It is inaugural. It is where Proust begins.

Émile Mâle, therefore, describes the closed system of medieval society, centered around the Church and its cathedrals. Art has no place there other than the one assigned it by theology. Its only function is to provide a perceptible representation of religious dogma and to illustrate the faith.[36] The content of works of art is only the reflection of the content of discursive knowledge. Thus, in order to draw up an inventory of their iconographic material, Émile Mâle is able to follow the same plan as Vincent de Beauvais in his *Speculum majus:* the two correspond point for point.

But this iconographic inventory bears on painting or sculpture and, of necessity, neglects architecture—which is not representative in the strict sense of the term. Architectural analysis, in fact, no longer brings in any consideration of subjects represented, or of content, but rather it works with forms and relations. This is the study to which Erwin Panofsky devoted his *Gothic Architecture and Scholasticism.*[37] He brought to light a structural homology (one valid even in their historical variations) between the construction principles of Gothic cathedrals and the structure of the *Summae* that were the required rhetorical form for works in which, starting in the twelfth century, the Church took stock of its wisdom—the form whose most famous example is provided in the *Summa theologica* by St. Thomas. The homology between these two ideological productions (contemporary but belonging to their own specific domains) can be found even in the detail of their respective structures, focusing on three essential points:

1. The Gothic cathedral and the scholastic *Summa* are two products of a synthetic spirit; they are bound to an identical systematic undertaking, to an identical ambition to sum up the assets human knowledge had acquired. Indeed, the thirteenth century, in a way that may remind us of Hegel, lived itself as a period of the completion of knowledge, as if its task were merely that of organizing an acquisition considered as definitive and very nearly complete. This aspect of a synthetic totalization can be seen in the very word *summa,* used by scholasticism to define its epistemological project. In regard to cathedrals, it appeared in the iconography this synthetic spirit welcomed onto the portals, capitals, and stained glass windows. Panofsky here is content with repeating Mâle's analyses: "The classic cathedral, in its imagery, seeks to embody the totality of Christian knowledge, theological, natural, and historical, by putting everything in its place and by suppressing whatever no longer found a place."[38]

2. Their internal structure is governed by homology: just as the *Summa* is organized so that the parts composing it and the subdivisions of these parts are laid out in relationship to each other according to a constant relationship, so does the organization of the volume of the cathedral obey a single principle: the ogival, ribbed vault (whereas the romanesque constructions combined ribbed vaults, groin vaults, barrel vaults, domes, etc.), a principle that will be found throughout the edifice, each time repeated according to proportions modeled on the homology of the whole.

3. Finally, both are organized hierarchically. They are composed of elements that are clearly distinct from each other, but this individuation must also imply their articulation with the other elements. With the result, for example, that the organization of the vault system can be completely deduced from a transverse section of one of the piers. Another example of this expressive articulation of the part with the whole is the relationship of the external aspect of the cathedral to its internal structure. The portal, or rather the Gothic facade, in fact, offers itself as a sort of plan (or cross section) of the totality of the edifice that it is intended to manifest, or externalize; just as, at the

beginning of a book, there is a table of contents or a "summary" to give one an idea ahead of time of what one is going to read. This example demonstrates very well what characterizes Gothic architecture: it is, like every other architecture, structured; but what is more, one might say it is structuralist, because it announces its own structure and exposes it in a context that gives this gesture a didactic intent not to be underestimated. The plan and the facade duplicate the structure.

This didactic intent is the same thing that brought the form of the *Summa* into scholastic practice. Panofsky demonstrates the transformations in the material presentation of texts that came to correspond to this concern with teaching, transformations that were so decisive that most of the features making up the idea of the book as we know it today came into existence with them. "We find it natural," he says, "that the major works of discursive knowledge, particularly philosophic systems and doctoral theses, are organized according to a scheme of division and subdivision that can be condensed into a table of contents or a summary. . . . Nonetheless, this type of systematic articulation was absolutely unknown before scholasticism." [39] The idea of the book, before it was made widespread by the printing press, was born at the same time as the cathedral; it was another version of the cathedral, different but profoundly homologous.

God's temple, God's book, the book of the world: the book and architecture are mutually supportive and foster such a monologic systematicity that, with one glance, it should be able to be grasped as a whole, concentrated entirely in the simultaneity of a facade or in a table of contents demonstrating the unity of its plan, outside of time, synchronically, in a space reduced to the order of the homogeneous, accomplishing the summation of everything in a single point, in a single thesis.

To make this homology between the structure of Gothic cathedrals and that of the *Summae* stand out Panofsky employs a process that bears looking at briefly. "It is necessary," he says, "to put the notional content of doctrine in parentheses and to concentrate our attention on its *modus operandi*, to borrow a term from the scholastics themselves." [40] The notional content, in fact, is found more in the iconographic material whose ground is the cathedral but which is not specifically architectural. Note that Panofsky justifies his method by means of a term borrowed from scholastic language itself. Thus, from architectural practice, he retains only the *formal* features of its method without bringing in the material and ideological content (the construction work proper, then the ornamentation, but also the religious intent) that it conveys; the *Summa* in the same way is seen as a form of didactic exposition, independent of the material on which it focuses. Now, this way of seeing the architect's work entirely from the formal point of view as the construction of a plan, or as a conception (as opposed to the realization), is no different from that of St. Thomas himself, for whom the architect is the man who "conceived the form of the edifice without himself manipulating the material." ("He is said to be wise in any order who considers the highest cause in that order. Thus in the order of building he who plans the form of the house is called wise and architect, in relation to the inferior laborers who trim the wood and make ready the stone: *As a wise architect I have laid foundations* [I Cor. 3:10]." *Summa theologica,* Question 1, Article 6.)[41] The architect is only concerned with the fundamentals, the foundation (*fundamentum* or *archè*), that is with the most elevated element: the form of the building and not the material conditions of its realization. Now this distinction between the formal conception and the material realization is in no way ideologically neutral. It is essential to the Thomist argument (not to say all of philosophy). Panofsky's structuralist method here is content with repeating scholastic concepts themselves, and specifically the scholastic concept of architecture.

Which is not a concept, but a metaphor. Or, to stay within Thomist vocabulary, an analogy (*similitudo*). Architecture is even one of the most frequent analogies to which the *Summa* has recourse to demonstrate Catholic doctrine. As just one example of the many times it appears, it serves to justify the hierarchy of all creatures in God's work. ("For just as an architect, without injustice, places stones of the same kind in different parts of a building not on account of any antecedent difference in the stones, but with a view to securing that perfection of the entire building, which could not be obtained except by the different positions of the stones, even so, God from the beginning, to secure perfection in the universe, has set therein creatures of various and unequal nature, according to His wisdom, and without injustice, since no diversity of merit is presupposed." Question 65, Article 2.)[42] St. Thomas also uses the architectural metaphor to illustrate the procession of divine persons, which must be conceived so as not to break the unity of the first principle, consequently, an internal procession: the divine persons are no more external to the first principle than the architect's art is external to the architect's concept. ("To proceed from a principle so as to be something outside and distinct from that principle is irreconcilable with the notion of a first principle, but an intimate and uniform procession by way of an intelligible act is included in the notion of the first principle were the builder the first principle. God, Who is the first principle of all things, may be compared to things created as the artificer to artificial things." Question 27, Article 1.)[43] Whence it is apparent that the architectural conception *does not leave* the spirit of the architect who does not become alienated in his works. There are multiple examples of such recourse to architecture. Let us mention just one final one pertaining to the existence of ideas, the necessity for whose existence St. Thomas demonstrates starting from the fact that the form or idea—"*Idea* enim graece, latine forma dicitur" (For the Greek word Ἰδέα is in Latin *forma*)—is the goal of all generation—"In all things not generated by chance, the form must be the end of any generation"—which implies that the agent of this generation already has in itself some analogy or resemblance ("similitudo") with this form. A resemblance in accord with natural being ("secundum esse naturale") such as that produced in mankind's engendering mankind, or fire engendering fire. Resemblance in accord with intelligible being ("secundum esse intelligible") such as is true of anything with intellect as its agent: "as in those that act by the intellect; and thus the likeness of a house pre-exists in the mind of the builder. And this may be called the idea of the house, since the builder intends to build his house like to the form conceived in his mind." (Question 15, Article 1.)[44] Consequently, the architect himself is caught up in the Thomist argument, where he occupies the position of the clearest analogy one can offer men of what God is.

The *Summa theologica* proposes to show, that is to make clear to reason, the dogmas of faith. Not to demonstrate them but to produce analogies that will make them comprehensible. The analogy, the essential component of its argument, puts an end to the conflict between reason and faith by assuring a continuity from the known to the unknown, from the creature's attributes to the being of God. No doubt these attributes are not in a one-to-one, univocal relationship in every case; God's justice is not the same as man's and God cannot be called an architect in the human sense of the term. He can, however, be called an architect or just, etc., because this nonunivocity is not equivocal for all that, and it is this relationship that the technical term *analogy* specifically designates.[45] And one of the most frequent analogies in the works of St. Thomas is architecture itself.

Architecture is, therefore, already caught up in the theological argument. Which makes it hard to conceive of it as simply parallel—as Panofsky's analysis would have it. Architecture is just one way of dealing with the relationship with God. Which, at a level no longer doctrinal, but historical and social, is confirmed by the function of the cathedrals themselves, which are analogies of Christian doctrine, serving to manifest it through material forms to the crowd of the faithful.

But we are still at a substantial distance from Bataille, who no more wrote *Summa theologica* than built a cathedral. The sums he produced were intended to subtract more than add. Subtracting, quite specifically, a cathedral: this initial *Notre-Dame de Rheims*.

Bataille reverses the roles.

The architect saw his superiority guaranteed in his power to outline plans, to make projects. *Cosa mentale:* the forms he conceives must guarantee the domination of idea over material. Execution has only to abide by his program, to submit to it until it disappears into it. The project by nature is destined to reproduce its form, to assure its own reproduction by overseeing the elimination of anything it has not foreseen, and the noninscription of whatever time might oppose to it. The future (the realized edifice) must conform to the present (the design of the plan). Time is eliminated.

L'Expérience intérieure (Inner Experience), the first volume of *Somme athéologigue,* is an autotransgressive book: it is not a book. It took too long to write for that. So long that one might say that time itself wrote it—is inscribed in it. Bataille wrote it with time, and in defiance of planning. He put time into it, in the literal sense. Which precludes our reading this book in any way other than in the space of textual heterogeneity outside the book. The texts composing it are not contemporary: no simultaneity ever existed among them. Their juxtaposition makes us read the gap making them different from the project that gave birth to them.

L'Expérience intérieure is no more than a string of prefaces indicating something foreign to the book that, perhaps, plays within the book, but only as something making fun of it. In one of these prefaces written, says Bataille, after the fact, with the intention of presenting the texts that were supposed to follow it, one can see a plan coming to light. But this plan, precisely, only comes to light as a memory, at the very moment in which it stopped being respected. "The opposition to the idea of planning—which plays an essential part in this book—is so necessary a part of me that, having written the detailed plan for this introduction, I am unable to stick with it."[46] So much for the plan.

So Bataille reverses the roles: neither time nor matter is the servant now, the plan is. One must make use of it in order to erase it: "With a plan that leaves the realm of planning."[47] He used time, time uses him to set itself free ("the plan is the prison").[48] Nothing that has anything to do with plans counts, because plans fall short of desire and suppress it. And, precisely, what attracts Bataille about Proustian "construction" is not the mastery with which the author of *A la recherche* succeeded in completing his plan; it is, on the contrary, the veiled destruction that never ceases to undermine it, swept along by the force of desire: "What gives Proust's lesson a privileged character is no doubt the rigor with which he reduces the object of his *search* to an *involuntary* find."[49] Writing is the plan frustrated on its own territory. It destroys the book, precludes its closing up (and what is left of a book that could not close up again? Its opening . . . of which it is least in possession). Precludes its developing along a homogeneous and continuous line. Writing lays out the place for discord at the very spot where architectures are faced with their disappearance.

Bataille: "Harmony, like the plan, casts time to the outside: Its principle is the repetition with which anything possible is perpetuated. Architecture, or sculpture, is the ideal and immobilizing harmony, guaranteeing that motifs, whose essence is the canceling of time, will last. It is from the plan, moreover, that art has borrowed repetition: the calm investing of time with a repeated theme."[50]

"Architecture": The Article

The first article that Bataille published in the *Documents* dictionary is devoted to architecture. It came out in May 1929 in the second issue of the review and consists of three paragraphs.

1. This is the first:

Architecture is the expression of the very soul of societies, just as human physiognomy is the expression of the individuals' souls. It is, however, particularly to the physiognomies of official personages (prelate, magistrates, admirals) that this comparison pertains. In fact it is only the ideal soul of society, that which has the authority to command and prohibit, that is expressed in architectural compositions properly speaking. Thus great monuments are erected like dikes, opposing the logic and majesty of authority against all disturbing elements: it is in the form of cathedral or palace that Church or State speaks to the multitudes and imposes silence upon them. It is, in fact, obvious that monuments inspire social prudence and often even real fear. The taking of the Bastille is symbolic of this state of things: it is hard to explain this crowd movement other than by the animosity of the people against the monuments that are their real masters.[51]

Set in place here is the structure of infinite regression best described as a mirror-trap, that is, a structure identifying in advance the object confronting it. Bataille starts with an expressive relationship that he transforms into an imperative relationship. Architecture begins by saying what society is (indicative mode), it expresses the soul of society and is, consequently, a simple sign of a transcendent reality that, for its part, would be what it is in its own behalf, independent of this image; but behind this descriptive neutrality there appears progressively an active intervention of the symbol in the very field that it expresses. Architecture, formerly the image of social order, now guarantees and even imposes this order. From being a simple symbol it has now become master. Architecture captures society in the trap of the image it offers, fixing it in the specular image it reflects back. Its locus is that of the imaginary understood at its most dictatorial, where the cement of faith confirms religions and kingdoms in their authority. "Society," says Freud "from then on is based on a common wrong, on a crime committed in common," but it covers up the site of the crime with discreet monuments to make it be forgotten. Architecture does not express the soul of societies but rather smothers it.

This smothering of social life under a stone monument is the constant theme of Bataille's earliest articles. In 1928 it appears in "L'Amérique disparue" (Extinct America), where it is integrated with a description of Inca civilization in Peru that contrasts its imperialist system of state control with the bloody madness of pre-Columbian Mexico—that is with the Aztecs. For Bataille the world of the Aztecs will remain the model of a society that does not repress the sacrifice that forms it. Ephemeral, at the height of glory and at the peak of its powers, this society neglected to put in place the institutional structures that would have secured its future, but, when the time came, offered itself as heedlessly as it sacrificed its victims to extinction and death when Cortez's army landed in Mexico. It presents the only image of a society based upon death and faithful to this basis to such an extent that it was somehow defenseless and died out. The pyramids it left behind were not used to cover up death but to display before the eyes of all people the spectacle of the death of the sacrificial victim. "Their knowledge of architecture," writes Bataille in the chapter of *La Part maudite* (The Accursed Share) devoted to them, "served them in the construction of pyramids on top of which they immolated human beings."[52] Architecture here is returned to the destructive interaction that its initial function was to interrupt. Inca imperialism, on the contrary, is a civilization of *hidden* death. Victims are strangled deep within the temples, whereas the Aztecs turned their sacrifice into a bloody spectacle. According to the law imposed by the death drive, tombs cover up death. Inca civilization is only an immense tomb, organized bureaucratically by civil servants in the state that remains "the most administrative and orderly ever formed by men."[53] Bataille describes it as a system of defense against death as the unforeseen itself, against its own unprogrammable otherness. No doubt one must connect the very small part, according to Bataille, that artistic activities occupy with the paralysis imposed on society by this defensive network: there is nothing brilliant about this drab world. Conversely, the architectural remains of Inca civilization stand out because of their considerable quantity, which makes them appear literally dominant—the cause and simultaneously the sign of this paralysis.

"Cuzco, the capital of the Inca empire, was situated on a high plateau at the foot of a sort of fortified acropolis. A massive, ponderous grandeur characterized this city. Tall houses built of huge stone blocks, with no outside windows, no ornament, and thatched roofs, made the streets seem somewhat sordid and sad. The temples overlooking the roofs were of an equally stark architecture. . . . Nothing managed to dispel the impression of mediocre brutality, and above all of stupefying uniformity."[54] There follows a description of the administrative apparatus that ends with these words: "Everything was planned in an existence where there was no air."

The question of the material and the structures of expression, therefore, is given political significance by Bataille. Architectural expression fulfills a "job" that certainly is not constitutive of society because, on the contrary, it obliterates that with which a society is constituted. Its job, rather, is to serve society to defend itself against that which is its basis only because of its threat. Society entrusts its desire to endure to architecture. Ideological production is inseparable from an entire system of oppression that it never merely reflects.

We have read "L'Amérique disparue" backward, starting from Aztec sacrifices and then returning to Inca architecture. But Bataille's text began with a description of the architectural system (and of all its ramifications for town planning and state control, etc.). The Aztecs come second, invalidating the first. Sacrifice can only be produced after accumulation.

The *first* period, uniting the cardinal and the ordinal, is the *time of one*, the time of unity. To this period belong all the systems that are monist, at least insofar as they seem destined to have a tendency to compose a homogeneous unit. Unity is an order: one must have it. The first period is therefore that of the logical—that is, monological—rule: only one voice must be heard. And precisely the *archè*— specifically the *archè* of architecture—expresses simultaneously commencement and commandment, it expresses the development to follow within the logic of unity. The defensive energy it deploys to eliminate otherness (which would introduce disorder) from what is to follow is what sustains it. Whence prelates, magistrates, admirals . . . It is better, for one (as opposed to the other), to begin with architecture; but it is also better for the other to begin with the architecture that it will destroy when it makes an appearance as the two that cannot be reduced to the logic of unity, as the two that does not answer its summons. Bataille's first text is this cathedral, *Notre-Dame de Rheims*, which the rest of his work will invalidate, reduce to zero, erase.—With which he will unsettle the three-part (Hegelian) logic that recuperated unity into a synthesis canceling the second instance, that of destruction (there is no unity of opposites, three does not unite one to two).[55] By the same token, in "L'Amérique disparue," transgression follows the description of the norm as *backlash* against its other.

The first article that Bataille published in *Documents* was governed by the same economy. Almost the only difference was that, whereas the destruction of architectural order by a disastrous disorder, in the case of the Incas and the Aztecs, only functioned inside the text

(since, historically, these two empires did not maintain any relationship, particularly not an antagonistic one), the Greeks and the Gauls
whose opposition is traced in this article, "Le Cheval académique"
(The Academic Horse), did actually confront each other. Moreover,
one should note that the Gauls' "barbarism" only operates in their
relations with "the" (Greek) civilization. Not in itself. Barbarism here
is defined only as that which eludes "systematic conquest,"[56] that
which they cannot successfully subjugate. There is more to it. The
article studies the deformation that a figure, that of the horse, under-
goes when the Gauls pick it up from the Greeks to decorate their
coins. That is, it only brings in barbarism as a disturbance in the academic expressive code. It is not, for example, a type of society that is
independent from civilization and specifically would be distinguished
from it by its lack of "culture." On the contrary, it is characterized by
a certain type of ideological expression (in this case figures traced on
coins), a phenomenon that, consequently, could not be more "cultural," but in a manner that *attacks* a social order rather than *defends*
it. Barbarism opposes to the defense system dominated by architecture and organized by it, to all these surrounding forms of expression—all the languages that confirm and reinforce each other—its
noncumulative *counterattacks*. The capital of the Incan empire was
dominated by an acropolis. Athens too. And the "architecture of the
Acropolis" joins "Platonic philosophy"[57] in the elaboration of this
social as well as philosophic hierarchy, by means of which idealism
paralyzes existence in the conservative reproduction of its own structures. Prelates, magistrates, admirals are back again, those levees
without which society would not last long, along with "everything that
can provide disciplined men with a consciousness of official worth
and authority."[58]

Imperialism, philosophy, mathematics, architecture, etc., compose
the system of petrification that waves of humanity, the crowd unleashed, will end up carrying off in its revolutionary uprising. "Up-
holding death's work," said Hegel, "requires the greatest strength of
all." But the relation between conceptualization and death is not the
same for Hegel as it is for Bataille. In the work of the mind, which
introduces divisions into the concrete, separating and abstracting,
Hegel sees the mechanics of death at work. Discursive knowledge is
thus the bearer of this "absolute power" of destruction that cancels
the sensuous concrete. It is not until later that science's abstract concepts, which initially liquefied the "sensuous being-there," become in

turn a unified whole of thought, "fixed and solidified," and are set rigidly into a system of abstract determinations. For Bataille, on the contrary, this petrification is the very essence of conceptualization (and here it is not yet necessary to make a distinction among the various sciences, mathematics, and others on the one hand, nor between science and philosophy): it is initially formalist. Conceptualization is *past* death, it is never death at work. Rather than bearing death and being preserved in it, as Hegel put it, conceptualization eludes death by keeping ahead of it, propelled by whatever in its terror over presentiments of the unknown takes refuge in the forms of sameness. Death fluidifies, it liquefies; mathematics paralyze. Architecture has not even a hint of motion. Its main purpose, as the article "Informe" said, is to provide what exists with a "formal coat, a mathematical overcoat": a form that veils the incompletion that death, in its *nakedness*, introduces into life. Concerning this point a paradoxical anthropomorphism of mathematics is outlined. In "Le Cheval académique" Bataille connects the harmonious proportions of human form (form being that which covers up nakedness) with "fright at formless and undefined things."[59]

2. The second paragraph of "Architecture" continues:

Moreover, each time that *architectural composition* turns up somewhere other than in monuments, whether it is in physiognomy, costume, music, or painting, one may infer a prevailing taste for divine or human *authority*. The great compositions of certain painters express the desire to force the spirit into an official ideal. The disappearance of academic construction in painting is, on the contrary, the opening of the gates to expression (hence even exaltation) of psychological processes that are the most incompatible with social stability. This, to a large extent, explains the strong reactions provoked for more than half a century by the progressive transformation of painting that, up until then, was characterized by a sort of hidden architectural skeleton.[60]

Throughout, this article is never concerned with architecture itself but with its expansion. Perhaps, apart from this expansion, architecture itself is nothing. It exists only to control and shape the entire social arena. It is constituted by this impulse propelling it to erect itself as the center and to organize all activities around itself.

Its ruling position, as old as Western culture (it made its appearance in Greece), according to Bataille, was weakened slightly more than a half-century ago by painting: Manet's *Olympia* dates from 1863, that is sixty-six years before these lines written by Bataille in 1929. Now we have dates. Already, in the preceding paragraph, there was mention of the taking of the Bastille as part of a system including modern painting in this critique of architecture. This contemporaneity is precisely what constitutes the locus of Bataille's writing.

Classical, academic painting, under the control of architecture, is limited to masking a skeleton. Painting conceals it, but the skeleton is its truth. In many primitive societies the skeleton marks the moment of the second death—a death that is completed, clean, and properly immutable: that which survives putrefaction and decomposition. The skeleton, as architectural, is the perfect example of an articulated whole. Modern painting rediscovers death in its first guise of the human figure's decomposition, an incomplete death, a mortal wound to form, a rotting corpse rather than a skeleton. Rotten painting.

In the same issue of *Documents* as the article "Architecture," Bataille had devoted a text to "L'Apocalypse de Saint-Sever," an eleventh-century illuminated manuscript. These miniature illustrations are the subject of his analysis. Note that in the eleventh century the great architectural impulse that was to be expressed by the construction of cathedrals was far from having been set in motion. This would take almost two more centuries. Also, we should note that the reading of these illustrations proposed by Bataille requires a foil to function (as the Greeks were the foil for the Gauls, the Incas for the Aztecs); here it is the illumination found on Rhenish manuscripts from the ninth and tenth centuries, miniatures in which he remarked a submission to an "architectural and stately mystique."[61] Commenting on the first illustration of the manuscript, he begins by demonstrating the freedom of this painting with regard to the system of architectural organization: "Although the two characters are inscribed within a frame, there is nothing *architectural* about this composition: the frame motif does not derive from the forms of monuments; the placement of figures inside the frame is itself free and not systematically organized, contrary to what happens in Rhenish manuscripts where the characters that are inscribed are reduced to the role of central elements of a monumental composition, a sort of arcade supported by two columns."[62]

Already, therefore, in the eleventh century, painting had transgressed architectural law. The article "Architecture" that traces this emancipation to the middle of the nineteenth century is contradicted in the very issue in which it appears. This chronological indecision formulates the problem of Bataille's reading of history, and at the same time the problem of the relations between transgression and history. (All the more because Bataille does not use these illustrations as an utterly isolated example; he integrates them into a contemporary corpus in which other forms of expression are encountered, such as "popular occasional literature," the *chansons de geste* [he cites the *Chanson de Vuillaume*] or poem-sermons in the common language.[63] Nor should one forget the "Fatrasies" of the twelfth century that he published in 1926 in *La Révolution surréaliste*.) But there is also the problem of something one could define as the geographical signifier in his text. Bataille, in effect, notes that the painter to whom the illustrations of the Saint-Sever manuscript are attributed, a certain Stephanus Garsia, "even if he was French by blood, belonged to Spain by his painting" (Saint-Sever is in the southwest of France, on the banks of the Adour river).[64] This is the second marker of a Spanish thematics (we have already had the bullfight in *Histoire de l'oeil*) that is to reappear on numerous occasions: from *Le Bleu du ciel* (Blue of Noon) right through the volume he edited on *L'Espagne libre* in 1945, from his evocations of Don Juan to the article on Cervantès's tragedy *Numance* and later on Goya. Spain is the locus of present death, the country of death agony. A sort of internal transgression of the laws of European geography.

3. These problems are taken up in the final paragraph of the article:

It is obvious, moreover, that mathematical organization imposed on stone is none other than the completion of an evolution of earthly forms, whose meaning is given, in the biological order, by the passage of the simian to the human form, the latter already presenting all the elements of architecture. In morphological progress men apparently represent only an intermediate stage between monkeys and great edifices. Forms have become more and more static, more and more dominant. The human order from the beginning is, just as easily, bound up with architectural order, which is no more than its development. And if one attacks architecture, whose monumental productions are at present the real masters of the world, grouping servile multitudes in their shadows, imposing admiration and astonishment, order and constraint, one is, as it were, attacking man. One whole earthly activity at present, doubtless the one that is most brilliant in the intellectual order, demonstrates, moreover, just such a tendency, denouncing the inadequacy of human predominance: thus, strange as it may seem when concerning a creature as elegant as the human being, a way opens up—indicated by painters—in the direction of bestial monstrosity; as if there were no other possibility of escaping the architectural chain gang.[65]

History tends to be thought of in terms of progress, in the perspective of a completion that provides meaning for it. The completion of history by man, the completion of man by history. History thought of as transitory, as historical in itself, because it must end, and this end will occur when man will have put his mark on the entire universe, when he will have appropriated it for himself, will have humanized it, and when every trace of inadequacy, of the initial lack of connection between the universe and himself, will have disappeared.

Alongside this rational account of history Bataille endeavors to produce another version suspending it, that of transgression. Despite the fact that here it is the transgression of history, transgression does not escape history. It is not thinkable in categories of progress, but even so it is not nonhistorical. It is seen through rupture-events whose discontinuous punctuation imposes suspense upon the continuous progression of a one-way track. During antiquity, therefore, as well as during the Middle Ages. Even at the origins of history. History, which is in this sense unfailingly theological, develops as an accumulation of masks to cover death, as a tomb that is always being reinforced. Bataille requires that one think of the historical nature of present death and not that of hidden death; that one think of that which overruns the defenses of history.

And yet the Aztecs did not threaten the Incan empire anywhere except in Bataille's text; and the Gauls remained outside of Greek conquest, even if they did come around to disturb them with their forays, etc. Whereas with the modern proletariat and its uprisings, as well as with the scandals provoked by contemporary art, it seems that law and transgression are in closer quarters and dispute the same territory.

Connecting the human form and architecture is not exclusively Bataille's idea. It appears already in Vitruvius, when he found the proportions of contemporary types of humanity in the different orders of Greek architecture. He, however (and everyone after him), used this metaphor to give life to the stone, to rediscover the caryatid in the column (see Poussin's letter to Chanteloup: "The beautiful girls you saw at Nîmes were no more delightful to your spirit, I tell myself, than the beautiful columns of the Maison Carrée, given that the latter

are only old copies of the former").[66] Bataille makes this a demonstra-
tion of the opposite, a petrification of the organism that is reduced in
advance to its skeleton. With man, the dialectic of forms that constitutes natural history approaches a harmonious stability, an immobility
that architecture will have little to do to bring to completion. From
human body to monument all that disappears is that which was per-
ishable, which remained in time's power: flesh that rots and its transitory colors. All that then remains is the skeleton, the structure.
Architecture retains of man only what death has no hold on.

Bataille will always define painting as the defacement of the human
figure, the defacement that constitutes man, in which he constitutes
himself as man. In contrast to architecture, painting does not ask man
to recognize himself in the mirror-trap it holds out to him; painting
confronts him with an image where he cannot find himself. Man produces himself by refusing his image, in refusing to be reproduced.

Reproduction, on the contrary, defines architecture. Nietzsche's
saying in *The Gay Science*, "Ich liebe die Unwissenheit um die Zu-
kunft" (I like ignorance concerning the future), could define the experience of historicity for Bataille, who quoted him on numerous
occasions.[67] He gives anguish political significance. Anguish is profoundly historical, but its historical nature is not progressive, it is revolutionary. In contrast with the "old geometric conception of the
future"[68] (Hegelian-Marxist for example) that would like to have assurances in advance through science about the future, without run-
ning any risk. History is lived when one does not know how it will
come out. Reducing the future to no more than the reproduction of
present, constructing the future the way the architect oversees a project, is to put the formal "mathematical overcoat" on it that stops time.
The revolutionary movement liberates the future from the prisons of
science. It faces it head on in its heterogeneity, as something unknown. Bataille speaks rarely of political *action,* but frequently of revolutionary *agitation.* The revolution destroys the authorities and
imaginary dictatorships that work only because they tap the support
of some faith. Including the authority of science.

"Man is seen as a bureaucratic-looking prison."[69] Architecture
functions as the fantasy that man identifies with to escape his desire
(to escape it is to control it). Man is confined: *conformed* within himself.
Nothing of him escapes the group's encoding synthesis, whose enclosure he himself guarantees. Because he, in fact, believes in his prison.

Shortly before July 14, 1789, the Marquis de Sade who was imprisoned at the Bastille had screamed and shouted so loudly that he claimed his cries had caused the popular uprising that was to destroy his prison before going on to decapitate the king. That was more than half a century before Manet's *Olympia*. And yet these two events mark a space that Bataille requires us to think of as contemporary. They shake up the period of edifying submissiveness. This is the space his writing will describe, working to elude faith-traps.

The critique of architecture will be accomplished through a polyphonic deconstruction, the result of intertextual play, of a dialogue of multiple writings and signifying practices, insofar as this play and this dialogue produce history: a history made up no longer of succession and the engendering of synchronic homologies, but on the contrary—breaking the seal on all synchrony—a history made up of the noncontemporaneity (both internal and external) of systems.[70]

The Labyrinth, The Pyramid, and the Labyrinth

After all, did not Icarus fall because he forgot the other *element?*
G. Picon, *"La Chute d'Icare" de Picasso* (Geneva: Skira, 1971)

The Labyrinth and the Pyramid

All of existence, as far as men are concerned, is specifically bound up with language, whose terms decide each individual's vision of it. Each person can imagine his total existence, even for his own eyes, only by means of words. Words rise up in his head bearing all their multitude of human or suprahuman existences in relation *to which his personal existence exists. The individual being is, therefore, only something mediated by words that can present a being only arbitrarily as an "autonomous being," though very profoundly as a "related being." It is only necessary to track for a little while the routes repeatedly taken by words to discover the disconcerting sight of a human being's labyrinthine structure.*
Bataille, "Le Labyrinthe"

The legend of Dedalus representing the labyrinth as a human creation must be forgotten. No man (especially not an architect), no men ever created it. The labyrinth has no inventor, no author, it has no father. The father question is a labyrinth—Dedalian already. But it is not simply a product of nature either, despite the diverse organo-telluric connotations that would connect it with Old Mole's tunnels, with the underground networks of chambers and corridors of caves (like Lascaux), with the "world of the womb," with the "infernal and maternal world of the depths of the earth." [1]

That would be too easy. Neither father's work nor maternal womb (neither human nor natural), the labyrinth is basically the space where oppositions disintegrate and grow complicated, where diacritical couples are unbalanced and perverted, etc., where the system upon which linguistic function is based disintegrates, but somehow disintegrates by itself, having jammed its own works.

The labyrinth we discuss cannot be described. Mapping is out of the question. Or, if it is described, it will be like the trajectory described by a mobile; not described as an object but as a traversal. The labyrinth is the traversal described by Bataille's writing to the precise extent that this writing did not stop describing itself (de-inscribing itself), that is picking up on itself and starting over, losing itself and reproducing itself in a movement one could call self-referential, if it were not simultaneously the loss of self and of referent. Writing that does not refer back to self, that does not fold back on self, but continually strays from the straight, expected route. The labyrinth, therefore, is not an object, not a referent. It does not have a transcendence that would permit one to explore it. Wanting to explore the labyrinth only confirms this further: there is no getting around it. But neither the category of subjectivity nor the category of objectivity can exist in this space, which, having made them unsound, nevertheless has no replacement to offer. Distance like proximity, separation like adhesion remain undecidable there. In this sense one is never either inside or outside the labyrinth—a space (perhaps that is already too much to say) that would be constituted by none other than this very anxiety, which is, however, incurably undecidable: am I inside or outside?

This then is the labyrinth, through which this study "on" Bataille initially began, and which precluded this being simply a study on Bataille that would begin with it (the labyrinth). Because the question of beginning is already a labyrinth itself where one gets lost by asking. Because it is impossible to follow Bataille in "his" labyrinth: one cannot adjust one's gait to that of any guide in labyrinthine space; one only goes there alone; one enters it at the same time one enters a certain solitude. Inside the labyrinth, on the contrary, one must confront the absence of Bataille, an equivocal absence that refers to Bataille only as a lost object. The labyrinth is not safe space, but the disoriented space of someone who has lost his way, whether he has had the good fortune to transform the steps he is taking into a dance,

or more banally has let spatial intoxication lead him astray: the labyrinth is drunken space. N. B.: The drunkenness is not without vertigo; drunken words have meaning no more than the drunken man
has balance. The axes of orientation (up/down, left/right, back/forth)
are astray. The inner ear returns to the level of immaturity associated
with infancy: upon these bodily passages, referred to as labyrinth,
orientation and disorientation depend. The key to the labyrinth, if
there is one, is a drunkenness with Galilean cosmic implications:
"What did we do [asks Nietzsche's madman] when we detached this
world from its sun? Where is it going now? Where are we going? Far
from all the suns? Are we not just endlessly falling? Backward, side-
ways, forward, in every direction? Is there still an up and a down?
Are we not being borne aimlessly into an endless void?" Here,
vomiting.

The labyrinth both is and is not our Ariadne's thread: rather, here
we must think of Ariadne's thread as itself weaving the labyrinth.
What with all its crisscrossing back and forth, it ends up becoming a
veritable Gordian knot or, if you will, a shirt of Nessus—that is, cloth
that only covers a body by adhering to it, clothing and nakedness
identical, in the same place. We must, therefore, think of Ariadne's
thread and the labyrinth as identical. The labyrinth will be our Ariadne's thread, losing us as well as Bataille inside and outside Bataille.

Bataille offers the labyrinth and Ariadne's thread both at the same
time. "These notes," he wrote in *Le Coupable*, "connect me with my
fellow creatures like an Ariadne's thread."[2] The text, with the written
thread of its lines, would allow one to escape from the labyrinth, or
at least let one locate oneself in it, or follow Bataille in it: let one enter
it without risk of getting lost. Because it is already written, it would
no longer be a labyrinth: Ariadne's thread, cuttable and "culpable"[3]
though it may be, is not cut, communication is maintained—there are
kindred souls at the end of the line. But what if communication was
itself the labyrinth? What if writing expressed nothing other than
loss? What if the act of writing was, precisely, losing the thread? In
"his" labyrinth, moreover, Bataille was not alone. He too was following someone who had left him an Ariadne's thread so he would get
lost. Bataille followed Nietzsche, who, as he said, "never lost that Ariadne's thread *of being always aimless.*"[4]

Labyrinthine space is space where the future appears only in the
threatening and unrepresentable guise of the unknown; that is why

it is, quite literally, outlined (delineated and described) by writing insofar as writing plays precariously with the "old geometric conception of the future." One can no longer, therefore, see where one is going: labyrinthine night was produced by the irruption of the pineal eye. "Delight in blindness," as Nietzsche said, giving this title to aphorism 287 in *The Gay Science:* " 'My thoughts,' said the wanderer to his shadow, 'should show me where I am: not reveal to me where I am going. I love ignorance of the future and do not want to succumb to impatience or to savoring beforehand what is promised.' " (Bataille uses a stronger translation—"ignorance *that touches on* the future"[5]— which indicates how one must "feel one's way" through a labyrinth and also that the relationship to the future does not enter into a theoretical, optical perspective, cannot be taken as a horizon. Delight in blindness = Gaia scienza.)

Bataille talked about the labyrinth. He even used the word as title for one of his texts. However, the labyrinth is not merely a word, it is especially not the "key" word (the one that would let us in on Bataille, or, to put it another way, one that lets us get to the end of this). It is not a theme either. It cannot be isolated.[6] The labyrinth does not hold still, but because of its unbounded nature breaks open lexical prisons, prevents any word from finding a resting place ever, from resting in some arrested meaning, forces them into metamorphoses where their meaning is lost, or at least put at risk. It introduces the action of schizogenesis into lexical space, multiplying meanings by inverting and splitting them: it makes words drunk.

Bataille reverses the traditional metaphorical sense of the labyrinth that generally links it with the desire to get out. Just as philosophy allows one to leave Plato's cave, the labyrinth (from Bacon to Leibniz)[7] is where those without access to the thread of knowledge are condemned to lose their way. Knowledge always takes the form of something to end all error and errantry. Bataille, on the contrary, denounces ("Icarian") solutions. Above all, he denounces the wish that it lead somewhere, have a solution (whether a scientific one, praising the merits of the "ancient geometric conception of the future," or an artistic-utopian one, dreaming of escape), because the only result of this wish is that, far from being a real exit from the labyrinth, it transforms labyrinth into prison. To will the future (and not to desire it), to submit it to planning and projects, to wish to construct it, is to lock oneself into a devalorized present that is airless and unlivable. "The project," according to Bataille, "is the prison."[8] To want to get out of the labyrinth, making this into a project, is to close it, to close oneself inside it.

One never *is* inside the labyrinth, because, unable to leave it, unable to grasp it with a single glance, one never *knows* if one is inside. We must describe as a labyrinth that unsurmountably ambiguous, spatial structure where one never knows whether one is being expelled or enclosed, a space composed uniquely of openings, where one never knows whether they open to the inside or the outside, whether they are for leaving or entering. The same structure characterizes language, whose words enclose me while I use them, nonetheless, to transgress the closure they build: "Denying the order in which a coherent discourse encloses me, still, within me it is the coherence of discourse that denies it."[9]

The structure of the labyrinth tests the pertinence of the diacritical couple man/animal, shaking rather than steadying it as does the "closed" discourse of science. Moreover the labyrinth is the basis of a myth whose stakes are the same. Theseus, destined to be king of Athens, kills the Minotaur: Athens is born by freeing itself from its archaic past (Crete), symbolized by this hybrid, simultaneously man and bull—the Minotaur. Deep within the labyrinth at Lascaux, in the most famous of its wall paintings, Bataille saw a minotauromachy: a man lies, dead on the ground, and beside him is the animal. *Les Larmes d'Éros* describes the bison as "a sort of minotaur," and connects the question of the difference between animal and man with the question of painting, to the extent that, for man, painting would be the refusal of reproduction and the assertion of nonspecific difference with himself. Minotauromachy—posited as a myth of the birth (death) of man and the birth of painting, breaking with the classical tradition that, since Alberti, had claimed that the assertion of human form expressed in the Narcissus myth was the original pictorial urge. Man (and Athenian humanism) asserted himself by denying all participation in animality (Oedipus also leaves childhood and gains his father's throne by killing another hybrid—the Sphinx). Bataille reverses the traditional interpretation of the myth there as well: just as he does not want to leave the labyrinth (on the contrary, he wants to set it up as the locus of an *excess without issue*), the desire he brings into play is not the desire to return, or to get out, but specifically the Minotaur's desire, consequently the desire to set free man's animality, to rediscover the monstrous metamorphoses repressed by the prison of projects. (Recall that Bataille proposed the title *Minotaure* to Tériade for the review he started in 1933.) In the heart of the labyrinth, Bataille-Theseus has no thought of return, he is not worried about getting out, he anxiously desires the Minotaur. When this desired contact occurs he will have to be metamorphosed into his absence (vanish, lost in it, winner or loser), into this animality where the human being absents himself when he no longer respects human forms or the human form; for example when, during a sacrificial battle that evokes bullfighting (tauromachy/minotauromachy), his triumph over the animal-victim comes only after he has identified with it.

We got into Bataille's labyrinth, therefore, through the labyrinth one neither enters or leaves. Door, arch. Madame Edwarda vanished beneath just such a doorway; one never knows in which direction one is crossing it. Above its pediment let us inscribe the two faces of Janus, god of prefaces. Let us follow the ancient ritual of the *praefatio: Jovi sunt summa, Janu sunt prima* (the highest for Jupiter, the first ones for Janus). Let us invoke (because this is where we first began) the god whose temple doors are opened as a sign of battle: to mark the entry into war.[10]

Our invocation will recall also, in this place, that Janus was simultaneously the god who presided over beginnings and the one who watched over passages. Etymology traces the name's derivation from the stem *ia* which is connected to the root *ei-* (to go), whence the notion of passage. The same root, in another Indo-European language, Irish, gives *ya-ti*, which is found in the Gallic *Ritu-* (see *Ritumagos* [Riom], which means the fording- or passage-field in place names such as Riom-ès-Montagnes).

Numismatists invoke Janus as well. According to popular tradition Janus was the first king of Latium, and, because he offered hospitality to Saturn, the god thanked him by teaching him agriculture, the building of boats, and also how to make coins (Plutarch, *Numa Pompilius,* 19).

Janus is also the *Diuum Deus,* or the *Divinus Deus.*

The month of January is consecrated to him. First month of the year, it is above all the new year itself, the anniversing moment that belongs simultaneously to the old year, whose annulus now closes, and to the new, annual, annular opening. A moment escaping temporal order, suspending this order with no assurances that the future will reconfirm it—here Janus rules over carnival disorders. A nocturnal moment piercing the yearly ring, it is also the "solar ring" of *L'Anus solaire*, because Janus has come to be the patron not only of the new year, but of the whole year, and consequently of time (he has been identified with Saturn and with Kronos-Chronos, Uranus's castrating son).

And finally (although Latinists today reject this assimilation) we will invoke him here by the name Bataille gave him, Dianus.

Frazer's *Golden Bough* opens with the invocation of Dianus, who was priest at the temple of Diana in the woods at Nemi. This temple was established by Orestes (the first Dianus according to the legend), whose flight led him finally to the banks of Lake Nemi, in the Alban hills (Bataille went there in May 1934). Dianus served as Frazer's model for his theory of primitive kingship, in which Bataille found considerable supporting evidence for his own concept of sovereignty. In fact, the priest at the temple of Diana bore the title *Rex Nemorensis,* king of the woods. The mocking title (this king ruled no one) gave him no power; it was given to the criminal who, having eluded Roman justice, had found refuge in this temple by forcibly seizing the sacred, golden bough from the present king and killing him in single combat. This king is, therefore, by definition a criminal (twice criminal, at the very least, owing his kingship to the second crime). But his rule is limited to an agonized waiting for the next criminal who will, in turn, come to seize the golden bough: it is limited to waiting for death.

Bataille took the pseudonym Dianus when he published the first section of *Le Coupable,* "L'Amitié," in the review *Mesures.* When this text appeared (although it was still possible that it would not come out because the Abbeville press that printed the review had been bombed by the Germans), Bataille wrote this note from Riom-ès-Montagnes, on June 1, 1940: "All that is left for me is to die. I have my reasons and it seems useless to give them. They are as enclosed and complicated as my life. I do not curse life at all." [11] This, to my knowledge, is the only text in which Bataille adopts a suicidal tone—certainly not unrelated to the chosen pseudonym.

Bataille at first wanted to publish "L'Amitié" anonymously. He proposed to Paulhan, the director of *Mesures,* a collection of notes from a book he was preparing "on the relations between the erotic and the mystical," and asked that the author's name not be mentioned if they were published. "Perhaps these texts are of interest at *Mesures*? But I would not want them published under my name. If they were to appear, it would be easy, I suppose, to publish them anonymously (they are taken from a book that I would not like to have published during my lifetime). I would even rather my name not be mentioned in conversations concerning what I am sending you today" (February 26, 1940). Both the notes and the principle of anonymity were accepted. On March 29 Bataille returned the proofs and asked Paulhan to change the way they were to appear: "I am sending you the proofs. I have decided that, rather than leave the text anonymous, I will use a pseudonym. If you see no difficulty with this we could publish these pages under the name Dianus."

In *Le Coupable* "L'Amitié" begins with a date, the date of the Second World War: "The date on which I am beginning to write (September 5, 1939) is no coincidence." It ends with this aphorism: "These notes bind me like Ariadne's thread to those who are like me and all else seems to me futile. . . . I would like for them to be published after my death, but perhaps I will live a rather long time, and they will be published during my lifetime.

"THE ONE NAMED DIANUS WROTE THESE NOTES AND DIED."

Labyrinthine structure imposes a simultaneous ban on the immanence of the ego and on the transcendence of the other. It separates me from myself without turning me loose. This ambiguity is due to the loss of the Archimedean point that used to provide orientation and direction. Labyrinthine structure is acephalous: antihierarchical (anarchic); one never moves ahead, rather one loses one's head there. Losing one's head opens prisons. "Man has escaped his head as the convict escapes from prison." [12] Labyrinthine discourse is decapitated discourse, uttered by the absence of a head.

A meditation on the drawing of "Acéphale," André Masson's headless man. This image of a human figure without a head rejects both identification and adoration; it is neither immanent nor transcendent, neither man nor god. It is an alteration of the human form that eludes every identification and draws the meditating subject into a labyrinth where he becomes lost, that is, he metamorphoses, is transformed in turn, rediscovers himself only as other, monster, Minotaur himself. "It is not me but it is more myself than myself," says Bataille of the "Headless Man." "His guts are the maze in which he has become lost himself, losing me with him, and where I rediscover myself being him, that is—monster." [13]

I am endlessly separated from myself by the labyrinth structuring me according to a law of intestinal exteriority (an interiority that is excluded, an exteriority that is included): the labyrinth is never simply *the* labyrinth.

Human beings have a labyrinthine structure, the labyrinth is the structure of existence because existence is unthinkable without language ("man existing entirely through language"),[14] that is, it could not take place without the mediation of words ("words, their mazes . . .").[15] Language makes man into a relationship to, an opening to; it prohibits his withdrawing into utopian self-presence, cuts off his retreat toward closure. It dispossesses him of his origins. Language is the *practical* negation of solipsism. The impossibility of finding a basis within oneself. Like a negative umbilical cord (one that would attach a person not to the origin but to the absence of origin), an umbilical lack that must be produced through writing, and in writing, until death comes to cut the thread.

This is the first version of the labyrinth, the one describing the nontranscendence of words as the impossibility of being cut off from words, and as the destiny of a subject who is not self-immanent.

There is a second version, also bound up with language.

It is obvious that the world is purely parodic, that is, that everything we look at is the parody of another, or even the same thing but in a form that is deceptive. Ever since phrases have *circulated* in brains absorbed in thought, a total identification has been produced, since each phrase connects one thing to another by means of *copulas;* and it would all be visibly connected if one could discover in a single glance the line, in all its entirety, left by an Ariadne's thread, leading thought through its own labyrinth.[16]

This second version of the labyrinth in effect expresses the collapsing action, the movement of parodic dissolution of beings and words swept along by their own inadequacy. We will give this process the name of labyrinthine copulation.

Hence: *The labyrinth and the pyramid* . . . second act: or the war between copula and substance. Language is made up of vocabulary, a lexical base composed of different words each of which has a "proper" meaning attached to it. It does not function, however, that is it does not speak and produce phrases, unless the words are assembled in a series put together around some verb form. And this is always, in a more or less derivative manner, based on the verb that is *the* verb: to be. (We should recall here, with Michel Foucault, that for classical grammarians if, on the one hand, "the verb is the indispensable condition for all discourse," if the threshold of language "is the point at which the verb makes its appearance," on the other hand, "the entire verbal species can be reduced to the single one that signifies: to be. In reality, there is only one verb, the verb to be, compounded, for all other verb forms, with attributes: I sing = I am + singing.")[17] This verb has no meaning but only a function, which is to allow meaning to be produced by an interplay of attribution, by relating words to each other. But it is not all so simple. To be is, no doubt, a verb, even *the* verb, and in this sense it is sufficiently distinguished from substantives as to be able—almost—to be outside of vocabulary, outside the lexicon, and to be a word empty of meaning: having only a syntactic function. However, this function as a copula is in itself already charged with a meaning that, although undetermined, is nonetheless determinant for the entire language it allows to function. Foucault points out that for classical grammarians this reduction of every aspect of verbal function to forms of the verb to be was meant to attribute to the verbal form the representative function of language. In other words, the copulative function of the verb to be is caught up in a system of language or thought that superimposes a semantic value on it: the verbal form that, precisely, could be defined as nonsubstantive becomes substantive in turn and *being* becomes the horizon of meaning. That which had no meaning becomes the sign of the transcendental signified.

Therefore, one must distinguish between two functions of the verb to be: one that is strictly verbal, its *logico-grammatical function* as a copula, which is limited to allowing attributive interplay; the other its *lexical function*, in which the verb form would only represent a fall from the eminence of a substantive position. These two uses of to be are in constant rivalry: a systematic and lexical reading that, by analogy, has words participate in the "last word," beyond words (a pyramidal reading); and a metonymic reading where it is the interplay of combinations, agreements, and splits that is brought to light (a labyrinthine reading). "Although it has always been disturbed and tormented from within," writes Jacques Derrida, "the fusion of the grammatical and lexical functions of 'to be' has, no doubt, an essential relationship with the history of metaphysics and with all of its coordinates in the West."[18]

First of all (first of all?), copulation is the name of a sexual activity connected to the reproduction of sexual beings, that is, animal species who are submitted to sexual difference. In this sense it is possible to say that copulation is the *subject* of erotic novels, specifically Bataille's erotic novels. But eroticism and literature are connected by implications that go infinitely beyond this simple naming of sexual activity in a genre of the novel that would, otherwise, remain minor. One must, in fact, understand literature itself, the practice of writing and reading initiated by Bataille, as an erotic practice: henceforth there could no longer be an erotic literature, literature and eroticism being now inseparable and utterly coextensive. Everything Bataille develops surrounding the theme of communication is intended to establish precisely this "communication" between eroticism and literature. An intransitive communication, this is not the communication of a message, but the rupture of individual limits enclosing those beings it brings into play, and even, if need be, the implied destruction of any message. For Bataille, communication does not submit to the structure imposed on it by linguists (sender, receiver, message, etc.); it destroys this structure. It is never the transmission of a message existing independently, as a signified, between two subjects whose identity remains intact and untouched by the process: communication is loss of self in the absence of message on both sides, in the nonsense that is the absence of a transcendental signified. Eroticism and literature are two names for the experience of communication that Bataille proposes: communication whose decisive character, perhaps, stems from the fact that it is produced less by a fusion of the beings brought into play by it, than according to an opposite strategy whose principle, irreducible element is the separation of these beings. It operates less by attraction than by repulsion (in romantic terms, what is called "allure" marking the opposite inductors of repulsion): "the theme of reciprocal repulsion focused on sexual parts is present as a mediator, like a catalyst increasing the power of the communication."[19] Communication is nothing other than this operation of repulsion, merely the production of repulsion as one of the terms of attraction. The matrix of communication is the *principle of inadequacy* that Bataille formulated in these terms: "Man is what he lacks." Consequently, it is the production of this lack (not its suppression) that is the issue. If a being exists only through communication, then communication itself is nothing if not the sacrifice of a being: "I propose to acknowledge as law that human beings are never united with each other except through tears or wounds, an idea that has a certain logical force in its favor." [20]

Writing and copulation are bound up with a problematic of traces that Bataille generally introduces through the counterexample of the reproduction of asexual beings.[21] Asexual beings, in fact, reproduce themselves by scissiparity; they multiply by dividing. The absence of sexual difference, consequently, implies the exact identity (the concomitance) between the appearance of the products of the operation on the one hand and the death of the initial individual on the other—this individual disappearing completely without leaving the least trace behind him, with nothing remaining. Between the products' appearance and the disappearance of the parent there is no room for the least difference, or for the least distance. The phenomenon of scissiparity thus would realize the unity of eroticism and death if, precisely, the fact that sex does not intervene in the process did not make it impossible to speak of eroticism. There is no eroticism without copulation (no more than there is copulation without sexual difference), but the truth of eroticism is the unity of copulation and death: copulation as orgasm—the little death. But copulation, precisely, is not death. Which is why Bataille always brings the model of scissiparity as a governing fiction into copulation (and does it, precisely, through *writing*). An anti-Platonic governing fiction that is antisymbolic: *sumbolon* designates the reunion of two parts calling for and espousing each other; scissiparity describes the division, the severing of an organic whole.

Copulation, therefore, is not death; it is what makes the difference between reproduction and extinction. The birth of children is not the death of the parents (though sometimes the mother's death, it is never the father's). Copulation entails a delay in the parents' extinction, which is bound up with a delay in the child's appearance, which is not contemporary with copulation: a period of gestation is required. This system of delays that sex produces is propagated right up to the individual's death, which is somehow not contemporary with itself, that is, not contemporary with the extinction of an individual, who, unlike an asexual being, leaves remains at death; what remains of the departed is the corpse. The entire system of traces is, therefore, coextensive with this series of interlocking delays, starting from the differed (or parodic) identity between copulation and death, between the little—or orgasmic—death and death. The trace is this *little* difference that literature (as an activity—or game—that could thus be defined as a perverse operation of the trace) will go to great lengths to dispose of in turn by guaranteeing the return of scissiparity inside copulation's space.

More precisely, we must make a distinction here between eroticism and sexuality—a distinction that is no less important than that between copulation and scissiparity. Eroticism is the presence in sexual reproduction (insofar as it produces traces) of its other, scissiparity (insofar as it implies the absence or, here, the obliteration of the trace). Life approved even in death. Obliteration of the trace or loss within the trace comes down to the same thing. It is not a question of a regressive return to scissiparity (which would be illusory), but rather a return *of* scissiparity—its return into the midst of complex beings, sexual organisms, whereas simple scissiparity happens in simple beings—single-cell organisms. A return, therefore, of scissiparity into composition, which henceforth becomes complexity—where one become lost: the labyrinth is the place of scissiparity's return into sexuality.

There is no way of choosing. And yet the labyrinth is a place of violent oppositions. It is the locus of the debate between the copula and substance. Between lexical and syntactic functions. A debate in which sense is always threatened but nonsense is never triumphant. Where substantives try to entrap being with their servility whereas the copula disseminates its sacrificial movement throughout the lexical system. This is an asymmetrical struggle, however, because only one of the two antagonists—substance—expects it to lead anywhere, giving it *sense and direction*. And, thanks to this expectation, substance will have the upper hand: going up, in fact, is how to escape the labyrinth. Icarus, seduced by Apollo's sunny invitation, took off—up.

Substance, thus, scores a few points and firmly attaches lexical function to the copula, by ennobling it with the title supreme being: henceforth sentences will be organized around it and clauses subordinated to it. Being as copula kept play alive; being as substance, from the top of its pyramid, stops it dead by a network of concentric subordinations (grammatical, ontological, ideological, logical, social, etc.). By coming to terms with substance, the copula ends up providing the terms and structure of being. Being is set up as substance, erected metaphorically to assert, through ontological analogy, one sense, one direction, one meaning. It becomes the key to the labyrinth, a key that transforms the labyrinth into a pyramid. The pyramid stands out. Clearly, decisively. It rises above confusion, towers above it. It is an edifying monument, one that turns meaning into a one-way stream.

That this pyramidal elevation would be the way out of the labyrinth was implicit in the labyrinth itself, insofar as it is constituted by the conflict between substance and copula—an asymmetrical conflict since one of its terms (and only one), substance, expected something to come of it (giving it some sense by risking one in it). Meaning is already at work in the labyrinth. Even if the copula rejects it. Because to reject it is only to postpone it, putting it off until later, this "until later" that is the very formula for meaning: substance could have hoped for nothing better. The very essence of meaning is to be put off until later. This extension of time transforms the to-fail-to-be that distinguished the copula into to-have-to-be. The substantial has itself acknowledged and the sovereign copula *mastered* there (exchanges its sovereignty for mastery) by lexical servility. Being that is put off until later subjects itself to the future (which is, from then on, its meaning) and to concerns about guaranteeing this future. The nonpresence of being is sublimated as the presence-to-come of a being freed from the game of time, a being made divine and eternal. The nonpresence of the being as copula can be read as a not-yet-present, and therefore as "putting off existence until later,"[22] which is the definition of work, nonplay, thus preparing its being defeated by sense-as-work.

And so now we are out of the labyrinth whose key, door, solution, whose term of excess was being. Unless there is a difference between repressing the labyrinth through sublimation, as it happens with the substantification of being, and finding one's way out; unless sublimation is not a way of crossing the threshold but on the contrary of sealing it off. Rather than cutting indecision short by an access to an unequivocal outside, this would have meant being enclosed oneself inside the labyrinth that is transformed into a prison and crushed beneath a pyramid.

In February 1936 Bataille wrote a text entitled "Le Labyrinthe."[23] He published it again in *L'Expérience intérieure*[24] with some modifications, among them the title, which became "Le Labyrinthe, ou la composition des êtres." Calling it *composition*, this text sets out a loose relationship between beings and being that outlines alternately a pyramidal structure and this structure's destruction in labyrinthine experience: the pyramid is, in effect, inevitable but impracticable (interminable), whereas the labyrinth is elusive (non-seizable) but impossible to circumvent—for reasons stemming from the economy of language.

1. *The labyrinth.* If, on the one hand, according to "Le Labyrinthe," men "act to be," if being is the aim of their existence, being, however, is "nowhere," it cannot be fixed in anything in existence. This is for two apparently opposite reasons.

The first reason concerns simple beings, like single-celled organisms that reproduce by scissiparity: they have no right to being because they are merely "transitory appearances" that, as soon as they are born, vanish without a trace. Being, therefore, is characterized by something Bataille calls *ipséité*, that is, whatever differentiating quality there is in an individual that is irreplaceable and incomparable, that is *itself* (*ipse*) and not another; this *ipséité* implies also that there is a self-identity preserving this individual differential through the changes that affect it. The least modification of simple beings makes them no longer the same, because they have never been themselves. Therefore, they always fall short of being.

But being is no less slippery for complex beings (such as humans), this time because somehow they are beyond *ipséité*, because the identity they attain implies a loss of their *ipséité*. Because of this very complexity, because they are constituted by relationships structuring, for example, a multiplicity of cells, a system of organs, etc., compound beings have a certain *ipséité* that allows them to remain themselves despite radical change in the elements composing them. Beings, therefore, through this structure constitute durable wholes. What they are is not limited to anything vulnerable to time. Nonetheless, precisely in this process of composition, being will now become lost: "One is compelled to reflect that, when an extreme level of complexity is reached, being is more than the precariousness of a fleeting appearance, but this complexity—gradually shifting—in turn becomes the labyrinth where that which has suddenly come on the scene strangely loses its way." [25]

The version in *L'Expérience intérieure* is even clearer in describing the way in which the supplement, somehow, gets lost inside itself, how no sooner is being itself attained, than it is transformed into a labyrinth and is lost. "I can acknowledge, if necessary, being compelled to reflect that, at levels of extreme complexity, being becomes *more* than a fleeting appearance, but the complexity—gradually intensifying—is for this *more* a labyrinth where it loses its way endlessly, is lost once and for all."[26]

What is not lost in time is lost in language or, more generally, in the system of traces. This "more" is, in fact, designated two paragraphs later expressly as the language with which "all existence, as far as men are concerned" is bound up. Words (in which self is caught) are what last, not the self itself. Language, thus, constitutes the labyrinth in which *ipséité* comes on the scene only to get lost, by presenting itself specifically as a *relationship*, through words, with other human existences. There is no being outside language, but because it is necessarily "mediated" by language it is reduced to a language being: it is the being of language that deprives me of *ipséité*; it is where "my" being gets lost.

2. *The pyramid.* The second stage: *ipséité*, denied the subject, is objectified: the way out of the labyrinth as the erection of the pyramid. "Being, in fact, is *nowhere* to be found, and it was easy enough for a mischievous morbidity to find it—divine—at the summit of the pyramid formed by beings forming themselves from the vastness of the simplest matter."[27]

This "mischievous morbidity" is caused by the philosopher, and more generally any practician of theory as the *function* of knowledge. Being and function are mutually exclusive. Bataille writes, for example, that "the master deprives the slave of a portion of his being,"[28] by reducing him to exist only as a function. And philosophers too "assume knowledge as their function." They do, indeed, make being the object of their concern, but by adopting the position of functionary, philosophers stop their participation in being. Being slips away "if someone simultaneously 'being' and knowledge is mutilated by being reduced to knowledge. . . . Everything would be visibly connected if, with a single glance, one could discover the line left behind everywhere by an Ariadne's thread leading thought through its own labyrinth."[29] A single glance. *Uno intuitu.* And one would have a map of the labyrinth. One would have escaped it. One would look down on it, like Icarus, from above. From the summit of the pyramid. The entire labyrinth would fit inside an optical cone. The pyramid is homologous to this optical cone, it is the very structure of vision, of theory that has at its summit the divine eye of being. But it is all conditional . . .

3. *And the labyrinth.* In fact, because of the copula's return, the pyramid is still mortgaged. The transformation of being as copula into being as substance is inevitable at a certain point, but it is illusory. The summit (sum) is the locus of the imaginary. Icarus flies away, but he falls down again. One of the labyrinth's most subtle (treacherous) detours leads one to believe it is possible to get out, even making one desire to do so. Sublimation is a false exit that is an integral part of its economy. The pyramid is only a product of the labyrinth itself, and thoroughly belongs to it. "This flight toward the summit (which, even dominating empires, is the composition of knowledge) is but one of the routes of the 'labyrinth.' Yet this route, which we must follow, false lead after false lead, in search of 'being,' cannot be avoided by us, no matter how we try."[30]

Therefore, in spite of their opposition, one is not faced with an alternative between labyrinth and pyramid. Each implies the other. If Western ideological discourses, caught up in the system of metaphysics, have valorized the pyramid (but without success in eliminating the labyrinth, despite all the Ariadne's threads they continually take turns in proposing), Bataille does not claim to speak for the labyrinth. Or if sometimes he may seem to, his writing, nonetheless, for reasons pertaining to the very nature of language—which he himself has mentioned repeatedly—must necessarily pass through a pyramidal moment. Like all writing, it is caught between vocabulary and syntactical play, between the tantalization of resemblances and the metonymic expansion of cutoff points.

The Caesarean

Incomplete

Eroticism is not a separate problem. For Bataille it was never one question among others, a question that would necessitate, just like any other, a preliminary approach by specialists. In no way does it evoke a "science of love" (erotology or sexology). (Eroticism undoes the theoretical space of the logos in which science maintained its processes. It falls under *heterology*, precisely, only insofar as it marks the impossibility of *erotology*, the impossibility of reducing something that can never be other than a practice to the unity of the theoretical logos.) Its function on the level of discourse is the same as on the level of bodies: it weakens the discontinuities that create individuals, ruptures limits and frontiers (both physiological and epistemological), and adds incompletion to completion. The erotic effect can be defined as the loss of what is proper: the simultaneous loss of cleanness in filth and of one's own, proper identity in an expropriating violation. Being is dissolved, carried away by the action of dissolute existence. Eroticism opens beings to a slippery action where they give themselves over and are lost, where their excess leaves them wanting.

The other does not have a name (it has none and it does not have just one), because it is that which is nameless (the unspeakable), and, in this sense, it is that with which language has no relation. That is why it could only have a multitude of names, could only be expressed by the lexical extravagance to which it inevitably leads heterological practice and, as such, does not escape the substitutive discourse. Eroticism is just one of the names of heterological impulse at work—

through the metonymic effect of the copula—throughout language. It is not the key, not the archimedean word, not the center around which heterology would be reorganized according to a unitary perspective. At a certain moment, relatively late in his work, Bataille said all his writing was governed by *eroticism;* on other occasions he had used different names: heterology, scatology, sacred sociology, interior experience, etc. Just as bodies lose themselves in an erotic slipperiness, the impulse to supply the word engenders a stream of *terms,* each of which, as such, is necessarily improper and destined in advance to be dismissed, rescinded, deleted. No doubt one should specify the conditions under which these lexical mutations take place. But at least, one can conclude already that nothing is more excluded by Bataille's texts than that eroticism be fetishized (and eroticism itself is, certainly, not fetishizing sex). Fetishism depends on objects and there is no object that is not partial. Eroticism requires an "overall view," a view of the whole, and only movement can be overall, specifically only the movement that leads to the destruction of the object. Moreover, eroticism is not linked in any privileged manner to sex, except to the extent that it is sex that, in a privileged manner, produces a wound in a being's integrity.

Bodies, Words, Books: every partial object is slowly and laboriously sacrificed in this endless movement (that is: the movement that cannot be reduced to some end one might wish to assign it, where one would like to fix it, to which one would like it to correspond) governing all of Bataille's production and, precisely to this extent, preventing all this work from becoming "perfect," "complete," and "separate" books that are "closed back on themselves." Never is their content independent of their context, or their composition. One must keep to these incomplete texts, distracted by blanks, these heterogeneous texts that intersect and emerge from a process of repetition, endless repetitions, texts that are formed from the redistribution of identical sequences. They lay out a whole that moves "like one wave lost in a multitude of waves."

There is nothing fundamental about eroticism: it is, like the labyrinth, the loss of a base and the irruption of parody. Eroticism is not everything, but it is above all not a simple element, a "part." It is what prevents the serious from being serious and the trifling from being trifling; what prevents the whole from being whole and the part from being a part; where everything is at a loss. Sacrifice of being, being as sacrifice, it makes every hypostasis, whether ontological or theological, seem a parody: *Eros is not a god.* It, therefore, prevents eroticism from being eroticism rather than its parody. Parody of ecstasy. Parody of death. Comedy of sacrifice. Comedy of tragedy.

Slaughter

> *It is still possible to take it out on the human body.*
>
> Bataille, "L'Oeil pinéal" (4)

Let us go back to the beginning. Continue its opening insights. To persist in whatever prevents its ending—or its controlling what comes next. One could say that our effort has only one aim: to displace that first tombstone deprived of future because it covered over death. So, once more, let us reopen our beginning until we arrive at anarchy. Until we reduce it to what it is: a bottomless pit. Until the whole edifice is no more than this pinnacle with a hole in it. So let us begin again until we are back to *zero,* until "one" is obliterated.

When we go back this time the question of beginning will take the form of the question of man.

Bataille says in his study of prehistoric painting that man is born with art, more precisely with painting, which can be defined as the refusal on man's part to recognize himself in the reproduction of his form. Which is one way of saying that man is defined by the self-denial in which he is produced: man begins there where he denies himself, he begins by denying himself. At the beginning, therefore, a refusal to (let himself be) reproduce(d).

Here I am going to discuss the article "Bouche" (Mouth) that Bataille wrote for the *Documents* dictionary.

In this article Bataille does not pose the question of beginning by taking a "diachronic" approach, by going back to prehistory, but rather by using, if we want to call it that, a "structural" problematic connected to an organic reading of the human body insofar as it poses problems that are peculiar to it, specifically ones not found in the reading of animal organisms. This difficulty is, in fact, strictly rhetorical: where does this reading begin? where does the introduction, the "head" go? "Man's architecture is not simple like that of animals and it is not even possible to say where he begins."[1]

(A surprising proposition: up until now Bataille has interpreted

man more through his analogy with architecture—borrowing the
simplicity and balance of his form from buildings. Animality, on
the contrary, appeared in inverse ratio to formal academicism: all the
more marked because it grew more and more distant from man in
the scale of beings and the dialectic of forms. But from one text to
another words change their "job," their "value": there is nothing
more unstable than their meanings. They are always at the mercy of
a writing move carrying them off in unbounded and unforeseen
metamorphoses: metamorphoses that are enough in themselves to
challenge the architectural project of a simple inscription in the lexicon, or even of an ordered polysemy. Here, therefore, man is no
longer inscribed within the architectural system of simplicity, in and
through which beginning is so simple: scissiparity torments vocabulary by multiplying meanings beyond the possibilities of any totalizing
project [no domestic copulation can collect its progeny under a single
name]. Everything divides in two. Meaning moves through cleavage.
There are thus two mouths, the "good" mouth and the "bad," the
open mouth and the one that stays closed. Just as there were two
Americas [on the map, with its central isthmus, is America not the
very picture of scissiparity in process?], Inca America and Aztec
America; two Greeces: academic Greece [the one with the Acropolis
and Platonic philosophy], founded by Theseus, and, looming behind
it, archaic Greece [the Greece of tragedy and the labyrinth]. The very
horse, the *cheval académique* presiding over the destinies of Athenean
civilization, would come back in the form of the "stupid DADA" that
kicked up such a fuss in European culture, the untamable animality
that man has not managed to destroy, but with which he is doomed
to form one body.[2] There is, therefore, no way one can take Bataille
at his word, except by trying to reconstruct the dictionary he never
stopped destroying.)

Alongside the article "Mouth," the *Documents* dictionary offered
one on "Eye."[3] And although it was never actually in the dictionary
(maybe because it is so big), the text on the big toe belongs to this
same impulse toward lexicographical organ removal that pinpoints
the way these articles operate.

The dictionary is already, in itself, a form of discourse that implies
a prior sectioning of the field of reference. It is an analytical and
anatomical discourse. Bataille makes use of the form itself for "anatomical" ends: so that it would no longer be merely the result of a

prior dissection, but, more precisely, a dissecting tool. Each article, in fact, dislocates the body, isolates the organ it treats and disconnects it from organic supports, by turning it into the locus of a semantic concentration through which the part takes on the values that are tied to the whole. The whole is disarticulated by the article, provoking insubordination in the part, which then refuses to respect the hierarchical relations defining it by its integration into the organic system as a whole. It affirms the part in its fragmentary obscenity rather than effacing it by its integration into the finality of a beautiful and living totality. The dictionary is a discourse that makes the organ suddenly emerge as a partial object, irrecuperable for the purposes of constructing a whole body image.

1. "The big toe is the most *human* part of the human body."[4] The provocative virulence of this first sentence stems no less from the decision to tackle man low than from its determined ignorance of anything not low. Upright stance is interpreted through what it stands on, not through its tendency to head for the sky, thus reversing the value-laden reading such a stance traditionally justifies. But, in other texts, Bataille will go back to this traditional reading—leading one to believe that more is here than a simple reversal. Deeply connected to reversal is the concentration (condensation) of all of humanity into this single spot of the human body represented by the big toe.

2. The eye represents an analogous condensation: that of the powers of seduction (also a play in the article on the big toe: "that which *seduces,* disregarding what poetry cooks up—which is eventually no more than a diversion."[5] An obvious sign of condensation is the naming of the singular of this double organ. It was already there in "the" big toe, but here, applied to the eye, this odd simplification of something double introduces multiple overtones when Bataille had already written *Histoire de l'oeil,* and behind the articles in *Documents* one can discern his contemporary development of the myth of the "pineal eye."[6]

This concentration of seductive values results in the organ's being isolated and considered in itself, without any reference, for example, to the system of vision (this is an eye that is *seen,* not one that sees: a blind eye) nor to any other organic area. This isolation in the "body" of the article takes the same form of enucleation reported in the two anecdotes: Lexicographical extraction calls for organic extraction.

Words are emancipated from lexical order at the same time as organs are emancipated from organic functions. The "critical" dictionary in *Documents* through semantic concentration produces a sort of symbolic erection of the described organ, an erection at the end of which the organ itself, as if by scissiparity, detaches itself from its organic support. A dictionary of organs is the place and means of fantasmatic automutilations through which it opens the tongue up to a space in which it can become a painting's contemporary. (Matisse: "There is no dictionary for painters.")

All of Bataille's texts in *Documents*, moreover, lay out a problematics of modern pictural space (problematics that, almost without transition, after the end of *Documents* and the article "L'Esprit moderne et le jeu des transpositions" will be replaced by the political question— dominating almost all his contributions to *La Critique sociale*) in the articulation characterizing this pictorial space with automutilation as the rejection and destruction of the human figure in *practice* (a critique of anthropomorphism). Painting, therefore, is not mentioned here because the eye as organ of vision is under discussion. The space of painting is space where someone who has torn out his eyes like Oedipus feels his way, blinded. Thus it is not to the eye but to the missing-eye that painting corresponds. In "La Mutilation sacrificielle et l'oreille coupée de Vincent Van Gogh" (Sacrificial Mutilation and the Severed Ear of Vincent Van Gogh) Bataille, we should recall, begins by telling about a young painter who bit his own finger off. The article then connects the solar obsession of Van Gogh's paintings with the automutilating act of cutting off his ear. It ends with a series of examples requiring that automutilation be read as a sacrificial act but also, conversely, every sacrifice as a more of less "transposed" automutilation. Now the connection between these two parts, one dealing with Van Gogh's painting and the other dealing with sacrifice, is provided by another case taken from the literature of psychopathology, which concerns a young woman who, precisely, ripped out her own eye, this "Oedipean enucleation," according to Bataille, constituting "the most horrifying form of sacrifice."[7] Moreover, painting not only comes into being through a refusal to reproduce the human body, not only deforms the body in the images provided of it, but painting, even at its origin, was in the most mechanical sense of the word the reproduction of mutilations actually practiced upon the body. That, at least, is how Bataille interprets the "stenciled hands" one sees printed as if with stencils on the walls of neolithic caves. These hands are always missing one or several fingers: he rejects Luquet's thesis of the "bent finger," finding it "not very convincing."[8] Automutilation, in fact, is not a simple accident of psychopathology victimizing, among others, a number of painters: besides the fact that the victim, because of the very nature of sacrifice, is also the "executioner" or sacrificer, automutilation needs to be thought of as a pictorial act, even *the* pictorial act, par excellence. For painting is nothing if it does not attack the architecture of the human body.

And this architecture is, precisely, not simple because it implies automutilation.

3. The mouth, however, is not an organ of the same sort as the eye or the toe. First because it is already, on its own, a unique organ and there is, thus, no need to reduce it to unity. Then because it is not an organ in the fullest sense of the term, but rather a cavity—a hole. As an organ, it is already an opening up of the organism.

Animal architecture is simple because it has an unequivocal beginning: namely the mouth—starting from which animality was to develop a structure according to a discursive, horizontal linearity. Whereas man, by standing, loses his beginning. He loses also his linearity and is laid out between two axes that can be described as the *biological axis* (now vertical), constituted by the polarity mouth/anus, and the *ideological axis* which lies in the couple mouth/eyes. The ideological axis remained horizontal: it is defined as *horizon*tality: the field of vision. The mouth belongs to both of these two axes, once as an alimentary organ, and once as the locus of emission of the word (the organ of symbolic excretion). But animal life did not know this division between two axes, and the organ of sonorous (vocal?) expression was connected to vital processes: the cry is not an intellectual phenomenon (it is not a consequence of reasoning), its cause is biological in nature (hunger, sexuality, etc.). Expression is separated from the biological axis by passing from cry to articulated language, which (like the big toe) is systematically connected to the verticalization of human beings. Articulate words are thus linked to being erect, but this fact is repressed because their functioning continues to develop according to the axis of discursive horizontality. Verticalization allowed the mouth to perfect its expressive potential, multiplying it and providing a relative autonomy to these possibilities, but at the same time it caused the mouth to lose its expressivity. The more the body becomes the complex *tool* of expression and signification, the less expressive it is on its own. If the mouth was, in fact, "the most living" part of the animal organism (which was what assured its initial position), in mankind it lost all its "prominence." And what is more, it is replaced by *nothing* in the new, vertical biological axis: "the top of the head is an insignificant part."[9]

The "Mouth" article is no more descriptive than the ones on the big toe or the eye. Like them it fulfills a formative or deformative function: all three operate a symbolic transformation of body image. But here the operation does not take the form of a reduction to unity (since there is only one mouth) nor of a removal (since it is already a hole; and despite the fact that this hole normally is able to be shut, "stoppered" [*bouché*]: articulate language as the vehicle of knowledge derives from this slightest opening—an anal evocation: "constipation"—the "*closed-mouth* face" is described by Bataille as "masterful").[10] It takes the form of *displacement*. The symbolic action consists in forcing the ideological axis up against the biological axis. Which is done with a revulsive turn of the head, thrown back in a spasm of pain or pleasure or in a burst of laughter, whose effects are first, to open the mouth (to really open it, not just halfway as in articulated speech, to open it irreversibly as well, in a rictus on the verge of paralysis, which cannot be closed); second, to put the mouth at the exact top of the body, a sort of symmetrical hole to the anus (a vertigo effect, disorientation: the high/low opposition does not function any more, nor does that of assimilation/excretion; in "L'Oeil pinéal" we find the following remark: "The phenomenon of staring fixedly at the sun has been considered a symptom of incurable dementia and alienist doctors rank it on the level of such symptoms as eating one's excrement");[11] third, to make the mouth utter, rather than articulate sounds, bestial cries (what it utters, consequently, is no longer a phenomenon of reason but an organic, material emission: laughs, cries, fantasies emerging from this gaping place opened up by displacing the mouth to the top of the biological axis have to be thought of in the henceforth infinite series of excrements, alongside vomit, tears, drool, sperm, and shit). The (complex) architecture of the human body permits it to contain and accumulate violent impulses that it only gradually lets out, bit by bit, and to keep shut up in the prison of its form the animality it has not succeeded in breaking completely away from. But this retention is possible only within certain limits whose overstepping implies a direct effect on this form, an effect attacking first its reproductive finality.

This destruction of the reproductive finality of the body, obtained here by the lexicographic isolation of organs, depends on what Bataille will (later) call eroticism ("what differentiates eroticism from simple sexual activity being a psychological quest independent of the natural end provided by reproduction and a concern for children").[12] Because jouissance also proceeds by breaking up a body's unity, literally dislocating it. It is first of all destructive and it dissolves body image. For Bataille, jouissance is always designated as loss of self-control; that is, first, a loss of self in a sacrificial chaos coming after the process of automutilation: "The violence of spasmodic joy," he says in *Les Larmes d'Éros,* "is the heart of death."[13] The body's form—by definition—holds back and represses jouissance. This is equally true both for the sublimated form of works of art and for the organic form of animal species. Eroticism eludes reproduction; it belongs to the same sacrificial regions as painting, those regions where the *Noli me tangere* ("Do not finger," don't touch, paws off!) demands to be violated, where one no longer merely looks, where the theoretical distance is reduced to *practically* nothing.

Jouissance functions, therefore, from this perspective, as the loss of an organ. *There is no organ for jouissance:* jouissance is produced where there is not (or no longer) an organ, in the interstices, the slashes, cuts, incisions, and other differential organic places. If genitality, subjected to reproductive finality, is accomplished on the basis of (genital) organs adapted for this purpose, sexual jouissance is inscribed in differences marked by active absences (or losses) of organs. It is not a question of unimaginatively reducing the sacrificial game staged in sexual relations to the assertion that the penis-knife relentlessly attacks its female victim: this version remains too dependent on organic structure, it subjects difference to zones that one can locate organically, it fetishizes sexual difference. Whereas this difference is only the point of departure for an infinite multiplication of organic differences inscribing themselves on the form of the body to loosen this form. The victim in this sacrifice could not be solely the feminine partner: otherwise, there would be no sacrifice (which always implies the identification between victim and "executioner"). Jouissance is cruel because it transgresses the human body, does not respect its form, and through a hundred metamorphoses sets free the animality that its penitentiary architecture contained.

The absent woman, put to death not by the man but by the bitch whose bestiality *she* (the woman) unleashed in herself: "as if some rabid bitch took the place of the personality of the hostess who received with such dignity. . . . It is even too little to speak of illness. For the moment the personality is dead. *Its death,* for the moment, makes room for the bitch, who takes advantage of the silence, of the absence of what is dead. The bitch—who climaxes with a cry—*has* this silence and this absence."[14]

Les Larmes d'Éros sets forth a history of painting and of eroticism, a history where the two are thought of as constituting a bifocal, dialectical whole. The book opens with a third approach (the first was proposed in the study on Lascaux, the second in *L'Érotisme*) to the enigmatic tauromachy whose fascinating image is offered at the heart of the Lascaux labyrinth: a man, dead, his penis erect, and next to him a huge bison. Then come the "mannerist" images (Dürer, Cranach, Baldung Grien . . .) in which the object of desire (the woman) only appears marked by the metonymic figure of death. In one place the figure is a skeleton, whose bones are outlined behind the generous flesh tones of a woman, as if, one might say, it emerged from them. In another Judith holds the sharp weapon with which she decapitated Holofernes in one hand, and in the other she holds his head by the hair. Elsewhere, Lucretia turns an identical blade against herself. This history of figurative representation concludes with a series of four photographs, taken in 1905, of a Chinese torture—the "hundred pieces." Unbearable pictures that record the torture of living organs being torn from a conscious body one by one.

(One should ask here, moreover, how photographic reproduction functions in the economy of a book whose illustration is, on the whole, borrowed from painting and occasionally from sculpture. This question incidentally pertains to the very project of a review like *Documents,* whose iconographic material was by no means limited to the reproduction of works of art. The article "Figure" depends entirely on the bourgeois wedding party that posed for the photograph illustrating it, etc. A note written to mark the publication in the United States of an album collecting various photographs of gang war murders in Chicago [*X Marks the Spot*] moves in the same direction: "It seems that the desire to see ends up winning out over disgust or fear,"

Bataille writes. The desire to *see:* to see "what"? Nothing. Or death. More than painting, the photographic image refers to an externality that has a backlash effect on the discourse it tears apart. A reality effect, if you will. But one that would shake rhetorical confidence. *Les Larmes d'Éros,* the tears of Eros, are proffered in anticipated dread of what the photographs offer as an unthinkable, ungraspable externality: the spectacle of death, spectacle's end. At the point at which tangency no longer provides space for the least transposition.)

"Since 1928 I have had one of these snapshots," writes Bataille. "It was given to me by Doctor Borel, one of the first French psychoanalysts. This snapshot played a decisive role in my life. I have never stopped being obsessed by this image of pain, simultaneously ecstatic (?) and intolerable." [15]

Adrien Borel was the psychoanalyst who treated Bataille around 1925 (or 1927). He is author of the study from which Bataille borrowed the case of a young painter's automutilation that begins his first article on Van Gogh.[16] Doctor Borel also participated, in 1938, in the Society of Collective Psychology that Bataille attempted to found following a symposium devoted to circumcision.[17]

One thing is sure: Bataille began to write with the image of the tortured Chinese man before him.

Between *Notre-Dame de Rheims* and Bataille's first writings a break was produced whose locus was this psychoanalysis, insofar as this nontransposed reproduction of torture marked it. The cathedral is deconstructed by means of the image of a body broken in a hundred bursts of jouissance.

Sacrificial slaughter: head thrown back, mouth twisted with pain/ jouissance at the body's pinnacle.

As Bataille mentions in *Les Larmes d'Éros,* just after recalling how he came into contact with this image, the tortured Chinese man was, several years later, also the occasion for what one can call his mystical experience. He evoked it a number of times. For example:

One of my first "meditations"—at the moment of torpor and of the first images: abruptly I feel I have become an erect sexual organ, with indisputable intensity (the day before in the same way, in the darkness, without wanting it at all, I was transformed into a tree: my arms were raised above me like branches). The idea that my very body and my head were no more than a monstrous, naked, and blood-swollen penis seemed so absurd to me that I thought I would collapse in laughter. Then I though that such a stiff erection could only end in ejaculation: the comic situation became literally intolerable. Moreover, I could not laugh because the tension in my body was so strong. Like the tortured man I must have had my eyes rolled up and my head was thrown back. In this state, the cruel representation of the torture, of the ecstatic look, of the bloody, open ribcage, gave me a rending convulsion, and from the bottom to the top of my head a burst of light passed—as voluptuous as the passage of semen through the penis.[18]

The contents of this "mystical" experience obviously make it particularly difficult to use it for purposes of sublimation. Bataille's text operates a symbolic act upon the body—from the articles of the *Documents* dictionary to the aphorisms in *Somme athéologique*—which, under the knife (the blades, rather than the tears of Eros, or Eros's tearing tears: "The cut has an erection"), produces the body as penis, or, in vulgar French, the *pine*.

"The Pineal Eye"

The sphinx, with its numerous and huge examples, is of major importance to Egyptian sculpture. The figure is composed of an animal body and a human (feminine) face.

On the road to Thebes, Oedipus meets a sphinx who asks him a riddle: what animal walks on four feet in the morning, on two at midday, and on three at night? He is the first to figure out the answer ("man"), and he causes the death of the sphinx.

(But, asks Bataille, "would not the answer be: 'I forget the question'?")[19]

In the *Aesthetics* Hegel interprets this episode and this answer as an allegory for the birth of Greece: man is the Greek answer to the riddle, an answer that eliminates any trace of animality when it takes the human form (the most spiritual form of all) as the perfect expression of "Know thyself" or, inversely, when it makes "Know thyself" constitute what is specifically different about the human species.[20]

1. *Homo sapiens*

Bataille does not go along with either Oedipus or Hegel. He "prefers" the sphinx. He refuses to have man be the answer. Instead he transforms man into a sphinx, into the riddle of his own contamination by animality.

Linnaeus, as we know, set forth in his *Systema naturae* (1735) the first scientific classification of the products of nature arranged by order, genus, species, etc. (each being placed in it according to its definition: its nearest genus and its specific difference). Man occupies the *first* place in his classification: nature's system begins with him, he is no. 1, *heading* it all. Linnaeus attributes to him, as his specific difference, the "Know thyself" (in Latin, *Homo nosce te ipsum*) that defines him as the only species that produces knowledge. (In the French editions of *Systema* this difference will be "translated" by another Latin formula that eventually is more successful: homo *sapiens*.) Science is, according to science, the definition of mankind: mankind, therefore, is introduced into science's object—the sum total of natural beings— as the subject of science's discourse. *Natura non fecit saltus. Homo sapiens* or *Homo erectus:* erection is just one of the names for knowledge or science, because without it there would have been no freeing of hands, etc., nor any of the organic system that science depends on (a system based ultimately on the big toe, because concentrated in this organ of the human body is everything making this body different from simian organisms—an organ unexpectedly inscribing the specific difference designated by *sapiens* or *nosce te ipsum* in the organic system. With the result that the article "Le Gros orteil" [The Big Toe] could be read as a text that indirectly describes the anatomical conditions of its own production). Man, therefore, is indeed the being that produces itself with science, as well as the subject of science. But at the same time Bataille denounces what little sense science offers mankind. As if science were constituted by a prohibition bearing specifically on sense, a prohibition bearing on what is *meaningful* for mankind. Here sense or meaning is defined as a being at risk.

Science develops as a process of pure assimilation an assimilation that would not be followed by any excretory phase. But if science is at work in this assimilation (with the names whose diversity would doubtless be worth examining on its own, even if, at first glance, they seem to say the same thing: homogenization, identification, reproduction), it is basically because assimilation provides an exceedingly fine definition for humanity's mode of existence. There is no more active assimilator than the human being: the outside world, anything there that might provide a welcoming structure for otherness is submitted to voracious conquest; the monotonous infinitude of technique has no other mission, no other vocation than this assimilation of the other no matter what the cost through a conceptualization threatened by anything that eludes it. The ravenous imperialism that reduces everything to itself, that keeps whatever it has assimilated (wanting neither to have to return it nor to be burst by it), is the very face of humanity. Just as, contrasted to the pure expenditure of energy that is the sun's entire existence, the earth seems the most avaricious planet of all, one that captures and profits from solar warmth strictly for its own internal purposes, a planet driven by a unilateral devouring action with no compensation,[21] in the same way the "master" of the earth, man, is the greediest being on *his* planet. More than any other species his existence is devoted to the conquest and voracious appropriation of whatever is not himself.

Natura non fecit saltus: or at least man devotes himself to preventing any leaps, breaks, or somersaults. He must be in control of every rupture, sewing up any rips that would threaten the homogeneity of *his* world. But this is only possible by homogenizing all material externality through a common "abstract" measurement—the idea, previously determined by science: "Aspectual homogeneity, realized in cities between men and their surroundings, is only a secondary form of a far more consistent homogeneity established by man throughout the external world, where he substitutes for external objects (*a priori* inconceivable) conceptions or ideas classified in series."[22] Science, having glazed the world over with the ideal, eliminates any difference that is not logical, or reduces it to a *specific* difference, a difference defined by the possibility of the species reproducing itself. Difference must be reduced, diminished, and strung together by logic.

Theory does not know or even encounter its other. The other escapes it. But it is primarily because this other does not give itself to being known, because it has nothing to do with theory. There is, in fact, only homological theory; a theory of the other would change nothing, since it would not break with the space of theory but just come down to the same thing once more. Moreover, in a certain sense, there has never perhaps been any other theory than theories of the other, as Jacques Derrida has suggested,[23] since all theory is deployed along the pioneer frontiers of assimilation, intervening at points where homogeneity perceives that it is threatened. This would be, for example, the purpose of erotologies that recuperate sexual bliss into discourse, etc. But Bataille never mentions erotology. On the contrary, one must think here of the gap forbidding the translation of heterology into erotology. In this gap the very possibility of theory sees itself threatened, as does the ancillary function of discourse, which in effect ceases to be a simple tool of expression to become the locus of a practice, the very material of an experience. Theoretical heterology does not exist; any project of heterological theory is just the most ordinary of ruses used by theory as a cover for attaining its own goals, which are the assimilation of the other. There is, on the contrary, no effective heterology unless it is produced as a practice.

"The heterogeneous itself is resolutely placed beyond the reach of scientific knowledge, which is by definition only applicable to homogeneous elements."[24] With this formula Bataille defines the two points constituting the heterological break: heterology is not a matter for science, on the one hand, for formal reasons (the opposition between theory and practice), but also, on the other hand, for material reasons that have to do with "content": heterology does not intervene in the same areas as science. These two points only constitute heterology by articulating with each other: because heterology escapes the status of theory (formal break), it focuses on contents (material break) that not only belong to other areas than those in which science normally develops, but that, above all, absolutely do not have the status in the sphere of heterology that science, in its sphere, imposes on its *objects*. Specifically, they do not have the status of object, they constantly overflow the category of objectivity. The "objects" produced by heterological practice are only defined by a certain virulence making them constantly overflow their definition. This virulence is one of refusal: they do not allow themselves to be subjected to concepts. Much the opposite, they reverse the action and, far from bending to lexical injunctions, they act back on the human mind, disturbing it with their stimulation. Theory, no matter what its contents, is thus, above all else, a place where the soul protects its peace. Whatever escapes theory hangs over it in threat. Theory can be boiled down to the project of "depriving, as far as possible, the universe in which we live of every source of stimulation."[25]

Philosophy's precise function lies, according to Bataille, in this empire of theory where all the ideological practices limiting language to an instrumental function are gathered. Philosophy's special domain is the trash cans of science. Philosophers, science's garbage men, eliminate or recuperate its refuse, reducing it to nothing or boiling it down to sameness. Science, in the course of its development, produces waste products that upset it (Bataille cites three concepts: nothingness, infinity, and the absolute). Philosophy's task is to demonstrate that there is nothing threatening about them, either because they are not, in fact, foreign at all, and do not escape science's jurisdiction; or because they have no reality, that nothingness, for example, is strictly speaking nothing at all, etc. What is essential is that nothing exists outside of a theoretical horizon; nothing escapes examination in the distancing that is the basis of theory; nothing exists that cannot be mentioned, that has no name, that cannot be subsumed into some conceptual abstraction. What is essential is to preserve continuity at any cost (*Natura non fecit saltus*), even, when necessary, crossing points of rupture, as, for example, by reducing the unknown to no more than a distant province of the known, or the infinite of the finite. Or even, when some apparently insurmountable contradiction arises, developing a theory of the "identity of opposites" that is the last word in theoretical heterology, indeed its method, the point at which the antidesire that controls it shows its real face: "a sordid craving for any integrity at all."

Ever since 1921, when Tristan Tzara recognized that "the absence of system is still a system, but the most sympathetic one," though this concession to trivial objections at that time continued, apparently, to have no consequences, it was predictable that Hegelianism would soon be introduced. In fact, from this statement to Hegel's panlogism is a very easy step because it conforms to the principle of *the identity of opposites:* one might even suppose that once this original cowardice had been accepted there was no longer any way to escape panlogism and its disgusting consequences, that is, a sordid craving for any integrity at all, blind hypocrisy, and finally the need to be useful to anything as long as it is well defined.[26]

The problem of the identity of opposites is, in fact, the decisive component supporting all homological strategy.

(A double parenthesis: First: Bataille firmly rejects this thesis. Nevertheless, he himself had recourse to related formulations. For example, in *Histoire de l'oeil,* the narrator defines "the completion of [his] sexual excesses" as a "geometric incandescence [among other things, the point where life and death, being and nothingness coincide]."[27] In "La Structure psychologique du fascisme": "There is, in a certain sense, an identity of opposites between glory and failure, between the higher and imperative [superior] forms and forms that are wretched."[28] These examples are not the exception. The entire book *L'Érotisme* may be read as an effort to bring out the "unity" in terms that are apparently contradictory such as saintli- and licentious-ness, or life and death.

Bataille, therefore, contradicts himself. We knew that. But doing so also shifts the question. Contradiction here, in fact, no longer seems to be a theme for philosophical reflection, rather it overflows theory's horizon to find itself caught in the very practice of writing, one would like to say as one of its figures, but first one would have to distinguish between the stylistic figures that constitute rhetorical technique as a mastery and those figures of writing that have a status far closer to that of lapsus or blunder. Because the territory covered by this practice of writing is constituted by language, there is the double, contradictory possibility of both affirming and refusing the identity of opposites. It is, in fact, the milieu where irreconcilables such as rules and irregularity, prohibition and transgression, are articulated. It is, if you wish, their unity, but on the condition that one read duplicity in this unity, on condition that one see unity as the main feature of points subjected to attacks by scissiparity. Language is, simultaneously, as a code, theoretical space [dominated by the signified] that, to protect its homogeneity, implies the identity of opposites, and, as writing, the space of a practice that on the one hand valorizes themes of rupture and on the other itself unfurls according to a rhythm of rupture, of destruction of sublimating unity. In *L'Érotisme*, Bataille writes: "The obstacles set against the communication of *experience* . . . stem from the prohibition on which it is based and from the duplicity I am discussing, reconciling things whose principle is irreconcilable, respect for law and its violation, prohibition and transgression."[29] Here, therefore, it is less a question of asserting the identity of opposites than of keeping them together as opposites.

Second: Bataille's "contradictions" may occur at the level of his formulations because, in other circumstances, Bataille will take as his own the terms whose use by Tzara he attacks. The fact that, for example, in 1929 Bataille was "not yet" Hegelian is not a sufficient explanation for this obvious inconsistency. He is therefore the same writer who, in 1929, sees the phrase "absence of system is still system" as acknowledgment of the identity of opposites making panlogism inevitable, and who publishes [in the catalogue for a surrealist show, in 1947] a text where all the sentences are constructed on the model of Tzara's sentence: "The *absence of God* is greater, it is more divine than God," "The firm absence of faith is unshakable faith," "The absence of myth is also a myth." [30]

However, there is a difference between these sentences by Bataille and Tzara's, a difference if not in words at least in mode. To say that "the absence of system is still a system" is to posit along a continuous mode the transcendence of system, it is saying that on the one hand the system is the system and that on the other hand that which is not the system is also the system. In such a formula, none of the words composing it excludes any of the other words; the system here is in no way at stake. Tzara's formula belongs entirely to rationality's expressive system because it can be reduced to an equation, an equation whose contents are perhaps paradoxical, but an equation just the same. Bataille's formulas, on the contrary, refuse to be recuperated in identity: they are not reversible. Unlike the system at work in Tzara's sentence, God here does not remain intact. Bataille does not say "The absence of God is still God" [a formula compatible with any rationalism—atheist, theist, Protestant, etc.], but "The absence of God is greater, it is more divine than God," or, elsewhere, "The sentiment of the *divine* is tragically bound up with the sentiment of the *absence of God*"[31] [a strictly atheological formula]. Far from confirming the identity of God with himself [God being simultaneously God and his opposite], divinity here is written as the nonidentity of God with himself, divinity is produced by writing that sacrifices the signifier attached to God, that sacrifices his transcendence outside the text [God being not God but his opposite]. In the first formula, God included even his absence, whereas in the second he is excluded from himself and is nothing apart from this exclusion.)

The final word as far as homology is concerned, the assertion of the identity of opposites, is described as "cowardice" that has, among other consequences, the effect of nourishing "the need to be useful to anything as long as it is well defined." Bataille continues in the same tone: "One sees, in fact, no difference between humility—the least humility—before the SYSTEM—that is, in short, before the idea—and the fear of God." Therefore, homology (theoretical discourse: science, philosophy, etc., and its "applications": implications of a technical order) has a dominant characteristic: servility. It serves someone. It serves something. It does not itself decide its own purpose. Does not ask itself what it means.

Bataille criticizes homology not because it is wrong, but rather because of the morally disastrous relationship to truth it presumes: in "L'Apprenti sorcier" (The Sorcerer's Apprentice), he speaks of "*moral* devastation" resulting from science's devalorization of difference (and parallel promotion of indifference) for which logic, science, and language in general are simultaneously responsible.[32] Difference, or what escapes logic insofar as it is ineradicably idealist, indicates therefore the locus of that which is not formulable in terms of an idea, of that which cannot be put into an equation: matter. "Matter," says Bataille in "La Notion de dépense" (The Notion of Expenditure), "can only be defined by *nonlogical difference*."[33] Matter is inequality (it is not even equal to itself). Making it equal is to abstract an idea from its materiality. Expenditure, in fact, is an *unequation*. And materialism, as the thought of unthinkable expenditure, effects a rupture in relation to everything composing the system of equal exchange that holds sway over scientific discourse as communication (the transmission of information from speaker to auditor). Expenditure is not thinkable in terms of exchange or of communication: because it is not measurable (it is so huge that one can only be lost in it) and communicates nothing (it destroys structures of communication; it is no longer possible to recognize a message, a sender and a receiver in it): The dissymmetry of the *potlatch* is Bataille's favorite example of such an unequation: he uses Mauss's phrase to describe it: "The ideal would be to give a *potlatch* and it not be reciprocated."[34]

Dépense: unthinking all-consuming expenditure: the thought of ripping apart / the ripping apart of thought. *Homo sapiens* wants to know nothing about this. *Natura non fecit saltus*. And, if it did (jump, nature), science is there to put it back together, laying bridges that will cancel out the rift. Because science is continuous. The future is all it cares about . . . as long as the future is not something different! Let's keep the continuous present going! The ideal would be for all our efforts to come back to us. Later. At the end. Let us build a future that will surprise the present, that does not startle it into jumping or blow it apart. This present that is only the anticipated digestion of the future, its assimilation in advance.

Philosophy, up to this point, has, as much as science, been an expression of human subordination, and when man attempts to represent himself no longer as one moment in a homogeneous process—a needy, pitiful process—but as a new rip inside a torn nature, the leveling phraseology derived from conceptualization is no longer able to help him; he can no longer recognize himself in degrading strings of logic, but recognizes himself on the contrary—not exactly with anger but in ecstatic torment—in the virulence of his fantasies.[35]

Practical heterology shifts the question and makes the homogeneous appear to be an accident of the heterogeneous. Man, precisely insofar as he is the point in nature where this strange organ of assimilation that is the mind appears, constitutes from this point of view a rupture with that nature whose law was to have no rupture, a rip in an order where ripping was the rule (if this word can still mean anything here, to designate, that is, precisely whatever has nothing to do with a leveling phraseology with words as its instruments).

In the sketches to "L'Oeil pinéal," Bataille opposes to the leveling phraseology of philosophico-scientific discourse, whose effect is the integration of man into a nature whose integrity he has taken charge of, something that he calls the virulence of "fantasies." ("A fantasy talks back, speaks as a master, not a slave: it exists like a son finally free after long suffering under an iron rule and who diabolically, remorselessly is ecstatic over the murder of his father; he exists *freely* and reflects none other than human nature unchained.")[36] Heterological discourse exceeds the possibilities of logic and breaks its chains. Here science finds itself literally outstripped. Bataille, however, never wanted merely to outstrip it: rather to make use of it. If science is servile it must serve. If it is not mistress of its ends, one must "use it for ends that are not its own," "subjugate [it] with arms borrowed from it."[37] This attitude—which, therefore, consists less of outstripping than hijacking—will be especially noticeable in the relationship Bataille will maintain with various incursions attempted by scientific method into the "human sciences" (for Bataille, these designate a mixture of psychoanalytic anthropology, Durkheimian sociology, phenomenological description of lived experience), into the human domain as such, that is, insofar as it is not integrated into other spheres of reality. The entire project of the College of Sociology is linked to this fragile and problematic category, the "human sciences."

Science defines mankind as *Homo sapiens*. With this gesture it constitutes itself as a biological phenomenon and integrates human beings into the animal order. But this gesture also, because it does not exceed theory (it confines itself to scientific objectivity), is no less one that preserves man from animality. If science, indeed, constitutes man's specific difference, it is as a *logical* difference, that is, an abstract, sublimated (already humanized) difference, which masks the face of difference that cannot be conceptualized: science, as specific difference, puts itself in the position of a fetish meant to cover up the animal face of difference, that nonlogical, material difference, constituted by prohibition or sin.

Nothing comes out of conceptualization, the organ of assimilation with no opposite. One must, oneself, leave—through a nontheoretical break with theory. Either leave or let the nameless animality that is at the heart of the labyrinth enter. "There is thus, in each man, an animal shut up in prison like a convict, and there is a door, and if one cracks the door the animal tears out like a convict finding an exit."[38]

To write would be to search for the silent "Sesame" that would allow this door to open.

2. *La tache aveugle:* The blind spot

TACHE [STAIN/SPOT] (not to be confused with *tâche* [task, work]): Initially designates a "mark," whether it is good or bad (cf. *Zeichen,* sign). Today its sense[39] is exclusively pejorative: a stain makes something dirty; spots are not clean (ink spots, stains of sperm, blood, etc.). Used figuratively in religious language, it designates the results of the fall, which for mankind is an indelible stain, condemning him to a maculate conception.

AVEUGLE [BLIND]: 1. without eyes (*ab oculis*) 2. deprived of sight, whose eyes cannot see. 3. offensive to reason; that which troubles the mind's vision, destroys the theoretical faculty (cf. blind passion). *Aveugler* is also used to mean stop up, as in stop up a hole, block a window (with window blinds). (Blindness is a stain: "Nota igitur generaliter percecum intelligitur peccator" [Petrus Berchorius cited by Erwin Panofsky, "Blind Love," in *Studies in Iconology*].)

In the mind there is a blind spot (tache aveugle) that recalls the structure of the eye. In the mind, as in the eye, this is difficult to detect. But, whereas the eye's blind spot is unimportant, the nature of the mind means the blind spot will, in itself, make more sense than the mind itself. To the extent that the mind is auxiliary to action, the spot is as negligible there as it is in the eye. But, to the extent that man himself is what is considered in conceptualization—by man I mean the exploration of the being's potential—the spot absorbs attention. It is no longer the spot that vanishes into knowledge, but knowledge that gets lost in the spot. Existence in this manner comes full circle, but it could not do so without including the night from which it comes only to return there. Just as it went from the unknown to the known, at the summit it has to turn around and return to the unknown.[40]

The mind unfolds into theory, that is, it functions by submitting to the model of optical perception: what remains of this model, essentially, is distance, which separates the subject and the object, which constructs the *ob-jectum* and allows the subject to consolidate while sheltered from contagion by the other. Knowledge without contact, knowledge where life is not threatened by the necessity of entering into contact with that which it knows.[41] By bringing the blind spot into this aphorism in *L'Expérience intérieure*, Bataille, with a single gesture, *acknowledges* the optical model in which thought, as theory, finds itself caught, and pushes this model far enough to *overturn* it—to this final point of lucidity that is blindness (blind-blinded, dazzled, for example, by too strong a light, such as that of the sun, etc.), to the final limit of day, which is night. Oedipus did indeed leave the animal night where the sphinx guarded the way out, Oedipus did indeed arrive in the broad daylight of anthropomorphism, the Greek miracle, but in the end it was only to tear his own eyes out, falling back once more by his own action into the labyrinthine night where he can only grope his way forward (touching the future with his ignorance). He no longer knows where he is heading: he has lost knowledge. Knowledge gets lost in the blind spot, just as day gets lost in the night.

The blind spot "recalls" the structure of the eye. Bataille no longer (the aphorism dates doubtless from the first years of the Second World War) speaks of the eye except by comparison: he is no longer naming this spot the pineal *eye*. But this is unimportant, what is at stake in the operation is touch, putting one's finger on the point of totalization-revulsion of the intellectual edifice: on the point of this edifice that, on the one hand, is part of it, but a part that, on the other hand, completely embraces it. The result is that the part as such is greater than the whole: it goes beyond it, exceeds it, transgresses it. The process of assimilation transforms the unknown into a part of the known, the infinite into the fringes (or margins) of the finite; but this part, where all hangs, reverses the action: it is the summit where the sum (the total) comes undone, the point at which inequality throws equations into disequilibrium. One might see in this action one of the "rules" of Bataille's "method." When, in the foreword to *L'Érotisme*, he says that "a separate question in this work always embraces the entire question,"[42] one should not read this formula in the sense of a Leibnizian type of expressionism. The reinscription of the whole in the part causes at the same time a deformation of the totalizing space. This deformation is apparent in the fact that the whole, by being reinscribed in the part, is not confirmed but annihilated, nullified. "There remains a point that always has the sense—or rather the absence of sense—of the whole. Now a description, from the point of view of discursive knowledge, is imperfect, if, at the desired moment, thought does not open up through it into the very point where the totality that is its annihilation is revealed."[43] In the area of "notions," this point is occupied by the *notion de dépense*, the notion of unthinking expenditure, the blind spot of rationalist, utilitarian economy, the whole where the edifice of thought is spent, swallowed up, ruined; where notions, upset by a nonlogical difference, open up beyond themselves. This is the blind spot (or pineal eye) that is the basis for the optical-theoretical relationship but that does not enter into the field of vision. It is blind because it does not see; blind because, from the moment it intervenes, it prevents the (mind's) eye from seeing; blind also because it is not visible.

And Bataille says "the nature of the mind means the blind spot will make more sense than the mind itself."

Science (and everything that comes out of the mind), in any case, makes little sense, has very little meaning. "The truth that science pursues is only true on condition that it be meaningless, deprived of sense."[44] Here one must distinguish between two notions of meaning: the meaning that guards itself against nonsense and the meaning that accepts the risk. The first corresponds to the scientific ideas: a conception of meaning that implies the foreclosure of the subject (meaning must not bring the subject into play, it must be no more than a mechanical effect of language, a product of linguistic functioning: language would make sense as a machine produces objects), the image of meaning that science proposes is, in reality, completely senseless. Because by wanting there to be only meaning, wanting sense without risking nonsense, one paradoxically obtains only nonsense. Meaning is meaning at risk; cf.: "A corrida without killing is nonsense."[45] Nonsense is meaning's meaning. "Nonsense is the outcome of every possible sense."[46] But the second conception of meaning, the one that ties it to the risk of nonsense, in reality therefore, quite simply, destines it for nonsense. For that which is nonsense both for science ("An unproductive expenditure is nonsense, or even *countersense*")[47] and also outside of science. There is no more meaning outside of science than there is in it, even if the meaning of science is outside of itself, is that which escapes it. These two alternatives do not, however, constitute a dilemma. The two nonsenses are unequal: one is the nonsense of nonlife ("Losing the meaning of life to stay alive"),[48] the other is the nonsense of life itself.

Conceptualization is senseless, because its (non)sense eludes it, its only sense comes from that which eludes it: specifically the blind spot that it must cover up. Intellectual assimilation is senseless because it is limitless, has no desire to come to an end, has no desire to know where it will end up. It interiorizes even its outside. Whereas it is never possible to interiorize sense, it is not a "content," the most intimate core of words or things. Moreover it is not exactly outside of them either. But in their opening up, in the sacrifice that dissolves them, in the presence within them of their absence. To have a sense, for Bataille, is to be constituted by that which negates one. Nothing is meaningful, nothing makes sense, until confronted by its negation. (See "Festival is the negation of actions, but it is the negation that provides a SENSE for actions [as death provides a sense for life]."")[49] A thing's sense is the rupture of its identity, that which exceeds it, that by means of which it exceeds and is not itself but that which is beyond it, or its absence.

Science does not make sense because the aim of its propositions is to enclose beings inside their identities. This blind spot, where it sums itself up by going beyond itself, is the sense of science, this blind spot that constitutes not-knowing as excess knowledge. This blind spot that is both the support and undoing of science; without which it would be nothing, yet which at the same time reduces it to nothing. The significant, therefore, is never rational: sense does not result from reason.

It is in this context (one he himself designates as an attempt to pass from a "scientific anthropology"—which would reduce the radical rupture man introduces into the rips and tears of nature to no more than a logical [specific] difference—to a "mythological anthropology") that Bataille introduces the *pineal eye,* defining it sometimes as a myth and sometimes as a fantasy. Things stemming from myth, like everything mythology offers (Bataille will borrow from it references to Icarus, Prometheus, the Minotaur, etc. as well), are not susceptible to reduction to the conceptual order: "mythemes" do not obey a monovalent logic of identities. The pineal eye is introduced as that which gives science its sense, and gives it because science rejects it and is threatened by it: "The fact that, according to reason, there is no valid content in a mythological series is the condition for its signifying value."[50]

3. Scatology

1. Heterology: *Science of the altogether other. The term* agiology *would be, perhaps, more precise, but the double sense of* agios *must be understood (analogous to the double sense of* sacer), *both* defiled *and* holy. *But above all it is the term* scatology *(the science of filth) that in present-day circumstances (the specialization of the sacred) retains incontrovertible expressive value, as the doublet of an abstract term such as* heterology.

Bataille, "La Valeur d'usage de D.A.F. de Sade."

2. The term heterology *as related to* heterodoxy *has the advantage of opposing this form of activity to every possible sort of* orthodoxy, *but it is appropriate, as an exoteric term, to prefer* scatology *as a term far more concrete and expressive.*

Ibid.[51]

So reason has to be given shit. It is a low blow, but this is precisely what it is all about.

In fact, this is all about something one can have *no idea of.* Something that is "like nothing else" (is submitted to no model, does not reproduce any specific difference), as the article "Informe" put it in the *Documents* dictionary. And for something one has no idea of, there are words that are not proper, not very elevated, not polite, gross and dirty words; they stain but hit the target; they are out of place (explosive) in philosophy's academic discourse. A simple change of vocabulary calls Platonism into question: a few scatological words in the midst of philosophical terms, and the ideal of idealism, the model of philosophical orthodoxy takes a beating (low down, obviously).

1. Anti-Plato. The question of the *formless,* however, the question of something one has no idea of is put by Plato himself.

In the dialogue bearing his name, Parmenides would like for Socrates to tell him what things, according to him, have an idea (or form, depending on the translation): for example, is there an idea of similarity, an idea of one and of many? Is there an idea of the just, the beautiful, the good? Is there even an idea of man, an idea of fire or of water? To the first two sets of examples offered by Parmenides, Socrates answers affirmatively and without hesitation, but faced with the last group, having to do with physical beings, he admits to some confusion, which Parmenides, with a new set of examples, will further increase. Here is this last, "scatological" set: "And what about these, Socrates—they would really seem ridiculous [γελοῖα]—hair and mud and dirt, for example, or anything else which is utterly worthless and trivial [ἄλλο τι ἀτιμότατόν τε καὶ φαυλότατον]. Are you perplexed whether one should say that there is a separate form (εἶδος) for each of them too, a form that again is other than the object we handle [χειριζόμεθα]?"[52]

The criteria Parmenides calls upon to characterize the type of object his question concerns mark off the scatological space in terms that will hold: these terms could perfectly well be repeated by Bataille. On the one hand, these objects are silly, ridiculous, laughable; on the other hand, they have to be touched, have nothing to do with visual, theoretical perception, but rather with physical contact. The question of scatology, starting with its appearance in Platonic texts, is introduced as an obstacle opposed to the theory of forms: Parmenides evokes hair, mud, and dirt, just as Bataille will evoke spit or spiders in the article "Informe." In both instances exactly the same thing is at stake: to determine the limits of Idea. Even if Plato and Bataille take different respective positions in relation to what is at stake, their difference, nonetheless, is incapable of being reduced to the logical form of contradiction: which would be too simple and would condemn the opposition to remain theoretical ("Platonic").

Scatology thus is (even if only as a question) inscribed in Plato's text: what of these ridiculous, worthless and trivial things, in relation to ideas (to forms)? What is it about these things that do not give themselves to being seen but to being touched, that are in their own way, that is to say negatively, *aeidès*?[53] What about those things not worthy of the light of day, better left unseen? That is how Plato put it later, in *Philebus*, this time apropos pleasure—also labeled ridiculous and grotesque [γελοῖον]: "But, as you know, pleasures—and I think this is particularly true of the greatest pleasures—involve the person experiencing [ὅταν ἴδωμεν ἡδόμενον ὁντινοῦν] them in a ridiculous, if not utterly repulsive display. This makes us self-conscious, and we keep these pleasures as secret as possible, reserving all such activities for the hours of darkness, as if they should not be exposed to the light of day."[54]

Just as philosophy unites what is serious with theory, scatology thus connects laughter and touch, which philosophy will have nothing to do with. But it is more important to see *how* philosophy manages to repress scatology, *how* philosophy speaks out as antiscatology (first of all by depriving scatology of speech), than to dwell at length on the *connotation* of the word *scatology*, even if the juxtaposition of filth, pleasure, and laughter is already in itself worthy of attention. This speaking out against scatology, at the same time as it deprives scatology of speech, constitutes the entire performance in *Philebus*, which can be read, in fact, as the decision to make pleasure speechless—a typically "homological" decision to refuse the Other, whatever is excluded, any place of inscription. Pleasure, in fact, must not be able to defend itself, because, to defend itself, it would have to employ language and be, therefore, no matter how slightly, on the track with philosophy, recognizing logos as a value. Pleasure (which "cattle, horses, and all animals" have as the goal of their lives) must remain silent, as animals are speechless. Pleasure is not a thesis defended by its partisan. Also, in the dialogue, Philebus, the partisan of pleasure, the worshiper of Aphrodite, is not the one who takes up pleasure's defense; Socrates designates Protarchus, an enterprising dialectician, as the appointed lawyer for silent pleasure. As a result, in *Philebus* (but also in all philosophy, in all edifying discourse), pleasure does not speak; one speaks in its name. Between Philebus's silence and the discourse Protarchus spins out in the name of pleasure lies a gap that is uncrossable (despite how easy it is to pretend it does not exist), between heterology and any sort of erotology. With the exception of a few interruptions, Philebus, about whom they speak and to whom they speak indirectly, remains silent. A heterological or scatological reading of the dialogue would consist in reading it no longer on the basis of what is said there, on the basis of its obvious text, but on the basis of this silence; bringing this silence into play as the heterological inscription of pleasure in a discourse that represses it. The light of day must not see the spectacle of coupling, and dialectical space must also be sheltered from the groans of bliss. Silence and night must absorb them. But precisely: what about silence and night in relation to ideas?

In an analogous way, in the *Parmenides,* Socrates is confused by the evocation of hair, mud, and filth, a confusion that is translated into the conflict between a repulsion and a desire. On the one hand, it would be indecent for a form to correspond to these things (repulsion) that only exist, Socrates concedes, insofar as we *see* them [ταῦτα μέν γε ἅπερ ὁρῶμεν, ταῦτα καὶ εἶναι]: *touch,* evoked by Parmenides, is not a criterion for existence. But, on the other hand, it is difficult to accept that the theory of ideas be limited; everything that exists should have its corresponding form (desire). A contradiction that Socrates finds frightening: he turns away "with all possible speed" and returns to his "refuge": those objects that have, without a doubt, a corresponding form. One must not think about things one has no idea of.

Nonetheless, it is the anguish of Socrates, his disgust and his flight that infer scatology. It was not there in Parmenides's question. The commentary of the latter following Socrates's reactions confirm this: he, Parmenides, knows that everything that exists has a form, that nothing that exists is contemptible: there is no filth, no more than there is scatology. That is what Socrates himself, with age and philosophy, will end up recognizing. If he would talk nonsense his disgust would disappear: neither hair, mud, dirt, or pleasure would make him laugh any more. No more than anything else: the philosopher no longer laughs, must not laugh. Laughter is not an "argument": in *Gorgias* one of Socrates's expositions is interrupted by a burst of laughter from Pôlos: "What's this, Pôlos? You're laughing? Is this now some further style of refutation, to laugh when somebody makes a point instead of refuting him?"[55]

Laughter is not the refutation expected by philosophy, that is the one it already has "in its pocket" in advance. Laughter is a practical refutation, more dangerous when unexpected, that refutes nothing. Bataille: "*From the moment in which the effort of a rational comprehension comes up against contradiction, the practice of intellectual scatology orders the evaluation of inassimilable elements*—which comes down to the vulgar statement that a burst of laughter is the only imaginable outcome, conclusive, final, and not the means of philosophical speculation."[56]

The different reactions Socrates has when confronted by the questions raised by Parmenides follow precisely the action of assimilation with no opposite, assimilation without excretion, that Bataille would describe apropos science. Socrates first is frightened by the formless (and science, discursive knowledge, is born out of the taboo directed at animality), then he surmounts (*aufhebt*) this repulsion to take refuge in the *proper* realm of ideas-forms (and science ends up, by the same token, forgetting the taboo that is its basis, being unable to think the irrational). Philosophy has to do no more than intervene to accomplish its function: tackling refuse, recuperating it and providing it with form. The garbage man of reason. We have to give it shit. With a few low blows about which it has no idea.

2. Low. Bataille's writing is only an effort to escape an ascendant idealization. An effort to think the low, to have the lowest possible thoughts, an effort by means of which this writing is produced as *sub*versive: it takes theory from underneath; like the "old mole" it digs invisible tunnels underground. The low starts where one can no longer see. Because the *low* functions for Bataille as that which is underground (where there are roots), as that which is always underneath, as that which gets lower and lower; the low lowers, weakening and toppling, it never provides solid ground. The low is too low—always getting lower—to be submitted to the common measure of the idea. In this sense, it is not even a thing, because every thing by definition is namable and corresponds to a concept. The low is (just as, according to *Philebus*, pleasure would be) essentially out of all proportion. It transgresses the limits within which the idea maintains its control. Lower, but *even lower than itself*, it marks an *absolute comparative*, a comparative with no referent, a comparative that in and of itself dissolves common measure.

The low is not the result of work. Work belongs entirely to the eschatological perspective of redemption. The thought of work, thought as work, has always been caught up in an effort at rehabilitation; work obliterates the results of the fall, it allows man to raise himself up. Scatology, on the contrary, is shot through with the desire to fall. Low can be a concept no more than it can be part of a project: thinking the low is simultaneously more and less than work, it is chance, the luck of the fall. Bataille rather rarely has recourse to proof by etymology. In *Sur Nietzsche*, however, it is etymology he asks to shape the series chance/ cadence/ fall (chute): "*Chance* has the same origins (cadentia) as *échéance* (falling due). *Chance* is what falls due, what falls, what befalls (at the beginning this was good or bad luck/ chance). It is *aléa*, how the dice *fall*." [57]

And cadence, in turn, evokes dance (disgusting to philosophers, according to Nietzsche); dance which is no more an argument than laughter, proves nothing, but which perhaps, along with laughter, is the only way out, the only excess eluding philosophical speculation. In 1943, Sartre had devoted an article to *L'Expérience intérieure*, an article in which as a philosopher he looks down on Bataille. Bataille replied in the "Défense de l'expérience intérieure," which makes up the fourth appendix in *Sur Nietzsche*. But Bataille's real response to Sartre is to be found elsewhere in the same book: in the episode of "dancing before Sartre" evoked by several fragments from February-April 1944: "Happily remembering the night I drank and danced— danced alone, like a peasant, like a faun, in the midst of couples.

Alone? To tell the truth, we were dancing face to face, in a *potlatch* of absurdity, *the philosopher*—Sartre—and I." [58]

Obviously, this is no argument. It is a heterological operation. A low blow. The fall/cadence/chance, the only transgression of theoretical ascension, is not the result of reason: it is neither the outcome of work, nor the conclusion of some reasoning. It is a difficult lapsus. "The hardest./ Touching the lowest." [59] *Lapsus:* in Latin, to slide, to fall. The fall, which we will come back to, is occasioned by a short circuit of knowledge and sexual bliss. It makes man leave the platitude of his horizontal and/or ascendant purgatory. Then he finds himself in Hell (a section of the library where the most troubling books are quarantined. On the cover of one this inscription may be read: Divinus deus). This is the realm of pagan gods. The *inferni*, the places below, are divine: *Eritis sicut dii*, said the tempter before the fall. Because the fall alone is divine. It is a divine pleasure to fall.— "But I must descend to *comfort* stations." [60]

What is low does not fall under concept but beyond its reach. It is only the uncontainable difference from itself of what is *lower* than itself. It has no identity and, at the same time, eludes transposition. Bataille's low blows are always meant to desublimate some metaphor.[61] He criticizes transpositions, therefore, paradoxically by means of the principle of identity itself, invoking it precisely at the point at which nonlogical difference intervenes, consequently, to play the part of a *simulacrum* of the principle of identity, as a fake principle of identity, which has to be called the principle of the simulacrum. For example, in "La 'Vieille taupe' ": "The earth is low, the world is world."[62]

"La 'Vieille taupe' " is an answer to André Breton's *Second manifeste du surréalisme*. This arrogant formulation of the principle of identity follows Bataille's citation of the rhetoric with which Breton's text ends: "May one use, despite all prohibition, the avenging weapon of *idea* against the bestiality of all beings and all things, and may one some day, conquered—but conquered only *if the world is world*—welcome the firing of its depressing guns as a salvo." One might be reading *Phaedo:* being surrealist is learning to die. The idea, thanks to which the world can not be world, transposes (transfigures) failure into victory, the fall into salvation. It permits revenge on the "bestiality" (animality) of those who would have the earth be low and the world be world.

This refusal of transposition is the leitmotif of pages collected in "Dossier de la polémique avec André Breton," in the second volume of *Oeuvres complètes*. It is composed of several completed texts not published at the time of their writing (which is an indication of effective even if indirect social censorship: for example, the bankruptcy of a review, which was the case for *Bifur* where "La 'Vieille taupe' " was to have been published). But there are also a quantity of incomplete fragments. This unfinished state is certainly an even clearer sign of the prohibition hanging over certain statements, to the point of preventing not only their seeing daylight, but also their even being formulated. The low, the untransposable is marked by these blanks, by these interrupted pages that remind us that Philebus, who took pleasure without defending pleasure, said practically nothing.

Bataille's scatological inscriptions are therefore not to the taste of the surrealist: they do not like the shit from which, in fact, it is not certain that the avenging weapon of the idea will manage to extricate us. Enter Sade: all the texts Bataille wrote on the occasion of these polemics with Breton refer to this sentence from *Justine:* "Verneuil makes them shit," writes Sade, "he eats the turd and wants them to eat his. The woman whom he makes eat his shit vomits, he eats what she throws up."[63] A sadistic scene echoed in Bataille by the sequence surrounding "L'Oeil pinéal": this eye (among other functions) is meant to look straight at the sun and looking at the sun is the equivalent of eating its excrement. But the "coprolagnic aberration," as Gilbert Lély so elegantly expresses it (regretting, however, Sade's abuse of this "paresthesia" in Les 120 journées de Sodome, "the result above all of mental alienation," an "error compromising in many places the didactic value of such a work"),[64] the coprolagnic aberration, then, is what Bataille in this period retains above all else of Sade's writings. No doubt this is because it is essential to the elaboration of practical heterology, of which scatology is the exoteric aspect, but also, certainly, because he anticipated Breton's disgust.

Let's just say that Bataille's Sade is sufficiently indigestible to cause Breton to perform, through his repulsion, typical scatological utterance. Certain of Breton's formulas, in fact, are a perfect rendition of scatological practice. For example, after having written that "when the 'unmentionable brush' Jarry spoke of fell into his plate, Bataille declared he was enchanted" (a somewhat doubtful phrase, since nothing would be less obvious than Bataille's "enchantment"), after this doubtful mention of Jarry, Breton inserts a note at the bottom of the page that is so accurate that it is hard to see his offensive intentions: "Marx, in his Difference between the Democritean and Epicurean Philosophy of Nature, reveals how, in every epoch, thus are born hair-philosophers, fingernail-philosophers, big toe-philosophers, excrement-philosophers, etc."[65] Bataille, or the excrement-philosopher. Scatology, in fact, has no other aim than to lower the seat of thought a few degrees, to make it, in every case, lose its head or, what comes down to the same thing, make the head lose thought. Return of the brute, back to headless animality. The philosopher-dumb-as-his-feet, the headless philosopher. The philosopher-prick. I desublimate. Bataille:—"to think the way a cock would think if it were at liberty to demand what it needs."[66]

("Cock": a dirty, obscene word. One might say that if metaphor always refers, at least in the definition given of it by rhetorical theory, to a proper name restricting in advance the field of its transpositions, scatological deconstruction of this sublimating process is produced by contact with an untransposable unspeakable: the search for the dirty name is a conclusive component of this tactic. The dirty word is a word exposing its impropriety, but, rather than doing it by moving toward some desired proper name, it exposes, on the contrary, what is not-proper and unclean about the proper name, exposing the transposition every name, by itself, is already, the transposition betraying the unspeakable, that which cannot be named.

"Cock," doubtless, is not a proper name, no more one than "prick," etc. But also no more, perhaps than "penis," or "phallus." This question has been studied by Ferenczi ["On Obscene Words"]. Whereas Freud recommended the use in analysis of medical [scientific] terms that do not wound the patients' modesty—already under great duress because of the sexual nature of the repressed representations—Ferenczi demonstrates the progress that is, however, accomplished by removing lexical inhibitions having to do with obscene expressions. The obscene is defined economically by its not-belonging to the verbal system as it is produced by education, that is to the system of verbal representations [*Wortvorstellung*] that are the basis for the secondary system [logical connections, etc.]. It does belong to "conceptual language," it is not an instrument of "communication" but an aggression. In the sense that, for Freud, children treat words as objects, an obscene word is a verbal representation functioning as a thing-representation [*Sachvorstellung*]. "An obscene word," according to Ferenczi, "has a peculiar power of compelling the hearer to imagine the named object it denotes—the sexual organ or function—*in substantial actuality.*" [67] Whereas scientific ["medical"] words are *signs* of obscene realities, obscene words are themselves obscene *realities.* They have a hallucinatory virulence. Lacan says: "At the place where the unspeakable object of such hallucinations is rejected in reality, a word makes itself heard, so that, coming in place of that which is nameless, it has not been able to follow the subject's intention, without detaching it from this intention by marking it as a reply." [68]

The obscene word therefore is the dirty name—the one that is not the proper name but a pseudonym: false name.)

An anecdote. One of Dali's paintings is entitled *Le Jeu lugubre.* The lugubrious game. In his autobiography, *La Vie secrète de Salvador Dali,* the painter mentions that Breton, who had come to his studio with Éluard and Gala, was shocked by a "scatological" detail in this picture: in one corner was depicted the back of a figure in underpants leaking shit down the person's legs. This was disturbing enough to the visitors in its scabrous detail that Gala went so far as to ask Dali whether or not he was in the habit of eating his excrement. Xavière Gauthier, who quotes the story, wonders if Dali did not make up the whole thing.[69] It coincides too much with the fundamental rejection of scatology providing the basis for Breton's behavior when faced with Bataille (one should recall Breton's reactions to a book later destroyed by Bataille, W.-C.).[70] The anecdote is all the more interesting because Dali's *Le Jeu lugubre* played a part in the polemics between Bataille and Breton. Bataille had written an article that it was supposed to illustrate. This article, which appeared in *Documents* in December 1929 (that is the same month in which *La Révolution surréaliste* published the *Second manifeste*), initially was supposed to serve as apology for Dali's painting, a painting that supposedly, according to Bataille, refused to capitulate to the playing out of antiscatological transpositions. Hence the original title of the article, "Dali hurle avec Sade."[71] In the meanwhile, Dali sided with Breton (should this about-face be connected to the sentence in his autobiography in which he mentions, still about the same picture: "I had to justify myself by saying that it was only fake excrement"?) and refused to have his picture published in *Documents*. There was even pressure not to publish Bataille's article. Finally it came out with the title "Le Jeu lugubre," the lugubrious game, accompanied by a sketch of Dali's painting. Bataille: "*some* sorts of carrying-on in the artistic/literary milieu are just as liable to make one permanently disgusted."

There is a weighty argument at stake in the counterpoint of Bataille's provocations and Breton's retching. What is the status of avant-garde writing? Once one knows where this all comes from can one keep on playing the sublimating game? Is something not definitively defused?

Sade had two values: an *exchange value*, imbuing his work and figure with messages of an aesthetic, scientific, and social order, involving him in those secondary processes that would permit him to be communicated, and a *use value* that reactivates his floating scatological untamed content and assures a regression to primary processes. There is the Sade one speaks about (and one should remark that Bataille, in "La Valeur d'usage de D.A.F. de Sade," precisely does not speak about Sade) and the unspeakable Sade. There are similarly two uses for Freud, two positions for literature in relation to psychoanalysis, each of which can be represented by Bataille and Breton, respectively.

The gap between them appears not only in the form of theoretical statements, in texts where one or the other expressed an opinion on the subject; it can already be felt in the biographical circumstances bringing them in contact with psychoanalysis. Bataille as a patient and Breton as a psychiatrist. Bataille: psychoanalyzed in 1925 by Adrien Borel. Breton: medical studies, assignment as a military doctor at the psychiatric center in Saint-Dizier, Val-de-Grace (at the same time as Aragon), then, in 1921, his trip to Vienna to meet Freud. In contrast to Breton's experience, Bataille's interest in analytical theory as such would be relatively weak, or at least reserved (he really preferred texts on the subject of collective psychology—*Group Psychology and the Analysis of the Ego; Totem and Taboo*—or texts that were at the time commonly rejected as being speculative—*Beyond the Pleasure Principle*). He would never have the intense relationship with Freud that he had, in a positive sense, with Nietzsche, or in a negative sense with Hegel.

The same gap is to be found in their respective theoretical stances. Bataille would speak out in favor of perverse practices that are not transposed, writing for him being not the locus of a theoretical negation of the distinction between normality and pathology, but a real practice of unbalance, a real risk for mental health. But "madness" is precisely what cannot be imitated. There is nothing more foreign to him than a project such as the one resulting in "simulations de délire" published by Breton and Éluard in 1930, in *L'Immaculée Conception:*[72] delirium and madness cannot be imitated; they are never produced without *spots or stains.* Madness, because it eludes the order of the idea, is no doubt as a result merely a simulacrum, a false appearance. But nothing is more foreign to false appearance than simulation. (The law of sacrifice: "in sacris simulata pro veris accipere," as Hubert and Mauss remind us.) The definition of the simulacrum can be boiled down to two propositions: 1) it simulates *nothing;* 2) nothing can simulate it. Whereas Breton proposes a use for psychoanalysis, Bataille proposes an inscription of perversion.

In the *Second manifeste,* moreover, Breton unloads all his medical knowledge on Bataille in a torrent of diagnostics: Bataille's theses "belong to medicine or exorcism"; "doctors would call this a generalized state of defective consciousness"; "a classic sign of psychasthenia."[73]

(Fifteen years later Sartre's article would conclude in the same tone: "The rest is a matter for psychoanalysis.")

Once again, for Bataille, it is a question of escaping from the idealist plot in which every position, from the instant in which it stops producing and maintaining itself within the positive virulence of some kind of practice, inevitably becomes paralyzed (no matter how revolutionary its content and aims might otherwise be) as a *theoretical* position.

There are four approximately contemporary texts that I will quote here, which will permit us to see in what terms this demand is formulated for Bataille in the framework of his opposition to surrealism. It is first of all a negative demand: the revealing of certain traps and the attempt to avoid falling into them. As for replacing whatever it is that this gesture breaks with, perhaps one should not think of this so quickly: the formula of replacement itself is already caught up in advance in the economy of transposition. Rather than replacing the overshadowing occupant, one should confront, as far as possible, the unfilled void, the unblocked void of a certain *place* yet unnamed. Raise a curtain, drop a name. Nothing *more*.

Covering up, repressing, are the mechanisms of neurosis itself— neurosis that, as Freud demonstrated, makes up every culture with its system of norms, its prohibitions, and its rules. Every civilization guarantees the security of those who accept its framework: anxiety has no place once one does not think about things one has no idea of. Freud says, "Neurosis is, so to speak, the negative of perversion." Whereas in neurosis most of sexual drives, particularly those condemned by moral and social authorities, are only manifested under the disguise of symptomatic transpositions, the absence of repression allows them to appear, untransposed, in the life of those who are perverse. In this sense, the absence of repression makes perversion a sort of return to or sustaining of infant sexuality. But only to a certain extent: whereas the child is ignorant of the law, whereas his or her innocent deviations are tolerated because there is no thought of evil, it is essential for the pervert to oppose the law.

It is in that gap between childish ignorance and the perverse rejection of the law that Bataille, in the following texts, strives to make way for his voice. This is the problem: if, on the one hand, language is, like any other cultural phenomenon, a sublimation, a process of neurotic transposition that covers over the desiring drive, and if, on the other hand, this drive certainly appears in infantile existence, but only on the condition of not speaking, of respecting the silence of the *infans*, under what conditions can what must not be said be, nonetheless, said? How can perversion speak out without turning into neurosis? What sort of practice would permit the word to be produced as a perverse *action*?

1. The first text will be "Le Gros orteil" (*Documents*, no. 6, November 1929). It is an article whose "sense" Bataille provides in the final paragraph: an attempt at antipoetic fetishism, a laying bare of what recognized sublimations veil: the foot with its big toe protruding is not the same as the foot of verse rhythm.

The sense of this article lies in the insistence upon implicating directly and explicitly *whatever seduces*, disregarding poetic maneuvering, which is, when all is said and done, only a diversion (most human beings are naturally weak and cannot abandon themselves to their instincts except in the half-light of poetry). A return to reality does not imply any new acceptance, but it means that one has been basely, and vulgarly, seduced, without transposition and badly enough to cry over, staring wide-eyed: staring thus wide-eyed at a big toe.[74]

(Implicating directly. . . . The foot *itself* is what is implicated in fetishism. A foot there for nothing else. A foot that is directly the object of desire, the object of seduction. An acceptation of fetishism that is different from Freud's, who shows the fetish to be a substitute: it is there in place of something else. I leave open the question of whether what is most important in Bataille's description is fetishism as such or the untransposable nature of the object of desire. Moreover, one must also ask oneself whether the refusal of transposition is equivalent to the assertion of something untransposable. If there is something *irreplaceable* for Bataille, it is a sense of the *place* itself, the place as something simultaneously empty and occupied. The fact remains that transposition is the common basis for both poetry and neurosis, both of which are in the service of counterdrives covering up the place at any cost [perversion would be the empty place, neurosis the occupied place]. See the first lines of the first version of the article on Dali: "The elements of a dream or hallucination are transpositions; the poetic use of dreams comes down to a consecration of unconscious censure, that is the consecration of a secret shame and of cowardice."[75])

2. One semidarkness for another: it is time for the literary hacks to abandon poetry's half-light for that to be found in the psychoanalyst's office. That is the theme of a review of an article by Emmanuel Berl ("Conformismes freudiens") published by Bataille in *Documents* (1930, no. 5).

> Berl starts making a lot of noise about the painters and literary hacks who are selling complexes, and yet there are very few painters and very few writers who have at this time any knowledge whatsoever of the complexes that their painting and their literature express unconsciously. Why not make the diametrically opposed assertion: that it is too bad these people have not yet gotten in the habit of going to stretch out in person on the analyst's couch and free-associating there under the cover of semidarkness.[76]

Artists, therefore, today are no more than the providers of "applied" psychoanalysis, they sell complexes. When it recognized the authority of psychoanalysis, contemporary art ended up with a compromise: whereas the logic implied in the Freudian discovery would lead, Bataille thinks, to the total and irreversible demystification of the artistic realm, artists (surrealists), on the contrary, find there one last resource, the material of one last burst of energy. Fearing to expose themselves "in person" to analysis, they offer their works to it— an intermediary protecting them against the effects of direct analysis. Literature survives as an object at the disposal of analytical science because writers, as subjects, fear the ordeal of a real course of treatment. Free association occurs only in books. Behind what are apparently autoanalyses there is, in reality, only a subject who is afraid to put his economy at stake—directly and in person—in a true analysis. The effect of psychoanalysis is a "reduction of repression" (a phrase that could describe perversion) as well as a "relative elimination of symbolism." Both of these elements are fatal to the mechanisms of sublimation, which they deprive of energy sources. Literature also (neurotic) is able to exist only through the exploitation of symbolic transpositions occasioned by repression.

Whether Bataille's description of the relationship between surrealism (which, moreover, is not explicitly named in the text) and psychoanalysis is correct or not, he raises an obvious question. For a literature to be no longer a field of application for psychoanalysis, it would have to have undergone this analysis itself directly. Yet, once conscious mechanisms are brought to light, certain springs run dry.

It is certainly no longer possible to continue as before. Petty indulgent attitudes (simulations of delirium, "critical" paranoia) lose all their resources. But what can be done to replace them? What can writing or painting mean *after* psychoanalysis? "One must move on to another type of exercise."[77]

3. Another type of exercise: one implying a desublimated writing, a writing that sustains (rather than covers up) perverse desire. This is also what is suggested, unnamed here as well (for "nothing really new can yet replace art"), in the article Bataille published in the final issue of *Documents* (1930, no. 8). The title here, once again, takes aim indirectly at surrealist aesthetics: "L'Esprit moderne et le jeu des transpositions" (Modern Spirit and the Game of Transpositions). The fact that *Documents* comes to an end with this text is double proof of failure: the text directed at surrealism proves it failed by allowing itself in the end to be almost completely assimilated by the cultural context (it produced works and these works sold, were exchanged), so that breaking with it was necessary. But it is also proof of the failure of the rupture itself for which *Documents* was an unworkable organ: only works can be documented. Shiftlessness has no place to go.

The "play of transpositions" mentioned in the article's title refers to the "symbolism" discovered by psychoanalysis and exploited by the surrealists. It is a minor form of play because, far from playing the game, far from playing with what plays out in desire, symbolism's only play is to transpose desire and turn it into works. Nothing artistic, nothing cultural can ever be on a level with desire. The only way out: a return to perversion in its most naked form, to perversion as play that is a refusal of transposition. In the social order, that which is exchanged under the name "works of art" is, no doubt, related to desire, which is its cause; however, works of art can never really replace the objects of this desire. They may claim to do so, but these objects are "irreplaceable."

Awaken perverse desire to counter neurotic cultural sublimation. In "Le Gros orteil," Bataille was already evoking foot fetishism. In "L'Esprit moderne": "I defy any amateur of paintings to love a canvas as much as a fetishist loves a shoe."[78]

The "use" value of works of art is condemned to remain equally negligible with respect to their social exchange value and to the sole use that could correspond to desire. The illustrations accompanying this article (like many of those Bataille published in *Documents*—for example, "Figure humaine," with its photograph of a wedding, or "Le Gros orteil" with all ten specimens of this organ to illustrate it—a certain incongruity apparently the guiding principle in the choice of iconography) represent on the one hand the Capuchin chapel in the church of St. Mary of the Conception at Rome (a chapel decorated with the bones of the monks buried there), and on the other hand flies stuck on flypaper. These incongruous flies recall another, hardly less incongruous fly that Bataille in "Figure humaine" landed on the orator's nose as a form of heterological aggression against his discourse. Both are instances of printing bodies foreign to the value system providing this same print with an exchange value—whether this value is philosophical, or, as here the case, aesthetic. The fly is neither an argument nor a work of art. "If one could ever imagine, along these lines, some sort of aesthetic intervention from flies, I assume that by now it is apparent that if someone did love flies the result would probably not be such a publication."[79] The object of perverse desire is not publishable. This sentence of the manuscript moreover (or therefore) was left out of the published text of the article. A symptomatic suppression (and its being symptomatic by itself indicates what is at stake: the symptom, in fact, is one of the mechanisms of transposition working in neurosis)—symptomatic, precisely, of the difficulties perversion has in being inscribed within the space of publication dominated by neurosis. (How can perversion speak out without turning into neurosis?) In fetishistic obsession, in the incongruous perception of *the improbability of anything at all,* there is immeasurable violence, violence that has no common measure, no means of comparison with the libidinal investments whose recognized objects are works of art on display and published texts. The gap between the object of desire and these works is the gap separating what is too shameful to confess from that which does not even have to be confessed: every trace of guilt having been obliterated.[80] The fly photographs, therefore, appear in illustration of a text evoking them in terms that are untenable in this place. They appear precisely as that which cannot give rise to publication. Consequently, the sentence providing this commentary was not published. There is, at the heart of perversion, an unpublishable kernel that makes inscription particularly difficult and always compromised: "It cannot," Bataille writes in another passage of this article (also suppressed) "result in any noise."[81]

4. The last of these four texts is Bataille's first contribution to *La Critique sociale*, a review of Krafft-Ebing's *Psychopathia sexualis*. This review occasioned an argument with Jean Bernier (see *Oeuvres complètes*, 2:625–28) one point of which is worth recalling: Bernier finds significant "the silence observed by Bataille concerning the process of sublimation." The rest of his remarks would lead one to believe that its significance is Bataille's a priori refusal to participate in any attempt to reduce the conflict between the imperatives implied in any social existence and the simultaneously limitless and irreducible nature of individual desires. Describing the tableau of sexual monstrosities Bataille wrote: "If one is seeking information about what human existence really consists of in detachment from any idealist aspiration, there is nothing, perhaps, to compare with this series of inordinately depraved and most often desperate studies, all of which aim at a satisfaction that opposes, to the extent such a thing is possible, every law, convention, and peace in humanity's possession."[82]

A formulation that stops any perverse (Fourier-type) utopia dead: it is not society that rejects perversion, it is perversion that is opposed to society. Or rather, two types of perversion must be distinguished, a minor ("neuropathic") form that is the object of social repression, and a major form in which the perverse individual actively subverts the order of common existence. Perversion that is not simply pathological, the object of science and judicial prosecution, but perversion whose very principle is that it cannot be subsumed by concept and escapes nosological taxonomy. An unformulatable abnormality, this perversion marks the locus of illegitimate jouissance—but is there any other kind? Modes of reproduction can, perhaps, like forces of production, be socialized. Desire cannot be.

Scatology does not propose an idea, even a new one, of matter, but produces matter as something eluding the idea. Heterological materialism is a critical practice in Bataille's two senses of the term: it is constantly in a critical position, to the extent that it does not accept the fabric in which, nonetheless, it is forced to produce itself; it is critical of this fabric but its criticism is by definition nonviable, its opportunities remain the *critical* thing. Heterology is the inscription in the logos itself of its other (*heteros*), an inscription that can only be sustained by insistently refusing its own mono- and homological reduction.

Reason excluded the exclusion that was supposed to take place without a trace. Scatological writing, one might say, introduces the exclusion. Introducing, for example, "a lawless intellectual sequence inside the world of legitimate thought,"[83] or "words into sentences that somehow exclude them,"[84] or "not as a phrase, but more exactly as an inkspot, this nauseating banality: *that love smells like death.*"[85]

Making the text immaculate of conception with . . .

4. The pineal eye

The most curious thing is that since that time a number of authors have pointed out that changes in the pituitary gland could be translated not only into macrogenitosomy, but also into a sometimes remarkably precocious intelligence.

Dr. Weber, "Descartes et la glande pinéale," *La Médecine scolaire*, November 1933

The pineal—or pituitary—gland—or eye—is a region of the brain that, ever since Descartes gave it the heavy responsibility of uniting soul and body, has never stopped presenting anatomists with problems of identification. A mysterious, enigmatic excrescence, science has often projected on it fantasies that owe very little to scientific procedures themselves. A mystery: which is how Descartes spoke of the union of body and soul that this gland was supposed to "explain." To which is added the mystery inherent in anything that, in an entity organized like the human body where every element corresponds to a finality inscribed more or less obviously in its structure, does not have a specific function connected to it: the mystery of the nonfunctional appendage, the useless organ. Into this picture yet a third element must be added, the mystery of the vanishing object, because the pineal gland would not (or almost not) survive the union of soul and body that it guaranteed. It is, therefore, observable only in the moments immediately following death; if one begins to look too late it is already gone. Descartes explains all this in a letter to Mersenne on April 1, 1640: "An old professor named Vacher who was performing this dissection confessed to me that he had never been able to see it in any human body; which seems to me due to the fact that ordinarily they take several days to look at the intestines and other parts before opening up the head."

These days anatomy distinguishes between the pineal gland (or epiphysis) proper and the pineal eye, which is only encountered among the lower reptiles. It does, indeed, seem that this eye constitutes a vestigial organ, but its connection to the ocular system, suggested by the name given it, remains for many extremely iffy. Nonetheless, not long ago it was commonly seen as the trace of a "third" eye, if not as an organ of the "sixth" sense. As to the pineal gland, it is encountered in vertebrates. An internal secretory gland, it is simultaneously connected to the development of sexuality and the development of intelligence. Removal of the pineal gland (or pinealectomy) performed on young chickens causes a precocious development of secondary sexual characteristics with, specifically, hypertrophy and hyperactivity of the genital glands. A connection has also been made between the particularly precocious intellectual development of certain children and a sarcoma of the pineal gland discovered in autopsy.

Let us end this brief picture with a return to the prescientific projections that took the pineal gland as their basis: a scatological return that we will borrow from Descartes's contemporaries, Gaspard and Thomas Bartholin, for whom this gland was only a mass of excrement from the brain.[86]

About 1930 Bataille tried on five different occasions to elaborate what he sometimes calls the "myth" and sometimes the "fantasy" of the pineal eye. A whole signifying network crystalized (or rather was shaken up, activated) around this fantasy of a practically infinite polysemic capacity, which therefore was to bring an end to the silence that followed *Notre-Dame de Rheims,* at the same time as it was to reduce this text to silence. With the pineal eye the return of writing was produced with which to shake and obliterate the edifying cathedral. The return of writing. Certain biographical data play a part: particularly the psychoanalysis with Dr. Borel during which Bataille became the possessor of the snapshot representing the Chinese man being tortured, a psychoanalysis that the decision to write, encouraged apparently by Dr. Borel, ended. "Except for the interpretation, the entire conception—and at the same time the obsession—expressed by the image of the *pineal eye* and set forth below go back to the beginning of 1927, exactly the period during which I wrote *L'Anus solaire,* that is one year before the *eye* seemed to me to be definitively linked to images of tauromachy."[87]

1927: the year Bataille wrote *L'Anus solaire*. *Histoire de l'oeil* would come out the next year, 1928, but it does seem that in 1927 it had not yet been written. It is, in fact, one year after having written *L'Anus solaire* that, according to Bataille himself, the association of the eye and tauromachy came to him, an association that prevails in a major episode of the *Histoire*. Bataille, moreover, recalled on several occasions that, before the *Histoire*, he wrote a text entitled *W.-C.* that he afterward destroyed. A text whose title and what we know of it makes apparent a strict affinity with the anal inspiration that constitutes the essence, the most active nucleus of the myth of the pineal eye. But was *W.-C.* completely destroyed? The introduction to *Le Bleu du ciel* first appeared in 1945 with the title *Dirty*, as a separate narrative. It bore an indication of its date: 1928. The title takes up again the scatological deformation of the name Dorothea by which the feminine character in the narrative is designated—Dirty. Finally, the narrative takes place in London and it is also in London, in July 1927, during a visit to the zoological garden, before the monkey cage, that the pineal eye flashed on Bataille. All this leads one to believe that this narrative, one thus prior to the *Histoire de l'oeil*, escaped from the destruction of *W.C.*[88]

The pineal eye, therefore, required the thirty-year-old Bataille to go back in writing on the bookish and pious architecture celebrated by *Notre-Dame de Rheims*.

However, despite the five repeated attempts, Bataille's work at elaborating the myth of the pineal eye came to a sudden end and was never completed. Failure, no doubt, but only from a certain perspective: from precisely the perspective with which he was attempting to break. Because it is also in accordance with a necessity inscribed in the pineal eye itself that these attempts at systematic exposition had to fail. The pineal eye cannot be exposed; all the more reason that it cannot be exposed in the spatial enclosure of the book whose hierarchical organization, on the contrary, it deconstructs. This incompletion, therefore, should not be taken as an accident. The failure of a project can also be putting project itself in check: a chance, an opportunity. (Which raises the question of posthumous editions of "drafts" left behind by a writer upon his death; of the publication of pages that their author did not wish to or was unable to bring to the conclusion represented, for a text, by publication. As far as Bataille is concerned, without insisting upon the fact that he himself preserved and classified the section of his *Oeuvres complètes* designated as posthumous writings, it is clear that these writings, as posthumous, as writings not published by their author—whether they seem finished or not—make up their own category in relation to which things published during his lifetime can seem the admissible results of a more secret, illicit work. Incompletion and failure from this point of view enter into the tactical arsenal of a writing that tries to escape the rules of mastery: they delineate the critical figures of a rhetoric of nonpower. One must also attribute the fact that Bataille did not publish any book prior to *L'Expérience intérieure* [dating from 1943 when he was forty-five] to this same negative tactic: both *Histoire de l'oeil* and the small editions of *L'Anus solaire* and *Sacrifices* were circulated too privately for one to think of Bataille's having "published" them. And finally, the meaning of the pseudonym Dianus should be recalled: the execution of the author by his work, so that the desired text would necessarily have to be only an object of posthumous publication: "One by the name of Dianus wrote these notes and died.") Bataille, therefore, published nothing under the heading pineal eye. Which inscribes its myth outside the space of published appearance, of things that appear. Publication, the term for the teleological maturation of the idea, constitutes the final stage of maturation of its germ. But if there is a hole in the germ, the maturation is abortive. This is what happens with the pineal eye.

Five times Bataille fails in his project of putting together in a book the "interpretation" of an image whose lightning flash had made him end his silence in 1927. This is certainly a case of abortion, that is to say an attempt that inscribes itself outside the economy of reproduction: this failure of the book, this failure to put together an interpretation of the myth were already programmed into the myth on which they focused. The pineal eye does not let itself be put together into a concordant discourse. This failure results from the excessive, disruptive energy turned loose by the pineal eye, to be dispersed outside the book in the writing of a text, whose law it will provide. This law, precisely, is one of dispersion, discord, disunity—the book's transgression as the impossibility of summing it up with a single point or of summarily laying out its contents. The pineal eye "appears" *in place of* summing up. In the place of: occupying the place but not filling it. The pineal eye, therefore, just as easily does not appear (is not published) in the place of summing up. The pineal eye is dismissed, following upon the failure of the book project.

This place, therefore, empties under the influence of writing that produces the hole at the summit. Following the logic of the *Aufhebung*, the realization of a beginning, the fulfillment of its promises is at the same time its negation; since, from the very fact that it makes the beginning end, this realization eliminates it as a simple beginning.[89] However, despite being eliminated as a beginning, the beginning at the same time is maintained as a foundation (*archè*). The beginning therefore is not an authentic beginning unless it contains, like a germ awaiting maturation, its own refutation, unless it is capable of itself producing its own refutation, pulling it out of itself. The operation of the pineal eye, in contrast, escapes this Hegelian logic: the hole at the summit undoes the beginning irreversibly, it prohibits it from holding its own, from continuing itself and confirming itself in its own refutation. The beginning here does not resurrect. Where it was, NOTHING appears. The result is a blank. To the inaugural element now is added that which prohibits its completion: the addition of the incomplete, the addition of an additional sign that is the sign of less. The operation of the pineal eye, in fact, requires that the sum be conceived as a subtraction. It makes the move from *Summa theologica* to *Somme athéologique*. It is, in fact, by a certain usage of the letter A, by imparting to this first letter of the alphabet (of the ABC's) a privative function, that the pineal eye produces the hole at the summit, in which what goes to one's head is absence (*summus, somnus: apex, sleep*). See Acephalus.

(This A can be heard twice in Bataille's name.

Jakobson claimed that it was a universal law of language that made the phoneme *a* the first vocalic phoneme used by the child in learning the language. [The first words everywhere are ones like *papa, mama*, etc.] The first letter of the alphabetic paradigm also designates the first phoneme mastered. For Bataille, there are a certain number of significant usages of *a* that refer, however, to Latin, where it is the mark of the feminine, as opposed to the -*us* of many masculine endings. Thus there is the -*us* of Dianus, the four *a*'s of Madame Edwarda. Latin here performs less as a dead, classical language, than as religious language. This is not Cicero's language, it is the language of the mass.[90] The same letter, therefore, designates [in Latin] femininity and [in French, going back to the privative *alpha* of Greek] ab-

sence: Edwarda is, simultaneously, a woman and the absence of
Edward, as atheology is the negation of theology, Acephalus the absence of a head, or Manet's Olympia the negation of Olympus. ["The
Olympia," Bataille says, "like modern poetry is the negation of this
world: it is the negation of Olympus, of the poem and the mythological monument, of monument and monumental conventions."][91] Edwarda is not the only feminine first name in Bataille's work that ends
in *a:* in *Ma mère* one encounters Réa and in *Sainte* Theresa. Many of
them end, rather, in *i* [a phallic letter written like the numeral of
unity]: there is Rosie [in *L'Abbé C.*], Dirty and Xenie [in *Le Bleu du
ciel*], Marie in [*Le Mort*], Julie [in the posthumous novel by that name],
Hansi [in *Ma mère*]. Whereas the rule in French would require femininity to be marked by a syllable that vanishes into the muteness of a
silent vowel [the mute *e*], Bataille, at least on the level of choosing his
characters' names, demonstrates a particular predilection for voiced
feminine endings. The feminine makes itself heard, just as in the *a*
one must see the additional sign of that which is less, the sign of pri-
vation. Lacan: "Suggestion for work: do prefixes of negation only
indicate, by replacing it, the place of this signifying ablation?"[92])

The *archè* is thus turned over to anarchy. The beginning, undone,
melts away. Scientific anthropology expressed the erection of man.
The mythological anthropology that Bataille wanted to develop with
the pineal eye made him lose his head, lose science. This loss of the
beginning was already under way in the articles of the *Documents* dictionary, in the article "Bouche" particularly, which stated of man that
"it is not even possible to say where he begins."[93] Homo erectus: but
the erection is cut off short. Science comes out of man's head: but the
head comes out of man's science, it tears his tissue to open an eye in
it, an absent eye. His erection makes him lose his head. If science put
itself forward as the logical difference on the basis of which the system of beings was organized, a difference assuring its subject (*Homo
sapiens*) the royal place in this system, the pineal eye breaks forth as
the nonlogical difference shaking up the symbolic system—the system of specific differences constructed by science. This transgression
of the symbolic system already made an appearance with the operation the article "Bouche" performed on the dismembered image of
the body, that is, with the production of the "pineal mouth"; since,
opened at the top, the summit of the body, the mouth ceases to be the
organ of linguistic articulated emissions, but serves only as an orifice

emitting bestial cries of pain or sexual pleasure. Body and language are simultaneously disarticulated. This disintegration of the symbolic system, for reasons that are by no means accidental, ends up in *L'Oeil pinéal*, which carries it to climax, to the failure confronted on five occasions of the project of writing a book that would have brought together the interpretation of its myth into organized theses.

The pineal eye is not an organ but a "fantasy" (or a "myth"). The fantasy is, in a certain manner, the discrete and essential component of all scatology to the extent that it escapes the economy of the idea. For, if the idea is the model of copies resembling it, the *phantasmon* on the contrary is neither a model nor a copy: it is an image with no resemblance.[94] "All the while appearing to resemble, it nonetheless does not resemble," says the Stranger in Plato's *Sophist*. The fantasy resembles nothing therefore. It is why one has no idea of it. Which prohibits one's making it the contents of a project of communication and, as a result, somehow inscribes it outside the structures of transmission of knowledge whose first rule implies that only the repeatable can be taught—only that which can be transmitted unmodified from a speaker (master) to a listener (disciple). The fantasy is what the bad student produces when, rather than replying, he forgets the question, or when, rather then (re)copying the answer (the solution), he covers the question up with graffiti. Rather than writing, he smudges and spots. Remembering school: "I spent," writes Bataille, "an entire class using my pen holder to smear the uniform of the boy in front of me with ink. . . . Later I drew less formlessly, relentlessly making up more or less comic profiles, but it wasn't just anywhere on just any old paper. Sometimes I was supposed to have been copying homework on my paper, sometimes I was supposed to have been writing the teacher's dictation into my notebook."[95] Scatology, with respect to psychiatric discourse, claims the status of a sick person's discourse; fantasy, with respect to science, occupies the discourse of the bad student. But the bad student here is also the one in whom the desire to know is not dead (because "science is made by men in whom the desire to know is dead").[96]

On five different occasions, during a rather brief period of time, Bataille wanted to "write *on*" the pineal eye. He wanted to write a book that would have developed the interpretation (his word) of this fantastic and/or mythical image. Of the five unfinished manuscripts that are evidence of these attempts, one is entitled "Le Jésuve" (a portmanteau word already appearing twice in *L'Anus solaire*) and the four others bear the name of "L'Oeil pinéal" itself. On the first page of one of these a note indicates that it consists of an "excerpt from an unpublished essay entitled 'Le "Jeu lugubre"'" (The Lugubrious Game).[97] However, it does not seem that, between the different versions of "L'Oeil pinéal" and the article Bataille published in 1929 in *Documents* (borrowing the title "Jeu lugubre" from the painting by Dali that was supposed to illustrate it), there is any continuity or even sufficient connection to allow one to see this as the prolongation of these—or their outcome. Nevertheless, a note of the same sort, at the bottom of the first page, presents the article "Le 'Jeu lugubre'" as, in turn, an "excerpt from an unpublished essay on the inferiority complex."[98] We know that the published text of this article is only the second version (rewritten after the painter's defection to Breton's side) of what initially was to have been a eulogy of the transgressions Dali contributed to the rules of the lugubrious, little literary game. The first version bore another title: "Dali hurle avec Sade" (Dali Screams with Sade). On the manuscript of this there is a note at the bottom of the page referring to the "essay on the inferiority complex," but crossed out we can see that Bataille first wrote "castration" rather than "inferiority." All this interlocking ("L'Oeil pinéal" with "Le 'Jeu lugubre,'" "Jeu lugubre" with the "essay on the inferiority complex" or "castration complex") gives an indication of how and why the book's failure came to cut things short.

The erection of the book comes up short and the pineal eye does not come to take the place of *Notre-Dame de Rheims;* it brings a heterogeneous void to the laws of the symbolic order. Henceforth, symbolic order will be unable to reappropriate this void for itself (by developing and putting together an interpretation of it, for example, or by offering its services in attaining "once again the unity of being"). The pineal eye leaves the fetish's place glaringly empty. It is simultaneously the irreplaceable and the unfillable. It is not transposable into any metaphorical fetish that would fill in the vacancy it leaves behind. It cannot be transposed into any book or other monument that would offer itself to the mother as the object of her desire and fill her lack. Replacing the keystone, from which hangs all the Gothic cathedral's architecture, the pineal eye's hole at the summit, opening Bataille's text, marks the gesture of a writing that, henceforth, will endlessly dismantle the traps of *Aufhebung.*

Aufhebung: translated here by castration. *Aufheben:* a word that, de-

spite not being primitive (that is, despite its not belonging to the category of words with opposite meanings studied by Karl Abel),
nonetheless is a word with opposite—not to say contradictory—
meanings, because it signifies simultaneously "eliminate" and "preserve."[99] But it contains this contradiction. The sole aim of all the
logic of the *Aufhebung* is to contain contradiction, to prevent its leaving the element of the same. The philosophical usage of the *Aufhebung* reduces this word's polemical polysemy by retaining, of the two
antagonistic senses, only the one that it puts in second place: the salvation, the preservation that comes after the fall, after elimination.
The negative value of the word only appears as a first moment that
will be repeated and surmounted in the positive value. The problematic of castration is set forth in the same terms: castration, no doubt,
makes the phallus disappear, but at the same time this disappearance
provides its real status, because it is the very essence of the phallus
that it be lacking. Lacan: "It can play its role only when veiled, that is
to say, as itself a sign of the latency with which any signifiable is struck,
when it is raised (*aufgehoben*) to the function of signifier. The phallus
is the signifier of this *Aufhebung* itself, which it inaugurates (initiates)
by its disappearance."[100] The logic of castration: the logic of the
Aufhebung. The phallus is produced by that which denies it. It is only
a reappropriation of the negative. An assimilation transforming otherness into "its" other. Although it menaces the phallus *in reality*, castration, thus, is what constitutes *symbolic* phallocentrism.

The production of "general equivalents" follows the same schema.
This is a term borrowed from Marx by J.-J. Goux to describe in
"Numismatiques" the homology assigning the phallus its place in the
system of sexual economy, gold its place in the system of commercial
exchanges, and the king his place in the system of political representation. (NUMISMATICS: the first articles written by Bataille are articles
on numismatics. There is doubtless no reason to attach excessive importance to these articles, which seem, really, to originate in professional zeal. Bataille, in fact, was working in the office in charge of
medals in the Bibiothèque nationale—his first job after the years he
spent at the French School in Madrid—when he contributed to the
review *Aréthuse* between 1926 and 1929. However, his article on "Les
Monnaies des Grands Mogols" contains the portrait of a Grand Mo-
gol, Djehangir, many of whose characteristics—his superstition, his
"childish cruelty," his immoderate pride—bring to mind already
those that will fascinate Bataille in the character of Gilles de Rais. One

should also remember the numismatist's perverse position with regard to money, contemplating it not for what it is [the means of commercial exchange] but focusing on it an interest that is either strictly
aesthetic or else documentary and historical. Finally, Bataille's first
contribution to *Documents* will be an article on numismatics: "Le
Cheval académique" is devoted, after all, to a study of equestrian representations on Gallic coins.) In the sexual economy the phallus functions as a general equivalent because around it, in the final stage of
infantile sexual development, all the partial drives that sprang up
during earlier stages come together. General equivalent: to the extent
that it is *valid for* (the equivalent of) all the partial objects to which it
applies its standard of value. Starting with the phallic phase, partial
objects corresponding to the earliest stages of infantile sexual organization fall prey, therefore, to the standardizing phallus, which thus
takes charge of the synthesis of various drives henceforth subordinated to the primacy of genitality. But this privileging of the phallus
implies at the same time its exclusion from the system of partial objects themselves, a system over which it rules only on condition that it
not (no longer) be part of it. "The object that functions as the equivalent, the sexual organ," writes Goux, "is necessarily excluded from
the imagined body and from the realm of objects of drives, with a
logical 'operation' whose fantasy side *castration* stages. Castration, or
the 'elision of the phallus,' no matter what (more or less bloody)
dramatization the usual ritual dictates for it, is none other than the
syntactic exclusion of the general equivalent of relative values (of partial objects)."[101]

The law is excluded from the system over which it exercises jurisdiction. The common measure, paradoxically, has an uncommon origin: in a transcendent place whence all its power is drawn. The
homogeneous is therefore, by definition, under the domination of
the heterogeneous and the law is outside of the law: it is only sublated
(*aufgehoben*) crime. At the heart of social existence, assuring the
group's cohesion, rules a repulsive crime.

All this description of the genesis of general equivalents corresponds to one of the most recognizable moves of Bataille's text. Specifically his analyses of fascism, whose political structure he uses to
reveal "the heterogeneous foundations of law."[102]

Here, then, POLITICS makes its appearance. (a) Bataille, after the failure of *Documents*, participated in the activities of the communist dem-

ocratic Cercle, a communist opposition group with Boris Souvarine at its head. The organization published a review, *La Critique sociale*, to which Bataille would contribute various articles between 1931 and 1934, most of which concerned straightforward political questions: the problem of the state, the psychological structure of fascism, etc. This change of ground is no doubt linked to the failure of *Documents*, which, in spite of everything, had remained a traditional art review, at least as far as its method of functioning and its audience (even if the intent was to scandalize) were concerned. The shift was linked also to changes in the historical context: the freedom of the earliest postwar years was a thing of the past; there had been the monetary crisis of 1929; the upsurge of fascism was creeping into more and more European states, etc. (b) Politics, however, had not been absent from Bataille's texts preceding his contributions to *La Critique sociale*. "One must move on to another type of exercise," he had declared in his remarks about E. Berl's article "Conformismes freudiens," and the end of the note locates this other type of exercise explicitly on political ground, because it denounces the adherents of surrealism as "decadent aesthetes, totally deprived of even the possibility of contact with the lower social strata." This expression did not denounce what one could call, before the term was coined, surrealism's political "nonengagement": surrealism has a political position, but it is addressed to the "higher spheres" of political milieus, not to the "lower social strata." (c) The shift of Bataille's writing in the direction of politics is itself a heterological gesture. But it is heterological only on condition that it follow the subversive route (the old mole's route), that is, on condition that it be addressed to a proletariat defined by its total and unopposed exclusion (its "abjection") from the balanced system of social exchange. The proletariat, therefore, would be expelled yet, just the same, still not constitute a general equivalent or represent the society that does the expelling. It is to the *Lumpenproletariat*, the non-representative waste product, that Bataille's political texts refer. The shift toward a political ground is useless as a transgression of the rules of literary activity unless it is backed up with political scatology. (d) The fascist political structure brings to light the unconscious basis of all political systems to the extent that they are based on representation (which has monocephalic tendencies). The heterogeneous, as here constituted by power, has no other function than to guarantee the homogeneity of the entity it commands. By contrast, the *Lumpen*—which, unlike an organized proletariat, represents nothing—

would be a heterogeneity that, turned loose, would bring on the disintegration of all the structures guaranteeing the homogeneity of the social edifice. (e) Finally we should mention, beyond this rupture constituting the movement into politics, that there is a possible articulation between the problematics of the pineal eye and that developed for the studies on fascism. The interpretation of the pineal eye referred to the inferiority complex. After defining fascism as a "condensation of power," Bataille explains the phrase with a note: "Condensation of *superiority*, obviously connected with a latent inferiority complex: such a complex has equally deep connections in Italy and in Germany."[103]

Fascism is the clearest example of a centralized, monocephalic structure in which the nation is represented by a head at the top. But the same excluding action that produces general equivalents was already present in the pineal eye texts themselves, where it made this image occupy a phallic position produced by the dialectic erection/castration.

1. The human form lends itself to complete erectness. The military command to attention is the closest approximation of this. When complete, the sense of this erection would be a flawless virility. The command to attention comes near but does not attain this: eyes on the horizon are excluded from the movement of vertical erection. Man's gaze is "emasculated."[104] It is this failure of virile verticality (Bataille speaks of "the common nature of functions as distinct as virility and verticality")[105] that the pineal eye would come to fill in for.

2. And yet the pineal eye is described as the experience of castration. This is what Bataille wrote: "In the course of every castration complex, it would be possible to determine a solar point, a luminous, almost blinding resplendence that has no other way out than through the blood of cut flesh and in the nauseating unsteadiness, just at the moment when the face becomes livid. . . . For the child who, terrified of being cut, tries to bring about a bloody outcome, is in no way proof of an absence of virility."[106]

A castration, which, therefore is not an absence of virility. On the contrary. It is, rather, something that constitutes virility. Sexual emasculation comes to atone for the emasculation of the gaze.

This phallocentrism appears in others of Bataille's texts, particularly in the first fragment of *L'Anus solaire* where it is associated with what is perhaps the most general form of general equivalents: being. "Each sentence, with the help of a *copulus,* connects one thing to another. . . . But the *copulus* of terms is no less arousing than that of bodies. And when I scream: I AM THE SUN, the result is a complete erection, for the verb *to be* is the vehicle of the amorous frenzy." [107]

The word *copula* in French is feminine. Is Bataille's making it masculine a lapsus? Is it an intentional mistake? Ignorance? Be that as it may, the masculine copulus erects the male sexual organ as the standard: it is the middle term of reproduction just as the verb *to be* is that of the identification of terms. It is, therefore, being that is in a phallic position (cf. "Being, it is true, is scarcely imaginable without gender— by general consent the absolute has male attributes").[108] This first— phallocentric—movement of the pineal eye constitutes the being-phallus in accordance with the logic of castration.

However, this formal homology is not all. The equation of pineal eye and phallic general equivalent will be short-lived. (Karl Abraham suggests that "the middle of the forehead, corresponding to an imaginary eye, can just as easily represent the sexual organs of a man as those of a woman.")[109] Bataille exposes the genesis of general equivalents so he can transgress it. Their formation is linked to the distinction between use value and exchange value, a distinction whose result is that only that which no longer has use value gets exchange value. On the economic scale exchange value is represented by a metal that has no immediate use value (gold), something extra. An excess, a surplus. Similarly, the phallus is put on reserve, rather than destroyed, by castration. It ceases to be an organ one uses and becomes a signifier.

Bataille's operation on general equivalents whose system is governed by the (masculine) copulus consists precisely in taking them out of reserve and placing them in the use circuit. Refusing to make them regulate their trade so that, on the contrary, their exchange will be disturbingly unruly (by means of *dépense,* unthinking expenditure: this non-equivalence). Refusing the sublimating transposition that makes them equal something else. The general equivalent is a surplus held in reserve, practical heterology puts the surplus back in use, it destroys the reserve that was guaranteeing it as an exchange currency. Practical heterology asserts the use value of that which is good for nothing, serves no purpose. If mastery had its moment with the general equivalent (the master let himself be mastered by what he measured), practical heterology transforms mastery into sovereignty.

For example: Sade. Bataille, proclaiming the use value of Sade in "La Valeur d'usage de D.A.F. de Sade," sets himself in opposition to the surrealists who want to turn him into a sort of general equivalent—currency for literary exchange. He immediately diagnoses the exclusion that this false recognition attempts to mask. "These days it has seemed appropriate to set these writings (and with them the author's character) above everything (or almost everything) one could possibly oppose to them: but there is no question of making any room for them at all, either in private life or in social life, in theory or in practice. The behavior of admirers with respect to Sade resembles that of primitive subjects with respect to the king whom they adore while execrating and whom they cover with honors while strictly paralyzing." [110]

The exception makes the rule: that was the rule of general equivalents. That is the rule transgressed by heterology, but this time in a manner that absolutely does not, as an exception, make it. Exception only makes the rule, in fact, insofar as it is kept at a distance and on reserve. Scatology puts an end to this distance. It ignores the fact of representation making possible the distinction between use values and exchange values. The obscene word has no exchange value, it represents nothing, is not a sign of something (sign of an obscene reality, for example) but is itself a scatological reality.

And here the pineal eye, caught up in the heterological game, breaks with the phallic place where the logic of castration wanted to conjure it up. Though its place, indeed, is in a certain way the phallic place provided by castration (the place where the [masculine] copulus was supposed to appear as a transcendent substance, supreme Being), it does not fill this place. It is a hole in the real—that which refuses symbolic suture. It cannot give rise to the phallic reappropriation of castration.

Moreover, whereas the phallic stage guaranteed that the partial drives awakened during the infantile development of sexuality would become centralized around genitality, in contrast, what might be called the "pineal stage" dismantles the corporal synthesis, sacrifices its integrity.

Science sets man at the head of nature by setting itself up, in the system of beings it lays out, as his specific difference. Science defines man by science: *Homo sapiens*. But the head has a hole in it. The pineal eye, the organ of not-knowing, is the undoing of science. If science thought up man, the pineal eye unthinks him, spends him extravagantly, makes him lose the reserve in which, at the summit, from his head position, he was guarding himself.

"Man is what he lacks." Bataille drops this on the back of one of the manuscript pages of "Le Jésuve."[111] One of the versions of "L'Oeil pinéal" ends with this description of a human being: "He is surrounded by a halo of death when, for the first time, a creature who is too pale and too big arises, a creature who is none other beneath the sick sun than the celestial eye it lacks."[112] Unlike science, the pineal eye is not man's "essential" attribute (his specific difference) except through negative action: the lacking attribute where the being of the one marked by it is swallowed up. These two phrases are not simply equations, not even what one might call paradoxical equations, they are actions producing something Bataille called "nonlogical difference" or "nonexplainable difference,"[113] that is, nonspecific differences that inscribe "man" outside of the logic of identification.

This other logic is the logic of the *dépense*, the expenditure that interrupts the reproduction of the homogeneous. This expenditure, this *dépense* is not reducible to terms of exchange and communication that only involve quantities preserving their identity at every moment of the process. *Dépense* cannot be formalized. An unknown unavailable to equations whose reckoning would make it possible to give it an identity. In such equations it is not the x that would disappear, replaced by a known numerical value, it is the $=$ sign that would take off. X marks the spot.

The logic of *dépense* is the opposite of that of conservation of energy. Bataille: "Generally speaking it appears that the sum of energy produced humanly is always superior to the sum necessary for production."[114] Bataille: "An unproductive *dépense* is nonsense, even *antisense*."[115] The pineal eye is the organ of nonsense.

5. The blue of noon

"When I carefully seek out, in deepest anguish, some strange absurdity, an eye opens up at the top, in the middle of my skull."[116] This is the first sentence in the first of fourteen aphorisms published by Bataille—in June 1936, in *Minotaure*, and later in *L'Expérience intérieure*, among the "Antécédents au Supplice"—with the title "Le Bleu du ciel." The aphorisms, initially accompanied by André Masson's illustrations, are dated August 1934.

This title, *Le Bleu du ciel,* would also be the title of a novel that Bataille finished writing in Spain the following year: the manuscript is dated "Tossa, May 1935." It was, however, not published until 1957. "I decided back in 1936 to give it no more thought," Bataille wrote in his foreword to the published volume. The novel is dedicated to André Masson.

Besides the foreword the volume is composed of an introduction, a first and a second section. The introduction (which appeared separately, in 1945, with the title *Dirty,* dated 1928), is, to all appearances, none other than a chapter from *W.-C.* that escaped destruction. As for the next two sections (the first printed in italic, the second in roman type), they are astonishingly disproportionate: the first fits into two pages, the second occupies forty times more. The fact that the text of *Dirty* is presented as an introduction, that it had been written several years before the two parts that follow, that it was published independently, all tends to make it a sort of initial appendix of a *Bleu du ciel* mainly composed of these two, strangely disproportionate sections.

This disproportion is worth our attention—the slimness of this first section whose heterogeneous typography also contributes to its somewhat extratextual status. As with the multiplication of openings (foreword, then introduction, then first section), there is an impression of impossible, interminable beginning that comes out of this disproportion. This is only confirmed by examination of the typed manuscript, which reveals an important cut made at the beginning of the second section, which skips from page 17 (first page of this section) to page 34: Bataille contents himself with noting by hand that "16 deleted pages are missing."[117]

But there are other reasons to pause over the first section. In the first place, it is composed of aphorisms (whereas the rest of the novel adopts a classical narrative form). One of them evokes a scene, presented as real ("Several days ago I arrived—really, and not in a nightmare—in a city that resembled the stage set of a tragedy").[118] It is true that the terms of this reality are rather enigmatic: night, intoxication, dance, and two old pederasts all leading to a mysterious appearance of the Commander. The same scene would reappear as a memory in *Sur Nietzsche,* which mentions the place where it happened: "The horrible night at Trento (the old men were handsome and danced like gods—a wild storm seen from a room where hell . . . —the window overlooked the dome and the palaces around the square). Night, the little public square in V., at the top of the hill, *for me* resembled the square at Trento."[119] This scene, therefore, took place at Trento. Bataille would write two texts using the pseudonym Louis Trente: *Le Petit,* whose first edition is (falsely) dated 1934, and *La Tombe*—though in the latter Trento is written not like the French name of the Italian city but this time in Roman numerals (*trente* in French means thirty) to evoke some parodic royal genealogy: *La Tombe de Louis XXX.*

When I carefully seek out, in deepest anguish, some strange absurdity, an eye opens up at the top, in the middle of my skull. This eye opening up onto the sun in all its glory, to contemplate it in its nakedness, privately, is not the work of my reason: it is a cry escaping from me. For at the moment when the flash blinds me I am the splintering brilliance of a shattered life, and this life— agony and vertigo—opening up onto an infinite void, bursts and exhausts itself all at once in this void.[120]

Le Bleu du ciel, in which this is the first aphorism, opens therefore on (and at) the pineal eye.

The pineal eye "is not the work of my reason." It is not, like a concept, produced by the calm workings of conceptualization: on the contrary, it is aroused by anguish, infinitely restless and anxious. Its introduction into the discourse that is, or should be, itself, the work of reason (it is at school that the child is taught to speak, to write), sets the heterological practice of writing in motion.

When he chose the expression "heterology," Bataille had hesitated among several terms such as "heterodoxy," "scatology," or even "agiology." This last, constructed from the Greek *agios* (synonym of the Latin *sacer*), would have indicated, better than "heterology," the ambiguity of something one hesitates to describe as the *object* of this *science;* since, by refusing to let itself be set up as an object, it at the same time prevents a scientific attitude's finding the basis necessary to develop in its presence. The sacred, in effect the "object" of agiology, is ambiguous: it simultaneously designates that which is the object of the greatest respect and that which respects nothing. It is one of those words with the responsibility for opposite values that interested

Freud, following Abel's thesis.[121] Freud found there one of the characteristics of dream logic, which he had shown completely ignored contradiction. As a result of this ambiguity, the sacred can be *high* (which is the sacred as an object of religious veneration, a royal or divine sacred) or *low* (as an object of disgust, repulsion, the sacred emitted by crime, by certain particularly repulsive illnesses, etc.). High/low: Freud cites this example just before mentioning the semantic ambiguity of the work *sacred* itself: "in Latin, *altus* means both high and deep; *sacer*, holy and damned." [122]

Like dream logic the pineal experience introduces a polysemic scissiparity into the lexicon. 1) The *sacred* is already the product of the splitting of a whole (social, physiological, etc.) into a series of homogeneous (i.e., profane) elements and another series heterogeneous to this: the sacred. 2) This *sacred,* then, is itself split into a *high sacred* and a *low sacred:* the low sacred is produced by scatology (the bit toe, base materialism, low social strata), whereas the high sacred is only the ideal image that the profane projects of itself. 3) But the high sacred itself does not stay frozen in this specular fixation. It, in turn, divides into an *acknowledged high sacred* (the height of erections, military power: this is the ruling sacred insofar as it is the sacred controlled by the profane, and set up by the profane as the rule, the ideal) and what one could call the *ever higher sacred,* making use of an absolute comparative, that is a comparative dissolving the reference of its comparison: the ever higher dissolves the high and thus rejoins the low. This final split is precisely the one accomplished with the pineal eye. The pineal eye is the "highest" insofar as it is no longer opposed to the low, but, on the contrary, moves onto the same side as the low in opposition to the "very high." The opposition is no longer between high and low, but between a stable, Archimedean point of reference (here the high), and the comparative that makes it lose its footing.

Two transgressions of the discourse of reason enter into complicity at this point in heterological writing. The first introduces into the discourse low elements (like "a spot of ink") that should have been transposed, introducing the unassimilated exterior of discourse into itself (see the cry, the silence, the failure of discourse). The second transgression, by opening up notions beyond themselves, upsets the symbolic code from "within" and dissolves the diacritical gap guaranteeing that words make sense. Joining these two transgressions (the "low" transgression and the "high" transgression), as independent accomplices in the pineal experience, results in dissolving the gap that would guarantee the distinction between high and low.

With the pineal eye's "unhealthy" representation, the human being "suddenly arrives at the harrowing fall into heaven." [123] The fall has lost its sense, its direction (down). But it can only take place if it is senseless: it is not a real fall if it follows the categories of sense, for example, if one falls toward a low that is only down in opposition to a high. Falls happen when vertigo no longer permits one to distinguish between the low and the "highest." Disordered sense, in every sense: insane, disoriented discourse. In an article devoted to the paintings of André Masson, where he points out the extent to which the ferment and expansion characteristic of these paintings, far from authorizing one to consider them from the point of view of their exchange value, demand an osmosis with a cosmic bacchanalia to be seen, Bataille writes: "The immobile object, the established ground, the celestial throne are illusions in whose ruins human pettiness childishly lives on; when daybreak brings the omnipotence of time, of death and headlong movement toward the great falling cry; for it is true that no ground exists, nor any high or any low, but a flashing festival of stars spinning forever and ever the 'vertigo of bacchanalia . . .'" [124]

(This article is entitled "Les Mangeurs d'étoiles" (Stareaters). [To eat stars. Put your head back. Open your mouth farther than possible. To the point of screaming.] Psychoanalysis has shown us the excremental meaning of heavenly bodies. It is mentioned explicitly by Bataille [see *Histoire de l'oeil:* "the milky way, a strange hole of astral sperm and celestial urine"].[125] Eating stars is eating excrement. Along with the opposition between the high and the low, the opposition between assimilation and excretion [inside and outside] is suspended.)

In the papers left by Bataille there were several manuscript pages from a rather laconic journal, kept between Wednesday, May 8, and Thursday, May 30, 1935, in Spain (at Barcelona), while he finished writing *Le Bleu du ciel* (the novel). On the twenty-ninth, the night before he was to return to Paris, he notes: "Finished the Bleu du ciel." [126] Other than noting visits to a few places, high and low, in Barcelona and its surroundings (churches, brothels, museum, two bullfights), other than noting a few rendezvous and parties, this brief journal is mostly concerned with André Masson, who had been living in Spain for several years. It is entitled "Les Présages," a title borrowed from a ballet by the choreographer Massine, performed for the first time at the Châtelet on June 9, 1933, with scenery designed by Masson. *Minotaure* would publish the ballet's scenario. As for Masson's drawings, they would be displayed at the Gallery Jeanne Bucher, between the thirteenth and twenty-fifth of June, 1934, along with five sketches meant for the album *Sacrifices* for which Bataille had written, during the summer of 1933, a text of the same title.[127] *Les Présages* is also the title Bataille planned to give a book, as we learn from a letter Masson wrote him from Tossa, in October 1934: "I would be very pleased if your book were called the Présages and I will tell you where you can find the photographs of the ballet."[128] Was it this projected book that ultimately developed into *Le Bleu du ciel?* The first chapter of the second section, in any case, is called "Le Mauvais présage."

Be that as it may, Bataille's journal entitled "Les Présages" tells of an excursion he made with André Masson to Montserrat:

Friday, May 10.
Slept little and left at 8:20 for Montserrat. . . . André makes the night he spent at Montserrat on a rock more and more clear to me. The landscape becomes more and more grandiose. I tell André what I think about the earth and the sky. Came to a place above the *Gigant encantado* (the spellbound giant): to the right a sort of rock shrine. The top: the first time I see the planet. The cathedral of Manresa seen through a telescope. Dinner at San Jeronimo. On our return André makes the night at Montserrat more and more clear to me. The fear of falling into the sky. The opening up of the sky: in the church like a fetus. I suggest that we write an account of our trip.[129]

Sinking into the blue of the sky. Falling into the sky, a sunless star thrust out of the world by the maternal church that gives birth to it. On May 17 Bataille notes a dream: "Very sad evening. Dream of starry sky under my feet."[130]

Scatology accomplished a first transgression of science: a transgression from beneath, or *sub*version. The history of modern science, the science begun with Galileo's discovery of the law of falling bodies, can be seen (at least at the beginning) as an effort to eliminate any valorization of the low. This elimination implies that falling, considered up to that point as the only natural motion (since it was how bodies returned to their natural place, their resting place, from which all other forms of motion distanced them more or less violently), is merely one instance of motion, an instance that is in no way privileged, that henceforth is no more "natural" than any other motion. This elimination would imply that there is no ontological difference between rest and motion (rest ceasing to be the natural state of heavy bodies as medieval physics had thought).[131] Galileo himself was far from being able to develop these consequences, yet they are implied by the project he initiated of mathematizing the world. In a mathematical world, governed throughout by identical laws, all points are homogeneous. There is no longer any place for the ancient cosmic hierarchy; all the oppositions (biological, psychological) originating in the senses, such as that between high and low, a reflection of the opposition between sky and earth, such as that between rest and motion, lose their value in such a world. Giordano Bruno, who conceived such a universe before Galileo, but was not successful in formulating this intuition in mathematical language, understood its infinity and homogeneity and the disorientation implied by these. (Koyré: "Motion upward! Motion downward! For Bruno, 'high' and 'low' are purely relative concepts, as relative as 'right' and 'left.' Everything is to the left or right of something, everything is above or below, however you like.")[132] The first transgression, therefore, undergone by science in Bataille's text could be defined as regressive: a return to the values science was supposed to have eliminated in its progress into the mathematization of the real. Return of the low.

Now there will be a second transgression, but this time a transgression that goes along with science. It will be connected to the first transgression to prevent its being set up as an ontological materialism, a vitalist ontology. Base materialism is not an ontology: matter—that is, that "nonlogical difference" produced by the notion of *dépense*—is not. There is no idea of matter. Matter does not come to take the place of the divine being that philosophical and religious idealism placed at the top of the composition of beings. It is neither a transcendental signified nor an ultimate referent, it is neither the final reality (the basis of things) nor the controlling idea: these two categories presuppose an assured status guaranteed objectivity as such, a status that only a theoretical position can provide. But there is no matter for theory. The sole consistent materialism must be practical, in the sense that practice would no longer be merely the application of theory, but on the contrary would transgress its horizon, and put it (and with it, its subject) at risk. The only definition Bataille provides of this materialism is that it is not subsumed by theory, that it is not submitted to the categories of reason. Matter is insubordinate. The last section of "La Notion de dépense" is entitled "L'Insubordination des faits matériels" (The insubordination of material phenomena).

Science and philosophy are completely caught up in servility: subordinated to the idea of that most general equivalent of all—being. Insubordinate, base materialism can only be "a materialism that does not imply that matter is the thing in itself."[133] That materialism's insubordination is more essential than the assertion of matter, that the low he asserts is less the ground for a realist footing than the transgression of an idealizing ascension, is apparent in the sort of grammatical fault that Bataille has to commit to express this. "Above all, it is a matter of not submitting oneself, and with oneself one's reason, to anything that can give borrowed authority to the being that I am, or to the reason this being is equipped with. This being and its reason can only be submitted, in fact, to something *lower*, to something that cannot, under any circumstance, serve to mimic any authority whatsoever."[134] To submit oneself is to put oneself under. One submits to that which is higher than oneself. When he criticizes the submissive attitude, Bataille is not content to replace it with its opposite. Insubordination, nonsubmission, is not a magical liberation that would replace the high with the low. Heteronomy is maintained, even confirmed by insubordination. To be insubordinate is not to submit to nothing, it is only to submit to that which is below, to that which is low. "The hardest thing, to go through the bottom."

The first transgression, opposing itself to the abstraction of concepts, an abstraction depriving concepts of any vital quality, identified that which made sense and that which can be sensed, valorized the qualitative differences that are revealed to sense perception (whereas science only retains, in a universe it has reduced to qualitative homogeneity, a system of quantitative equivalencies and abstract relations). The first transgression denounced, therefore, what little sense science made. The second will begin with this little sense and take it to the point of affirming nonsense. It takes science from being a minor (defensive) nonsense denounced by the first transgression with the label *insignificant*, to being a major nonsense—no longer a defense against sense but on the contrary the aggression (counterattack) of the senseless—the *insane*. There is no longer a high or a low, nothing makes sense anymore; but this senselessness is no longer the result of mathematization with its "grasp" of the universe, but of the vertiginous bacchanalia to which the universe now is prey.

Discourse of the Insane. In his table talk, Luther called Copernicus the "Insane One" (*der Narr*). Giordano Bruno was burned on the

Campo dei Fiori. Galileo, after several trials, was imprisoned. It is not, however, certain that the Church was wrong. It is not certain that if "it"—the earth—spins, everything else will not start spinning, and science itself, swept along in this vertigo, will fail to establish itself as the ground one could still rely on, since the earth is no use. Classical science destroyed the Church but had nothing to replace it with: reason is not enough to make a God. Henceforth, there is only room for the Protestant compromise: was Hegel an atheist or not? Bataille hesitates, replies in the affirmative or negative, depending on the circumstances. Hegel, in any case, was Protestant: the modern religion, he said. Between atheism and Protestantism there is, in fact, a reasonable difference.

(The pineal eye is the point at which diacritical oppositions are neutralized: rising becomes falling, excretion is just as easily assimilation, the low is higher than the high. This sort of reversion constituted one of the most characteristic "procedures" of baroque poetics [see the letter "Des miracles de rivière" by Cyrano de Bergerac: "Now we can lower our eyes to heaven"]. A reversal where reality becomes illusion, high becomes low, servant becomes mistress, etc. This practice has been linked to the confusion of a sensibility disoriented by the perceived paradoxes resulting from Galilean science. Baroque rhetoric, in this view, endeavored to gain control over these paradoxes. It would hence be the opposite of a heterology. Far from employing paradox to liberate otherness, far from dissolving the known in the unknown [as the blind spot does in Bataille's texts], it is, as Genette has emphasized, a matter of "mastering a universe that is enlarged beyond measure, decentered, literally disoriented, by having recourse to mirages of a reassuring symmetry transforming the unknown into the reverse reflection of the known."[135] Otherness only makes an appearance in symmetrical opposition. "Every difference is a surprise resemblance, the Other is a paradoxical state of the Same, let us put it more crudely, with the familiar words: the Other comes down to the Same."[136] It is true that this baroque reversion of the universe is produced around an axis, the mirror—generally aquatic—encountered when one lowers one's eyes, whereas for Bataille it is produced with no intervention whatsoever, in the fantastic change from gaze to ascending vertical: a reversion with no axis, reversion as loss of axis.)

The first transgression could be read as a return to the earth-mother stifled by Caesarean imperialism. But the earth is not where it should be. The second transgression in fact reminds us that the mother has been put to death. That there is no longer a cathedral. That nature died putting her *sapiens* offspring out of this world. All that remains is the vertiginous immensity of a sky, into which the one who can no longer know must fall and be swallowed up. Backward, sideward, foreward, in all directions? Is there still an up and a down? Here, vomiting: "And above all 'nothing,' I know 'nothing,' I moan it like a sick child whose attentive mother holds his forehead (open mouthed over the basin). But I have no mother, man has no mother, the basin is the starry sky (in my poor nausea it is like this)." [137]

Man's delivery was fatal to the cosmos: "Nature giving birth to man was a dying mother: she gave 'being' to the one whose coming into the world put her to death." [138]

Masson, at Montserrat, makes his nocturnal experience more and more clear to Bataille: "The fear of falling into the sky. The opening up of the sky: in the church like a fetus."

On the Place de la Concorde, at high noon, Bataille conjures up Nietzsche's Madman, who, lantern in hand—lighting the light—announces the death of God:

WHAT WERE WE DOING WHEN WE UNCHAINED THIS EARTH FROM ITS SUN? WHITHER IS IT MOVING NOW? WHITHER ARE WE MOVING? AWAY FROM ALL SUNS? ARE WE NOT PLUNGING CONTINUALLY? BACKWARD, SIDEWARD, FORWARD, IN ALL DIRECTIONS? IS THERE STILL ANY UP OR DOWN? ARE WE NOT STRAYING AS THROUGH AN INFINITE NOTHING? DO WE NOT FEEL THE BREATH OF EMPTY SPACE? HAS IT NOT BECOME COLDER? IS NOT NIGHT CONTINUALLY CLOSING IN ON US? DO WE NOT NEED TO LIGHT LANTERNS IN THE MORNING? DO WE HEAR NOTHING AS YET OF THE NOISE OF THE GRAVEDIGGERS WHO ARE BURYING GOD? [139]

The Caesarean

Children whose mothers die bringing them into the world are born under the most favorable auspices: Scipio Africanus the Elder, the first Caesar, was born in this manner and named for the incision performed on his mother.

Pliny, *Natural History*, Book VII

God is the keystone, a (closed) mouth on the temple roof, capping the pinnacle.

In the brothel on rue Saint-Denis, Mme Edwarda spreads her legs, with her hands spreads the lips of her vagina to show the narrator, and spread out on the open pages of the book one then reads: "You see," she says, "I am GOD."

Who knows?

First I will discuss what is conventionally called "erotic literature." This designation covers a writing genre not defined by formal criteria (generally necessary to characterize a genre), but rather defined merely by the subject treated: any text (whether, as is generally the case, novels, novellas, poetry, or—rarer—plays) that describes, in more or less crude terms, those areas of amorous relations usually passed over in silence in accepted literature. Similarly, there exists a type of painting described as erotic because of its representation of the human body in states and activities that for propriety's sake are not for everyone's eyes. This literature—and this painting—constitute, therefore, a genre apart, a deviating genre, one would like to say "the genre of deviation" if the phrase did not risk rapidly making deviation minor simply by making it a genre.

Genre, or genus,[140] is defined, in fact, by reproduction, whereas a deviation is first of all a reproductive deviation, reproduction outside of genus, a production of differences that are neither species-specific nor logical, but are unexplainable discrepancies. This is how a monster deviates from a genus and from that law of the genus—reproduction. On the one hand, the monster does not reproduce the structure of the genus, but on the other hand, the monster does not reproduce itself either, whether this is—as often the case—because it is sterile, or, if it is fertile, because its descendants revert to the generic structure from which it deviated. If its monstrosity became hereditary it would cease, for this fact alone, being monstrosity and would become the law for a new genus. The very definition of monster is that it eludes reproduction: like Plato's simulacrum it is neither copy nor model. Hegel himself provided no other definition for monstrosity: in paragraph 250 of his *Encyclopedia* (to which Bataille will refer, but from a slightly different perspective), which points, so to speak, *in absentia* toward heterology's place in his system, he uses monsters to illustrate "the powerlessness of nature to firmly maintain the concept in its realization."[141] If, in fact, "on the one hand, monsters must indeed be counted within the genus, " "on the other hand, they lack certain determinants that would have to be considered as essential characteristics of this genus." The monster, a deviation from nature, does not obey the law of its genus: it is, in the strictest sense, degenerate. "It makes no difference if biologists manage to put monsters into categories just as they do species. They are still no less positively anomalies and contradictions," writes Bataille in "Les Écarts de la nature" (The Deviations of Nature).[142] The same is true of literature's deviations: they only constitute a genre by losing all value as deviation.

Erotic literature, as a genre, therefore, has not much power to scandalize. It has its own place in the economy deciding the hierarchy of discourses. And the place it has is not exactly the finest. Science already condescends to literature, and erotic literature will, thus, be doubly scorned. But this scorn is the condition of its acceptance. By becoming a genre, erotic literature puts itself in the position of a minor genre.

The novels of Sade are the first ones to bring eroticism out of its worldly ghetto by charging it with real scandal. Before Sade, and even for a long time after, erotic literature, of all literary genres, would be the one with the most modest pretensions. Though some prefaces—such as that by Laclos for Les Liaisons dangereuses or even Sade's for Justine—appeal to a principle of utility, through a paradoxical, pedagogical value attributed by the author to the depiction of vice, it is all too obvious that these prefaces exist because pleasure alone motivates the novel itself. Moreover, these prefaces, with their somewhat unconvincing virtue, are themselves exceptions in erotic literature. Erotic literature is a genre without pretensions—either moral or literary. Literary pretensions are precluded because of a prohibition that is, no doubt, even more deep-seated and more serious than the moral prohibition. If there is description of a sexual referent, then the work of writing is necessarily set aside. At the very most, a few stylistic effects will be there, and only (like virtue in the prefaces) as a distraction. Never necessary. Because everyone knows exactly what it is all about. Everyone knows that this sort of literature, this literary genre, is defined only by what it treats. Formal invention changes nothing. In this sense erotic literature is the most monotonous genre of all. The one in which, paradoxically, repetition has risen to the level of law: the law of a genre one would like to pass off as the genre of deviation. Anonymous texts for the most part, they repeat each other, being themselves constituted only by the repetition of an episode that does not occasion an infinite set of combinations. "Erotic painting can never be new; eroticism, by definition, is a paradox that turns into pointless repetition and hence returns to the norm, becoming tedious."[143] The norm and tedium, that is to say, exactly those things repressing what is positive about deviation: its value as anomaly and contradiction.

It is never the erotic text as such that produces a scandal. It only becomes scandalous when it leaves the ghetto of erotic literature. It is scandalous for an erotic text no longer to be considered as minor in relation to the "great" texts (the ones that should represent the essence of literature). And yet, to consider Sade merely as a writer, on the same level as Racine or Victor Hugo, would not amount to much: everybody likes to clear names. Our culture is eager to locate those who were misunderstood so it can make reparation for its past negligence. The danger lies, rather, in the sense one has that literature itself will not remain intact after this sort of rehabilitation. When the barrier designating a reserved zone of tolerance for the minor freedoms of erotic writings, in the heart of literature, disappears, the very status of literature is called into question. *Les Fleurs du mal* and *Madame Bovary*, *Ulysses* and *Lady Chatterley's Lover* stand witness to this fact.

When eroticism refuses to obey the laws of a minor genre, it calls into question the economy upon which literature itself is based and shakes the hierarchy of discourses that make up a culture. To say that only the "great" erotic novels have transgressive power does not reestablish or confirm this hierarchy. On the contrary, transgression is only produced by an act affecting the rules themselves, disturbing the classifications that these rules establish, as here, for example, by associating a form and a content (the latter reputed to be "low" and the former of the loftiest sort) that are not supposed to come together. An anonymous writer can write erotic novels, but not Flaubert, not Joyce, not a Writer . . . otherwise the difference between just anybody and a writer would become much trickier to define.

Turning representations of sexual commerce into business, transforming sexual pleasure into a pleasure that functions as exchange value (as a type of aphrodisiac), transgresses no prohibition: anything whose development conforms to the structures of exchange merely confirms the transcendence of the general equivalents regulating all of commerce. Whenever Bataille speaks, as he often does, of *communication,* whether to designate the result of a sexual encounter or of a literary mediation, he is talking about an experience that cannot be transposed into the vocabulary of exchange. Communication does not use, but consumes (spends, *dépense*) the elements whose composition forms the structure of any exchange. It makes the separate poles (sender, receiver) lose any distinct identity at the same time that it disturbs the code they obey. Never could any subject of a narrative be scandalous as such (realism in some ways being the most conformist of literary ideologies). In any event, the subject will never be as scandalous as a narrative's calling into question the codes that determine the system of narration. Now, it is an attack on one of the most basic codes of our culture (a culture particularly avid for literature that can be taught in the classroom) when an erotic work does not bend to the conditions normally making it tolerable. This, in effect, is the scandal: that writings reveal such a tight connection between literature and eroticism that literature (suddenly having become a far more serious activity than one would have liked to think, more serious even than science, serious beyond seriousness, moving into the realm of play) seems to be the agency our culture depends on to determine the relations between knowledge and sexual pleasure.

In 1946 the French judicial system took Henry Miller to court. The *Tropics* (first published, in English, at the Obelisk Press, in Paris, 1936) stood accused of being contrary to accepted standards of good behavior. Bataille published an article in *Critique* on the subject of this charge, in which he specified very clearly what might be scandalous about a text that was simultaneously erotic and literary: "In the case of Miller, what is interrupted is not, as those who undertook these suits imagined, the trade in naughty books, it is the activity of the human spirit whose duty it is to express clearly and completely 'what it is.' "[144] Telling what the human spirit is . . . This is not a question of defending a moral position. Nor is it a question of defending aesthetic values. Literature, through the scandal of eroticism, finds it is invested with the power to determine infinitely more fundamental things at stake, things so fundamental that one has some difficulty recognizing literature there.

At any rate, eroticism is left to literature. Science, apparently, will have none of it. Before psychoanalysis, in fact, there had never been a place for an erotic theoretical discourse. Unless, of course, the discourse stays "theoretical," that is, unless it results in an erotology that replaces sexual pleasure with knowledge as the fulfillment of desire.

All theory is elaborated in opposition to sexual pleasure, for reasons connected to the very essence of the theoretical attitude. We shall recall how Plato stages the situation so that Philebus, the advocate of pleasure, is reduced to silence. The control exercised by science over all discourses has, at the very least, this one effect: pleasure is deprived of speech, it is forbidden to use words. The violent attacks Freud had to confront throughout his career serve to demonstrate the extent to which the separation of knowledge and sexual pleasure into different fields is essential to the equilibrium of our ideological system. Moreover, it is not certain that psychoanalytic discourse itself can be considered as a theoretical erotic text: since sexual pleasure cannot be constituted as an *object* of scientific investigation, erotic discourse as such only begins after a heterological break with theory.

THE CONCEPTION OF CONCEPTION. "How can the places we come out of be discussed?" asks Maupertuis at the beginning of *Vénus physique* (1745). There does, in fact, exist a spot—a blind spot—in conceptualization that precludes an immaculate conception of conception. In the mind, the organ of conceiving, everything one cannot conceive of, everything one has no idea about, creates a spot. And, just as in the structure of the eye, the blind spot (because it does not see) is basic to vision itself, similarly the mind has a blind spot, which is conception; there conceptualization vanishes.

1. It is a commonplace of old medical treatises to recall that mankind is condemned to ignorance of everything concerning his own origins. Blind Love, *caeca cupido*: love is a spot (*macula*), an inconceivable stain. With a single fall mankind was doubly condemned—to sexual reproduction and to the impossibility of conceiving of this. Generally speaking, even if the concept of an immaculate conception is mysterious in itself, this mystery is one that (perhaps because it has been set up as dogma) poses fewer problems for conceptualization than does sexual reproduction. In the seventeenth and eighteenth centuries, for those doctors, anatomists or naturalists, who tackled problems of birth the choice was between proclaiming it a mystery and some particular theories. Mystery, reminding mankind of their feeble conceptual capacities, sends them back to a divine and impenetrable omnipotence. The theories, however (some of which are linked to a theodicy, and others to materialist claims), are all merely pseudoscientific variants of an immaculate conception inasmuch as

they eliminate sexual difference. Proclamations of mystery first. From among innumerable examples, let us just mention one of the first sentences from the *Traité de la génération* by the anatomist Daniel Tauvry (1700): "No matter what tack the mind takes, one is incapable of understanding how even the least of things is generated."[145] As for the theories with explanatory pretension, the one of preexisting, nested germs (with its several variations from Malebranche to Leibniz) comes down to saying that God in the moment of creation placed the nested germ for all the human race in Adam's or Eve's loins. All men are already created; they exist in germ form from the beginning of time; copulation is not conception; the only true conception is immaculate. But the opposing theory of panspermia—or dissemination—is no different in that respect. It claims that germs are scattered throughout nature, in the air, in water, in food, and that, consequently, a woman could indeed "conceive" without having had sexual relations with a man, for example just through exposure to a breeze carrying a heavy charge of these tiny bits of spermatic material. Materialist though it claims to be, panspermia also eliminates any sexological component from the theory of conception. Coitus is merely incidental and optional in reproduction. *Lucina sine concubitu,* reproduction without lying together, according to the title of the pamphlet that this theory inspired John Hill to write in 1750. A final example of the domination of the immaculate conception over the earliest theories of generation: Réaumur, when he discovered the parthenogenesis of aphids, was surprised that nature had not pursued such a simple course everywhere.[146] Indeed, sexual reproduction as sexual difference is for conceptualization the mystery par excellence: a nonlogical difference. For "science" it is a question of lifting a theological ban by minimizing copulation, that is, by having copulation be merely occasionally causal in plans originating with an immaculate conception. No longer is it a matter of considering mankind on the basis of the fall and of sin: science must make reproduction *innocent.* This is primarily accomplished through a denial of sex.

2. There is no science of things that are banned. Science ignores the ban in the sense that it does not admit it is there. But, for the same reason, science does not transgress the ban.

Yet sex is banned.

The discovery of spermatozoa was made by Leeuwenhoek, an autodidact from the Netherlands, who liked to spend his time making microscopes and looking through them at all sorts of things. The story goes that one day one of the things he looked at was sperm immediately after ejaculation. In a letter addressed to the secretary of the Royal Society in 1677, a few years after this experiment, Leeuwenhoek reported that he had discovered the existence of what he called "spermatic animalcules": "I remember," he wrote, "having observed male semen three or four years ago, at Oldenburg's request, and having taken these aforesaid animalcules for globules. But because to pursue my research disgusted me, and I was even more disgusted at recounting it, I did not mention it then." [147] The linguistic prohibition is explicit. There are things that science should not, thus cannot, discuss. Moreover, this interdiction was not something Leeuwenhoek imagined: the publication of his observations in the *Philosophical Transactions* of 1679, in fact, ran into all sorts of difficulties, and their author was obliged to resign himself in the end to their being published "insofar as decency permits." [148]

Every interdiction, however, correlates with a desire, and Leeuwenhoek's laboratory—despite his indecent experimentation (or because of it)—was a very popular spot, honored by the most noble visitors. "Everybody still runs to Leeuwenhoek's, he seems the great man of the century," wrote Constantin Huygens as a young man in 1680. That was in Delft, but in Paris, too, this was fashionable. Fontenelle mentions it in his *Élogue de M. du Verney.* Everybody rushed to anatomy lessons, led by the royal family, and dissections of the body's most private parts only increased this passion. Sometimes people even returned home with "souvenirs." "I remember," wrote Fontenelle, "having seen people of this social set wearing dried parts prepared by him [the anatomist Duverney], for the pleasure of showing them off in company, especially parts that used to belong to the most interesting subjects." [149] And Bayle: "Only in the past century has there been so much digging around in man's body. But of all the parts examined with incredible curiosity, none have been more scrupulously dissected than those whose purpose is generation" *(Nouvelles de la République des Lettres,* July 1684).

But this curiosity (this desire to know) remained silent. Science had no reply—not until it found the language permitting it to answer, that is, a language lifting the interdiction.

In 1685 Charles Drelincourt, medical doctor, published a *Conception of the conception: De Conceptu Conceptus quibus mirabilia Dei super foetus humani Formatione, Nutritione atque Partione, Sacro Velo hactenus tecta, Systemate felici retequntur.* Science thus lifted the veil covering the places we come out of. According to Bayle's commentaries, science did so tactfully through Drelincourt, so that there was nothing an interdiction could fault: "He conducted his curiosity with such extraordinary skill that, committing the most felicitous violation ever, he entered the sanctuary of this good Goddess Nature without dishonoring her and without becoming lost" (Advertisement for the *Histoire du foetus humain* from *Extraits de M. Bayle,* published by M. du Rondel, Leyden, 1688). This "sanctuary" and this "violation" seem to have come straight from the period's rhetoric of gallantry. If the passage from a prescientific epoch to the scientific epoch is marked by the disappearance of metaphors in a discourse, and their replacement by concepts, these texts are still far from having left the realm of "literature." They do, however, prepare for a scientific approach because they "demystify" an interdiction. Only an excessive prudishness—the sign of a doubtful virtue—would take offense at Drelincourt's observations. That, at least, is Bayle's opinion: "Let no one tell me that such remarks would be more suitable in any language other than French, which is too modest and delicate. That is a mockery. Our language, just like any other, is only created from certain sounds striking the ear; and sounds, as everyone knows, are incapable of filth. Nothing is dirty except to nasty people, just as nothing is repulsive except to those full of distaste. This alleged delicacy of our language is the fantasy of some précieuse, whose stomach is turned by the mere suspicion of obscenity. . . . If naked men are nothing but statues for a good woman, could frank and natural words be anything other than words for a good man?" Curiosity, desire for desire, was looking for desire: science offered it a uterus. (See Hegel's discussions of the skull and phrenology in *Phenomenology.* Phrenology attempts to get at conscious individuality, it ends up merely reducing the spirit's existence to a bone.) Science only makes progress where the desire to know is extinguished. To get at sex, it has to desexualize it.

3. Sex escapes being rationally conceived because expenditure is unthinkable in the syntactic economy controlling conceptual interaction. If, in a pinch, sex is objectifiable in the form of dried organs worn to salons, even there, sex's opening up into *dépense* remains under interdiction. This unthinking, extravagant expenditure will constantly be the core of refutations of the theory of dissemination

or panspermia. These germs afloat in nature are lost in countless quantities; and these germs, most of which will never germinate, are no less frightening than was the silence of infinite space half a century earlier. It is the same vertigo as that aroused by Leeuwenhoek's discovery of the "spermatic animalcules." That there might be in man's semen such a quantity of germs, whereas one alone, at best, will occasion a conception! A thought whose economy is ruled entirely by the law of utility can only be scandalized by such total loss. Jacques Roger records these reactions: "Such waste is incompatible with divine wisdom," "All of that is incapable of fitting into the perfect harmony we remark in nature."[150] It is impossible to conceive of something that serves no purpose. This is a scandal for thought pertaining to such an important point in its economy that anything useless is immediately associated with crime. Those thousands of spermatozoa that are destroyed, that have no future, are seen as equivalent to abortions, of which God stands accused. "With this doctrine, the supreme organizer is accused of having committed an infinite number of murders and of having made an infinite number of useless things by creating miniature men who would never see the light of day."[151]

If sex escapes scientific discourse, it is through all of its ties to a contraceptive, unthinking expenditure. There is no concept for *dépense*. (Bataille will speak of the "notion" of *dépense*. But notions are not concepts. Bataille no doubt borrowed this distinction from Jean Wahl's book *Le Malheur de la conscience dans la philosophie de Hegel*, which had been published in 1929. In it Wahl demonstrates how the Hegelian notion is elaborated in the course of a "struggle against concepts.")

4. To conceive, in the strict sense, is for a woman to become pregnant. In the figurative sense the verb designates the mental activity that produces concepts. In seventeenth-century Latin the first meaning of *conceptus* is "fetus." It is through metaphor that this word acquires the sense of "concept." Metaphors are never innocent. And this particular one will be propagated throughout an entire system of exchanges and parallelisms to the point where we end up not knowing which one, thought or sexuality, functions as the metaphor of the other. The sexual organ or the head. The copulus for words and the copulus for bodies have to back similar syllogisms. In the eighteenth century this metaphor will unite the research of a budding embryol-

ogy with the essays of empiricist philosophers into the battle directed against the immaculate conception: there is no idea formed except through the channel of sensory experience, there is no pregnant woman without prior "experience." Innate ideas exist no more than do innate children. According to La Mettrie: "It is just as impossible to give a man deprived of all the senses a single idea as it is to make a woman pregnant if nature has been so far distracted as to forget to provide this woman with a vulva."[152] And Hume will ask: "Why cannot a well organized system be fabricated from the belly just as well as from the brain?"[153] But Aristotle already, as Canguilhem remarks, had followed this metaphor by importing into his logic the model he later elaborated in his theory of life. There are not two copulations, but only one. "There is perhaps more than a simple correspondence between the logical principle of noncontradiction and the biological law of specific reproduction. Because just any being cannot give birth to just any being, and it is also not possible to attribute just any property to just any being."[154]

5. This parallel, however, is not entirely parallel. Sexual difference skews it. In such descriptions the organ of conception is for man mostly the head, whereas for woman this will be the sexual organs. Women make babies and men make books. To each his own conception.

That the child is the concept produced by woman in the same way that the concept, in an intellectual sense, is man's product, that both are therefore products of the respective *mental* faculties of the woman and the man, is clearly apparent in the deep-rooted theory that would have the feminine imagination play a major role in the child's conception. It is desire that fires this imagination. Desire, therefore, through its intermediary, gives rise to active animal spirits whose effects will be felt by particularly sensitive sexual organs. In extreme cases these effects are enough to cause conception itself. (This power of imagination will have sufficient force to occasionally cause male pregnancies!)[155] However, these animal spirits will usually be limited in their effect to modeling the fetal structure, giving it their form. Which is why decent women have children that look like their father. But this is an explanation that is particularly favored for deviations in nature (and deviant women): a child born with the beef kidneys her mother coveted carrying her; another has broken bones at birth: when she was pregnant, his mother had been much moved by the sight of someone being tortured on the wheel; or else a lamb is born with the fur of a wolf because its mother was frightened by one. Claude Brunet reports in *Les Progrès de la médecine pour l'année 1697*, of a boy born with only one eye above which hung a penis. The explanation: "We have to suppose that the pregnant woman vividly, and with astonishment, imagined just such a penis dangling from his forehead by striving to connect the two parts before her own two eyes, either in a dream, or while joking with her husband, or else while closely observing some display at a celebration of Priapus." [156]

That the development of embryology will abandon this maternal imagination to the popular imagination is perfectly clear. The mother's desire is not a concept.

6. Are books created like children or not? How can the places we come out of be discussed? The psychoanalyst Karl Abraham once accepted for treatment a young philosopher whose topic was the most canonical problem of all, the origin of ideas. One day this philosopher said: "I compare the brain with the womb." [157]

To the extent that erotic discourse can be described as a discourse that would tell sex (desire, nakedness, orgasm) without transposition, a theoretical erotic discourse is inconceivable; theoretical discourse, in fact, is neither more nor less than a transposition of the forbidden erotic discourse. The concept is only a metaphor of a sexual process. To conceive is to transpose sexual *dépense* by subjecting it to one sense, by bending it to the norm of reproducibility. But despite Bayle's opinion, certain sounds are not incapable of filth. Particularly those sounds in a sentence that would elude the connections that the secondary process (that is, logical thought) would like to use for forcing them into a simple representative position, into being there only as a relay of meaning, to evoke something else. From the moment that a sound eludes theoretical transposition (escapes conceptual metaphor) the effect is filthy. The filth and waste are, in fact, everything not assimilated by the sense of the sentence. Erotic discourse, therefore, would be one that inscribed into theory sounds like inconceivable spots that corresponded neither to concepts nor to proper names: false names, names for the unnamable, pseudonyms, simulacra, etc.

The system of sublimation constituting a culture is based on the separation of knowledge and sexual pleasure *(savoir* and *jouissance)*. Science, on the one hand, is valorized and erected as the norm heading the hierarchy of discourses, whereas literature, for its part, is charged with regulating the question of pleasure in the best interests of science. The pleasure function. In this economy traditional erotic texts (those obeying the law of genre) occupy a very precise position. They are the *premature ejaculation* meant to save knowledge from pleasure. The phenomenon of premature ejaculation, male orgasm preceding the female orgasm, has been interpreted by psychoanalysis as the man's refusal of the *jouissance,* the orgasm of his partner.[158] Science must not be orgasmic and it is literature's task to watch out for that. The flirtations that science and sex indulged in during the worldly and licentious eighteenth century remain on an extremely equivocal level. They do not call into question the division of labor in which science requires literature to settle any problems posed by the pleasure principle so that, for its part, science will have its hands free to inquire into reality.

Bataille's erotic texts go after the system of sublimation itself. Not respecting the narrow limits of the zone reserved for the pleasure of cocky aesthetes, they reject, first of all, the law of genre, which would have an erotic novel defined by its subject alone. In Bataille's erotic narratives, the sexual referent is just one of the elements of textual play. (Which is why the "nonerotic" works of Bataille—novels that run no risk of legal interdiction, collections of aphorisms, etc.—despite the [entirely relative] absence of this referent, also belong to the general movement of this erotic writing.) Referential obscenity is nothing in itself, it merely triggers effects that are far more decisive, because they disrupt the hierarchy of discourses. There is, in effect, no referential obscenity unless it is able to *play,* and it cannot play except when the referent does not limit the work of writing, except when obscenity is not merely referential. In this sense, Bataille's narratives must be considered as obscene inscriptions (obscene by being inscriptions). From the outset they are obscene because they do not respect the rules of distribution. They juxtapose fiction and theory in a way that destroys the basis of the system of sublimation: the separation of knowledge and sexual pleasure.

(Beyond the pleasure principle . . . Neither *Histoire de l'oeil,* nor [with all the more reason] *Madame Edwarda* allow themselves to be confined within the hedonistic economy of frivolous novels. *Histoire de l'oeil:* "I do not like what are referred to as 'pleasures of the flesh' because they are, in fact, always so dull."[159] *Madame Edwarda* [in the preface]: "I am by no means inclined to think that voluptuous pleasure is what is essential in this world. Man is not limited to the organ of sexual pleasure." [160] Beyond the pleasure principle lies death—and sustaining death's work is what demands the greatest strength.)

Madame Edwarda . . .

"I wrote this slim volume in September and October 1941, just before 'Le Supplice,' which makes up the second part of *L'Expérience intérieure*. To my mind the two texts are closely interdependent and one cannot be understood without the other." [161] One would, no doubt, have to overcome all sorts of reservations to call "Le Supplice" a theoretical text: few theoretical texts indeed are as burning and as agonized. Nevertheless, *Madame Edwarda* was not published with "Le Supplice"; these two interdependent texts had to be separated, and the reasons for this are described by Bataille as "reasons of suitability." Reasons, thus, dependent on the compartmentalization imposed by the sublimation separating eroticism and theory. This separation, in itself, is enough to put "Le Supplice" in the position of a theoretical text (whatever reservations one must subsequently raise about such a designation). "If *Madame Edwarda* did not remain together with 'Le Supplice' it is partly, regrettably, for reasons of suitability. *Madame Edwarda*, of course, is a more effective and truthful expression of me; I could not have written 'Le Supplice' if I had not first provided its lewd key."

1941: that is, in the midst of the Second World War in Europe. Bataille was to live this second war in a completely different mode from the first. We could say that he *lived* it, whereas he refused the first. Between these two occasions his relationship with war had been subverted. In some ways it is this period between-two-wars that I have wanted to describe in this book—a space between-two-wars gaping more and more threateningly, where Bataille's writing forced its way through.

—Just before the end of the first war, probably in 1918, Bataille wrote *Notre-Dame de Rheims*, a call to victory and to peace, to the victory of peace, which would finally permit the healing of wounded souls and wounded cathedrals. Just before the outbreak of the second, in 1939, he began writing a text whose title, borrowed from Nietzsche, is enough to show the extent of his about-face: "Wars, for the moment, are the strongest stimulants for imagination." [162]

This between-war period is marked, in Bataille's work, by a number of different political positions. In 1918: the hope of peace. Then, during his involvement with *La Critique sociale:* opposition to the state and to any form of organization that would channel social violence, an exaltation of unplanned revolutionary (heterological?) uprisings— revolution being defined not as the means of the laboring classes' rise to power, but as the free eruption of the masses. With "Contre-Attaque" and the Popular Front, his opposition to war returned, but not in the name of peace (which, whether social or international, fools no one)—this time his opposition was in the name of revolution. Revolutionary violence would be opposed to warring violence, with the proletariat's violent refusal to serve as cannon fodder in the conflict between national capitalisms. Then with the College of Sociology— that is, at the moment of Munich, while the democracies were desperately trying to maintain the illusion of peace (going so far as to "beseech Mr. Hitler to consent to any settlement at all, providing that it be *peaceful*"),[163] he joined in denouncing the fetishism of peace, the sickly fear of war, whether these appear on the right or on the left, where revolution is no longer strong enough to oppose war.

Between 1918 and 1939 the myth of the "final" war collapses, at the same time as the myth of democratic harmony. The postwar period gradually reveals itself as what it is: a between-war period. For peace cannot resist time, whose essence is polemical. Time: war and tearing apart. Heraclitean time (Chronos = Polemos) bringing down the pyramidal peace.

—"Le Supplice," written in 1941, is one of the two sections of *L'Expérience intérieure* that were written, according to Bataille, "inevitably—responding measure for measure to my life."[164]

L'Expérience intérieure would be published in 1943. In 1944 it was followed by *Le Coupable* and in 1945 by *Sur Nietzsche.* These three books, constituting a sort of war triptych, were supposed to be collected in *Somme athéologique* (but only the first two texts were actually reedited for inclusion in this publication). *Somme athéologique,* published during the Second World War, obliterates *Notre-Dame de Rheims,* the cathedral that anticipated the Te Deum celebrating the end of World War I.

These three books are linked by more than their date of publication to the war. *L'Expérience intérieure,* with its tortured center written in 1941 (that the torture and the war are contemporary is certainly no mere coincidence), assembles in "Antécédents au Supplice" several texts from the between-war period. These antecedents date from as far back as 1920: a new version of "Sacrifices" appears with the title "La Mort est en un sens une imposture"; "Le Bleu du ciel" had appeared in *Minotaure;* "Le Labyrinthe" had been published in Wahl's *Recherches philosophiques. L'Expérience* is a book written with—not against—time; Bataille put time into it. This time that transformed the postwar period first into a between-war period, then into a second world war, is what Bataille began to write with.

In *L'Expérience intérieure* there is a premonition of war. The first aphorism in *Le Coupable* is dated the very day war was declared: "The date on which I begin writing (September 5, 1939) is no coincidence. I begin because of the events, but not to talk about them. Incapable of anything else, I am writing these notes. From now on I must let myself go into bursts of freedom and whims. Suddenly the moment has come for me to speak straight." [165] Bataille's first use of the verb "to write" is intransitive: he begins to *write* the day war is declared.

Thus the two texts that Bataille declares intimately linked (though one, *Madame Edwarda,* is fiction and the other, "Le Supplice," is a collection of aphorisms) are separated "for reasons of suitability." They were written together. They have to be read together ("one cannot be understood without the other"). But they could not be published together. It is in one of the projected prefaces of *Madame Edwarda* that we learn this from Bataille.

Because there is, in fact, a preface to *Madame Edwarda.* The erotic novel, in the final stage, will end up being accompanied by a theoretical text. These two discourses had to cross so that this novel would not function merely as an "erotic novel," that is, so that it would not remain a victim of sublimating mechanisms (for instance, "reasons of suitability"). Fiction by itself cannot be the locus of transgression; to be this it must escape its compartmentalized space, for example, by being linked to theoretical discourse. The internal transgression constituted by its erotic content would be defused unless linked to an external transgression calling into question the hierarchy of discourses, where what is serious is kept separate from literature.

That the theoretical text is a *preface* to the erotic narrative, that, consequently, it *precedes* the text in a diachronic reading, is an indication of the reversal of the relationship between sexual pleasure and knowledge. Pleasure no longer, as in a Platonic erotology, is the preparing ground for knowledge. On the contrary, it is theory that goes first, providing the preface. Sexual pleasure's place, therefore, according to this arrangement, is no longer that of a prescientific ejaculation. It is not just short of knowledge, but beyond knowledge. Bataille's erotic narrative is science that has been violated, penetrated and heated, white-hot, to orgasm. This orgasm comes within the very space of science and dissolves the shielding theoretical enclosure. The movement from theory to erotic narrative marks the dissolution of knowledge in its own blind spot. The pregnant enclosure, in whose very bosom concepts developed, has been eviscerated.

The final version of the novel opens, therefore, with a title page as follows:

MADAME EDWARDA
by
Pierre Angélique
PREFACE
by
Georges Bataille

Only the theoretical text is signed with the "proper" name. The erotic text denies the name of the father.

(For psychoanalysis, the child's desire for knowledge is the desire to know where it comes from. The child, resulting from maternal desire, would also like to have caused this desire. To secure its position, which is one totally subjected to maternal desire, the child wants to know the cause of this desire, wants to know to what desire on the part of its mother it owes its being. To guarantee its being, the child would like to be certain of mastering its cause. For the child, therefore, the mother's body, as the location of the desire producing it— the child—is the riddle it must penetrate. But, rather than responding to the child's desire with the desired desire, the mother's reply to the child is the father's name. The father's name is the key to her desire and the cause of the child's being. The name of the father replacing the mother's desire [of which it is the cause] is the first word given in answer to the desire for knowledge.)

Proper names are only for proper texts. But science does not satisfy the desire for knowledge. ("Science is created by men in whom the desire to know is dead," wrote Bataille.)[166] This desire, consequently, reemerges as the desire for the mother's desire, somewhere beyond science in a space opened up by erotic fictions that permit the name of the father to be absent. The pseudonym is not there merely for convenience—or suitability.

For psychoanalysis the book is a maternal symbol. Which gives activities such as reading and writing, and obsessions such as bibliophilia, etc., overdetermined, unconscious values. A book is never just a book any more than reading is just reading. According to Melanie Klein, "reading has the unconscious significance of taking knowledge out of the mother's body."[167] By metaphor, therefore, the place of knowledge is displaced from the mother's body into the pages of a book. This transposition constitutes the entire task consigned to education by society. Not only does this transposition displace the locus of knowledge, but by displacement it distances knowledge from desire; it separates knowledge from the desire it transposes. Through education the desire for knowledge must be split up into desire, on the one hand, and knowledge, on the other. What the child wants to know is what does the mother's desire consist of? But science is only developed by actively forgetting this origin, or, what amounts to the same thing, by constructing a metaphor of this origin.

Psychoanalysis works, in a way, on deconstructing this metaphor, with the result that its position in the field of sciences is unusual. This aim to deconstruct is particularly noticeable in Freud's first great work, *The Interpretation of Dreams*, where it is somehow the hidden thread.[168] This book reveals the omnipotence of desire in psychic phenomena, but at the same time reveals that this desire is necessarily unconscious and only capable of being revealed through transgression. To propose a sort of science of desire as the key for interpreting dreams is thus, in itself, a double transgression: science (only active on the basis of desire's repression, only as the repression and transposition of desire) is perverted and desire, from whom science wrests its secret, is transgressed. There are a number of elements drawn from the circumstances surrounding the composition of *The Interpretation of Dreams* (moreover, the book itself contains some of these elements) that confirm Freud's eagerness to accomplish this transgression. Freud began to write *The Interpretation of Dreams* during a period when he was obsessed by the problems of conception, and of conceiving of conception: how is immortality best achieved? by writing a book or by having children? (He was about to write his first book, his wife was about to give birth to his sixth child.) While writing this book upon which he placed all his hopes, all his desire for immortality, Freud was told of a dream in which a friend of his had seen the unfinished book lying on a table. The friend's story became the day's residue that, the following night, picked up the material of Freud's "dream of the botanical monograph." His interpretation of this dream sent him back to a childhood memory: his tearing a book given him by his father. Tearing a book, opening the maternal body; writing a book, wresting away desire's secret. These are actions disturbing to bookish metaphor, actions that challenge the economy of science whose primary function is the active forgetting of the maternal body. Nonetheless, every desire for eternity, as the desire to escape desire (everyone knows that, as Auguste Comte said, angels are sexless because they are immortal), can only restore the book to its place.

Metaphors stifle desire. Tearing out a book's pages, and even opening them to read, awakens it. The book is sealed with the name of the father. According to the rules it should bear the author's patronym on its cover. It is, in fact, the father's name that cuts short any desire for knowledge, separating the two terms and making them alternatives: desire or knowledge. Thus the book is born; thus the concept is born: metaphors cut off from their origin by the name of the father. The name of the father vouches for the book and kills the desire for knowledge. The birth of the concept is deadly for desire.

Kojève writes about Hegel's concept of the end of history—the final stone in the Hegelian edifice, the summit of the system's pyramid: "The end of history is the *death* of man, strictly speaking. After this death there remain: 1) living bodies with human form but deprived of spirit, that is, of time or of creative power; and 2) a spirit that exists empirically, but in the form of an inorganic reality that is not alive: as a book that, because it is not even animal existence, no longer has anything to do with time." [169]

Bataille, quoting these words, speaks of "strange texts in which speech itself seems stricken by death."

The book 1) puts an end to history, 2) kills man (who wrote it), 3) escapes time (the death of death), 4) is only spirit reduced to a pure, objective, inorganic, inert reality (see the exposition in the *Phenomenology* on the subject of the skull: "the spirit's being is a bone." [170] *Poor Yorick!*)

Nonetheless, let us open the tomb.

Let us open *La Tombe de Louis XXX*, a posthumous volume composed by Bataille around 1942. (Open it. Spread the pages in the middle. To the place where, as the handwritten instructions on the manuscript indicate, a photograph of a vulva was supposed to be inserted.) The final poem is called "Le Livre."

LE LIVRE

I drink from your slit
and I spread your naked legs
I open them like a book
where I read what kills me.[171]

Open, the book is no longer the inorganic, inert reality described by Kojève as the end of history. No longer a book of stone (or bone), but a book of flesh. Between the spread pages of the book the subject of writing makes an appearance.

The subject: the book is built upon exclusion of the subject. It rests upon the stifling of the subject. At least this is true of books of science (but is there any other kind?), which are the most restful of all books. The book is the subject's tomb: the subject rests below, subjectum.

All of Bataille's reading of Hegel takes as its main line that the subject and knowledge are mutually exclusive. This exclusion is implicit everywhere, in every project for knowledge, but only the ambition to absolute knowledge brings it out into the open. Its absoluteness signifies, in fact, that this is a knowledge that is relative to no subject. Their mutual exclusion constitutes a literally vital issue, an issue where life itself is at issue from the moment that the subject of science is entitled only to absence, from the moment that the subject's discourse denies it the right to biography. Bataille's reading of Hegel, therefore, will be haunted by some biographical supplement, something extra that science did not manage to suppress. (Something just as incongruous as "the appearance of an *I* in the metaphysical whole" discussed in "Figure humaine." But Hegel himself, in the important paragraph 250 of the *Encyclopedia,* made fun of Krug's demands, his requirement that "philosophy produce the tour de force of *merely* deducing the pen with which he writes.") The presence of this supplement, with its unmitigated improbability, causes a reaction in the philosophical construction. Bataille proposes a biographical reading of the concept. That is why, in a sense, Hegel's biography is

harder for him to deal with than Nietzsche's. It is a biographical decision for the subject of a writing to accept being transformed into a
concept or, if one prefers (it comes down to the same thing), to accept
being eliminated as a subject. Bataille returns a number of times to
the crisis (a crisis of "melancholy" or of "hypochondria") during
which Hegel, whose father had just died, "believed he was going
mad"[172]—a moment of tortured supplication almost immediately
canceled out by a system. But the object of this crisis was already
bound up with the system. The development of this system had just
been revealed to Hegel—a development so necessary as to be autonomous. It was so necessary that not only did it develop independently
of its subject, but this subject itself witnesses the system's completion
without vanishing into it. Hegel's crisis of 1800 corresponds, therefore, to his having been driven by the system to the necessity of letting
himself—the subject of his thought—be transformed into a concept.
"Imagining the necessity for himself no longer to be a particular
being, the individual that he was, but instead to be the universal
Idea—in a word, becoming *God,* he felt himself going mad."[173]

The concept requires that the subject be subjugated to such an extent that it is transformed into concept. This is never an abnegation
that goes without saying. It comes about at the end of a biographical
crisis, precisely, the crisis constituting the subject: there is no subject
except in crisis, the subject is only produced by being sacrificed. But
this elimination can take two forms: the proper name of a subject can
be transformed into a concept; or it can be dispersed into a simulacrum, a pseudonym. Books and science are produced according to
the first type of elimination. "Hegel's desire is thus resolved in a
knowledge that is absolute, that implies the elimination of the subject
who knows, because he is relative."[174]

The subject cannot be booked. Open the book; liberate the subject.

Bataille's poem "Le Livre" (The Book) does not develop a metaphor. It does not make literary use of those symbolic transpositions
that psychoanalysis revealed in unconscious psychic processes. No
longer, in fact, is it a matter of recalling what the book has been able
to retain of its association with the maternal body in the child's mind:
it is not the book that is like a mother, it is the woman who is "like a
book." The two gestures are not symmetrical, because, whereas the
first reinforces the idealizing action of metaphor, the second, on the
contrary, raises the issue of knowledge at the very locus of orgasm.

We might say that we are witnessing the deconstruction of metaphor, not its erection. The sexual referent, whose metaphor repression so thoroughly whitewashed that one forgot it was a metaphor—metaphor for what?—is completely laid bare.

The narrative of *Madame Edwarda* opens with an aphorism, a sort of foreword, which warns the reader and also asks the book's question, asking it in the book's own place, directly—since the one reading it (to whom it is addressed) has in his hands, before his eyes, the open book with its pages spread. "If you are afraid of everything, read this book, but first, listen: if you laugh it is because you are afraid. A book, you think, is something inert. That is possible. And yet suppose, as it sometimes happens, you do not know how to read? should you fear . . . ? Are you alone? are you cold? do you know the extent to which man is 'yourself'? idiotic? naked?"[175]

Read the book—the bound book. Perhaps, in fact, we do not know how to read because we do not know how, in our reading, to do anything other than close the books up on themselves. Rebinding volumes, shutting them up with their transcendent objectivity. A text is readable only if the contents are bound; it must be deliverable and is only so when covered with a modest cloak (a mathematical one, if possible): "All of philosophy," Bataille said, "has no other goal." The metaphor of the book (the book of the world, of nature, of the universe) functions by placing reading under this scientific cover. "The universe would have to assume a form," wrote Bataille in the *Documents* dictionary, in his article "Informe." Legibility, since the time of Galileo, is scientifically guaranteed only if it is expressed wearing this mathematical overcoat (cloaked in triangles, circles, and other geometrical figures).

Reading confirms a form by covering it with a mathematical cloak. But the mathematical garment, while providing form, covers up nudity. To read *Madame Edwarda* (to read Bataille, to read—if we knew how to read) would be to undo the book, to bare the absence of a ground, the absence of anything beneath things. To bare the formless nakedness of a slit.

In "response" to the foreword on the first page, the final page of *Madame Edwarda* is an end note: "I said: 'God, if he "knew," would be a pig.' The one who would grasp (I imagine when he did he would be unwashed, 'unkempt') the idea's logical conclusions, but what would

be human about him? beyond, beyond everything ... farther and
farther ... HIMSELF, in ecstasy above a void ... And now? I
TREMBLE."[176]

1. *Fear.* The narrative opened with these words: "If you are afraid
of everything, read this book." "I TREMBLE": these final words of the
narrative "conclude" a note that evokes "the one who would grasp"—
in the third person singular and in the conditional (that is, in a verb
form that expresses, though in terms that are not negative, the absence of a subject)—this reader invoked in the second person imperative by the initial aphorism. As if the reader had withdrawn during
the reading, as if the reader had been sacrificed. Because of not
"knowing how to read." Or rather because of thinking that one can
know how to read. (And one could only know how to read, in fact, if
books were inert things and did not open up.) The reader is, therefore, indeed, sacrificed during the time spent in the book. But the
book itself is also, simultaneously, sacrificed. It too is the victim of this
reading, it cannot close again, it cannot heal. From the first "If you
are afraid" to the final "I TREMBLE," the change in grammatical person
prevents fear from closing back on itself to provide the text with a
circular structure.

2. *The note.* The note at the bottom of the page is a figure of the
rhetoric of knowledge. It offers an erudite reference. Evokes some
possible connection, some supplementary confirmation that it has at
its disposal for further development. In any case, it tells something.

By its mere presence in fiction, therefore, this note at the end of
Madame Edwarda constitutes a transgression of the codes. It inserts a
piece borrowed from a foreign code into the development of the
narrative.

But there is more. Under cover of a form that is that of a supplement of knowledge, this note, while pretending to clarify an obscure
sentence, in reality only dissolves the utterance of this sentence into
the anguish of the subject uttering it. In other words, not only does it
transgress the narrative code by being a note, it does not even function as what it pretends to be. It is merely the simulacrum of a note,
providing no further light on the text to which it is attached.

On the contrary, it has the effect, rather, of bringing definitive
darkness down upon an obscure sentence. Especially because it dis-
members the linguistic structures that convey meaning. Instead of
explanation it offers only an incoherent sentence (a subordinate with

no principal, a conditional with no condition): a mutilated sentence that is interrupted by an incongruous parenthesis, that survives its convulsions to end with the crystalline purity of the simplest statement of anguish, uttered in capital letters: "I TREMBLE."

The note undoes language. The rhetorical transgression that constituted its presence is intensified by a linguistic transgression. At the back of the book, forms and overcoats are torn and something is stripped bare.

3. *Knowledge*. In this note, moreover, it is knowledge itself that is in question. The note refers to this sentence in the narrative: "Would God, at least, have known? GOD, if he 'knew,' would be a pig."

The capital letters isolating the word GOD in a sort of monumental majesty; the quotation marks setting this intransitive "knowing" apart as something strange, this literally absolute knowledge; the excretory energy of the word *pig* that refuses to be domesticated and to fill the role of attribute that the sentence would like to impose upon it; the absence of an answer, with the elusive sentence that, however, formally (by its position) answers the question preceding it. (Does God know? does he not know? No one knows whether or not God knows, but only that "if he 'knew,'" etc. Besides, what is there to "know"?) But should not the answer be: "I forget the question"? The sentence is really, violently, radiantly obscure. A note is called for.

The clarification initially evaded by the "answer" that the narrative text provides, will, nonetheless, escape once again in the text of the note pretending to clarify. Because the answer to desire eludes conception.

("God, if he knew": the words are found also in "Le Supplice," the part of *L'Expérience intérieure* that Bataille wrote at the same time that he wrote *Madame Edwarda* and that he said could not be understood apart from *Madame Edwarda*.[177] This phrase is followed by "And farther and farther," found in the final note to the narrative as well. There is also a "fall into the void" mentioned, whereas the note describes the reader as "in ecstasy above the void."

This aphorism from "Le Supplice" describes the experience of not-knowing as the performative experience of the answer's escaping, "and nothing is revealed, either in the fall or in the void, because revelation of the void is only a way of falling farther into absence." And that is also the function of the final note in *Madame Edwarda:* to excite the desire for an answer and to evade it, to reveal *nothing*. This diversion of figures borrowed from the rhetoric of knowledge produces not-knowing. ["Not-knowing strips bare" is the title of the next aphorism in "Le Supplice."])

"God, if he knew" in "Le Supplice" puts an end to knowledge and, in *Madame Edwarda,* puts an end to fiction. "Should I continue the narrative?" "I have finished." Knowledge and fiction live only on their dissociation, which guarantees the dissociation of knowledge and obscenity, and guarantees that there is no place where it is possible to say: "God, if he 'knew,' would be a pig." Knowledge, pig. Knowledge on one side, pig on the other. If one does not respect this division one enters a space of unspeakable things. The text becomes engaged in a space in which it is no longer distinct from its own obliteration. "I have finished."

The book is the subject's tomb. "I" tremble to open it.

End of *Madame Edwarda.*

End and sequel.

Because there will be a sequel to *Madame Edwarda.* I would like to pause over the fact that this sequel is entitled *Ma mère.* Pause over the amazing homonymy produced by this title between a book (an inorganic, inert reality, a volume of printed paper) and a woman (moreover, not just any woman: she is marked by the shifter of the first person singular possessive pronoun as the one who brought the author of *Ma mère* into this world).

But first I will summarize as far as possible this narrative, emphasizing the elements that make this homonymy important in its economy. Because this equation of mother and book cannot be read as some secondary result of a particularly salacious project—the project of an incestuous erotic novel. Activating this equation between mother and book, in effect, puts the established relations between knowledge and sexual pleasure at stake.

Moreover, in *Ma mère* there is no actual equation mother = book. Or rather, this metaphorical equation is one the narrative undoes. First, because the mother dies in the narrative, which is, in a certain sense, only the son's long killing of the mother by his desire to know her. But the equation mother = book is also undone a second time because *Ma mère* is not a book: it is an unfinished book. And incompletion in Bataille's texts must always be considered as one of the constitutive gestures of his writing, never as mere accident.

Besides, had *Ma mère* been completed, which is not unthinkable, incompletion would have been merely postponed, put off by shifting it toward those new sequels already sketched out with the titles of *Charlotte d'Ingerville* and *Sainte*, that, with *Madame Edwarda* as the first piece and *Ma mère* as the second, were to have made up a work called *Divinus deus*. *Madame Edwarda* cannot, in fact, be said to end unless one takes this ending as the beginning of its sequels, as the opening piece of *Divinus deus*. For Bataille, a completed book needs a sequel to prevent its settling, its being fixed. *Histoire de l'oeil* was supposed to have had a sequel too, for which Bataille sketched out a plan.[178] We see the same impulse at work in his essays. His collecting *L'Expérience intérieure*, *Le coupable*, and *Sur Nietzsche* (though this latter never found its way in) into *Somme athéologique* makes not so much a total statement, a "summation," as it makes an opening that connects future books to past books. It opens up the space of written books to unknown futures. The two projected books announced on the flyleaf of the first volume of *Somme (Le Pur bonheur, Le Système inachevé du non-savoir* "the incomplete system of not-knowing"—a title requiring no further comment) are no less essential to an interpretation of the sort of "summation" Bataille intended than are the three published books. There is once again the same impulse with *La Part maudite*. The book published with this title was initially presented as the first volume of a series; it was supposed to be followed by *La Souveraineté* and *L'Érotisme*. Bataille always saw publication of a book or a new edition as an opportunity to rearrange the texts (the reorganization of *Haine de la poésie* into *L'Impossible*, for instance). These projects inscribe an essential incompletion into Bataille's text; they prevent a book's ever having any real closure. A "completed" book is immediately inserted into a new organization, unwritten, that will play it through again.

Ma mère is a narrative written, as is *Madame Edwarda*, in the first person. Like *Madame Edwarda*, it was supposed to have been published, if it had been completed, under the pseudonym Pierre Angélique. But though it is written, like *Madame Edwarda* once again, in the past historic tense, it goes farther back to retrace a previous period in the narrator's life: the end of his adolescence.

Ma mère begins with the father's death. This event, one apparently just as gratifying to the son as to his mother, is the point of departure for the narrator's initiation into the knowledge his mother possesses and which makes her the object both of his desires and of his respect.

The narrator repeatedly emphasizes his position as the one who does not know. His mother, moreover, never stops reminding him of this, defiantly, to provoke him: "What do you know about it?" "You know nothing about my life."[179] The mother is desired and this desire, by itself, sets her as the locus of knowledge. The child's desire for knowledge thus appears for what it is: the desire to know what the mother's desire is, the desire to know what the mother "wants" ("Distraught, I said 'Mother, I want to know what you want'").[180] If it is true that sublimation is essentially the separation of knowledge and sexual pleasure, a separation implying that whatever is known is lost to desire, *Ma mère* depowers the sublimation, because desire and knowledge, on the contrary, never cease provoking each other, expanding and exacerbating each other, coming ever closer to an explosive exhibition of the obscenity of knowledge. "God, if he 'knew,' would be a pig." Because my mother knows, she is a pig. (In *L'Abbé C.* another "girl," Rosie, whispers something similar: "How beautiful, how dirty it is to know!" "No one is more obscene than I. I exude obscenity from KNOWING, I am happy from KNOWING."[181] The erotic initiation of the narrator of *Ma mère* has nothing to do, therefore, with the initiation of Socrates by Diotima, reported in Plato's *Symposium*. There knowledge and sexual pleasure are separated in the end. *Ma mère,* on the contrary, produces both in the same gesture. Committing suicide, the mother leaves her son a note sealing their closeness: " 'I don't want your love,' she writes, 'unless you know I am disgusting and unless you love me knowing this.' "[182]

The woman called "my mother" throughout the narrative is, therefore, for the narrator, the object of his desire. But the narrator-son, conversely, never stops describing himself as being his mother's object of desire. These two desires are not symmetrical. Whereas, for the narrator's desire, the mother is the epitome of the Other, the locus of the knowledge he is kept from, the mother's desire, on the other hand, finds nothing external to itself in her son: "What she loved [in me]," says the son, "was always the fruit of her womb, there was nothing more foreign for her than seeing me as a man she had loved."[183] Nonetheless, despite not being symmetrical, these two desires concur, each in its own way, in deleting the name of the father. The novel began with the father's death; the initiation into the mother's scatological knowledge that it next retraces could just as easily be described as a retroactive erasure of paternity. Because this erasure is only the other side of this knowledge. The nearer the revelation of the desire to which the narrator owes his existence comes, the more savagely is the father's name deleted, denied, refused.

And, in a certain manner, putting the father's name out of circulation constitutes the contents of this revelation—as we see in the great scene where the mother finally "speaks" to her son and tells him how he was conceived: "Pierre! You are not his son but the fruit of the anguish I felt in the woods. You come from the terror I felt when I was naked in the woods, naked as the animals, in an ecstasy of trembling. Pierre, I came ecstatically for hours, sprawled in the rotting leaves: you were born of this sexual pleasure." [184]

Ma mère was published not with the author's patronymic for its signature, but with the pseudonym allowing the author and narrator to be completely united.

The anguish, the terror, call into question the identity of the subject possessed by them and torn by them. And it is this literal scissiparity, this tearing apart, that, according to what his mother tells him, produces the narrator. He owes nothing to the paternal copula. His being eludes the family syllogism.

The book, here, refuses to be covered up by the name of the father, which would plug up its opening, shutting it up again. It does not close over or heal, because after eliminating the father, the agony of scissiparity brings the mother to her death. The book opened by the father's death never closes. The mother, in turn, disappears. Neither book nor mother survive the father's name. The father's death is the book's opening, the mother's death makes its closing impossible. What is at stake in the narrative, in fact, is not so much a return to the mother, incest as such, as the transgression of the system of copulation that creates substantives—that names. Inscribed here, in copulation's space, is the scissiparity its system represses, which can be defined in the same terms Bataille uses to characterize eroticism: the identity of life and death, their nondifference, their nondeferment.

The mother, no less than the father, is an important element in the system of a familial, copulative reproduction. Both are put to death by the narrator's desire to know in *Ma mère*. Bataille, moreover, makes a significant slip that shows well enough how inseparable the death of one is from the death of the other. Bataille's narrator comments on his mother's death in the following words: "I can say to myself that I have killed my father: perhaps she died because she yielded to the tenderness of the kiss I gave her on her lips."[185] Obviously, it should read "I killed *my mother*" instead of "I killed *my father*." But actually, does it make any difference?

Caesarean: the surgical operation that consists of opening the belly of the mother to take the child from it. This operation has long been performed on corpses, when the mother was already dead (for instance, see *Macbeth*). In any event, until not so very long ago, the operation implied the sacrifice of the mother.

SCISSIPARITY

Bataille's erotic writing transgresses the law of genre by not limiting itself to the description of copulations.

We know that *Divinus deus* (that series of narratives that began with *Madame Edwarda* and was to follow with *Ma mère*, then *Charlotte d'Ingerville* and *Sainte*) was supposed to end with an essay entitled "Le Paradoxe de l'érotisme." There are a few pages of notes giving some idea of what this was to be about. One of them treats the opposition between scissiparity and copulation. "Death and birth are only separated in the forms of complex animality most familiar to us. In the reproductive modes of the simplest animals these are merged. They merge with the result that we can never tell whether these animals are being born or dying."[186]

Death (if that is what we wish to call this unreality) is what appears—beyond the pleasure principle—in Bataille's erotic narratives. Death by its very definition requires that it be unknown. Death puts an end to the one who wants to know her and who, in the end, succeeds. To know death is to be sacrificed to her. Traces constitute a system allowing one to get around this difficulty. All the differences that the sacrifice brings in for the sole purpose of erasing them, are tied to this system. The first of these differences is that between the one performing the sacrifice and the victim, permitting distance to be taken (the distance that theory will be based on). Yet sacrifice excludes the possibility of maintaining this distance to the very end: there is no sacrifice unless the one performing it identifies, in the end, with the victim. Unless this distance is *sacrificed* as well.

Eroticism is the introduction into sexual reproduction, into the practice of copulation (insofar as it produces the system of traces, delays, and differences) of its other, scissiparity, which implies absence or obliteration of the trace, vanishing of (and into) the trace. Just as sacrifice implies a distance between the knowing subject and the one who dies, but only implies this distance to do away with it, to sacrifice it when the time comes. (This distance, constituting the sacrifice, is thus destroyed by it: in a sacrifice, it is what constitutes the sacrifice that is sacrificed. There is no transcendental sacrificed object. Sacrifice can only be self-destruction, self-mutilation.) Eroticism, similarly, implies the separation between life and death that gives its structure to copulation between sexes. But eroticism implies such a distance so as to erase it, so as to inscribe into sexual union the coincidence of birth and the death excluded by this union.

Eroticism is not the same as scissiparity. Because this form of reproduction does not allow one to do away with difference, because the question of disparity cannot even be posed: "We can never tell whether these animals are being born or dying." The life/death opposition makes no sense as regards scissiparity. Scissiparous cells are simple and there is no death (or life) for things that are simple. "Simple forms of life are immortal."[187] This is not scissiparity for its own sake. It is the return of scissiparity into copulation, preventing the copula from becoming substantive in the name of the (eternal) father.

THE SPECTACLE OF DEATH

In the church of Saint Mary of the Conception, in Rome, there is a chapel decorated with the bones of Capuchin monks buried there. Death itself material for a tomb.

On May 7, 1922, in Madrid (Bataille, who was present at the bullfight, which he describes in *Histoire de l'oeil*, was at that time at the French school for advanced Hispanic studies), a famous torero, Granero, was killed by the bull: "Death's theatrical entrance in the midst of celebration, in the sunshine, seemed somehow obvious, expected, intolerable."[188] In 1925 Dr. Borel gave Bataille a photograph taken during a Chinese torture known as the "hundred pieces."

At the end of a tumultuous discussion following a lecture he gave in 1945 on the notion of sin, Bataille described his position:

I feel I have been put in a position toward you that is the opposite of someone placidly watching dismasted boats from the shore. I am certain the boat is dismasted. And I must insist on that. I have a great time and I look at the people on the shore, and laugh, I think, far harder than anyone looking at a dismasted boat from the shore can, because, in fact, in spite of everything, I cannot imagine anyone cruel enough to be able to see a dismasted boat from the shore and laugh with much abandon. But sinking is something else, one can have the time of one's life.[189]

The spectator *touched* by what he *sees* (a knife blade, a bull's horn). Death appears, but it is in my gaze. I am part of what I see.

WITHOUT A TRACE

—Sade wrote in his will: I pride myself that "the traces of my tomb will vanish beneath the surface of the earth just as I pride myself that my memory will vanish from the memory of men." Bataille comments: "The meaning of an extremely profound work lies in the author's desire to *vanish* (to be resolved, leaving no human trace)." [190]

—About Kafka: "He did not die, however, before expressing his apparently conclusive wish: whatever he left behind had to be burned." [191]

—In the last of the texts that Bataille published, that is, the introduction to the second edition of *Le Coupable,* speaking about what he wrote, he said: these words "would only be fully meaningful when *forgotten,* falling suddenly and conclusively into oblivion." [192]

(Is Bataille forgotten here the way he wanted? or is he betrayed by our insistence upon keeping these traces? Does one trace only become erased, perhaps, by new traces? Does the trace only vanish, perhaps, into its own excess? Continuing until it is possible to speak of silence. Yes, tapping something like the echo of silence in words. Multiplying the trace, this reserved excess, until it is unreservedly excess. In the end, all I have meant to do is expand the anagram of Dianus, the criminal and powerless ruler, the king of the woods, who was also prey to scissiparian anguish. *Ma mère:* "You are the fruit of the anguish I felt in the woods." *Le Roi du bois:* "My anguish in the woods reigns supreme, in the woods I indulge in my royal extravagance. No one can take away death." [193] Death leaves no trace. Die like a dog. Like an amoeba. Like Dianus. Who, when he died, left these notes that would only really make sense, be fully meaningful when forgotten. These notes we make senseless by retaining. Death erases traces. Erases the tomb. "I am not talking about nothingness, but about the elimination of that which language adds to the world." [194])

In scissiparity "the" parent, the original cell (the "mother" cell), vanishes without a trace when the products of its scission appear.

THE CAESAREAN

A new life is, at the very least, the earliest version of killing the mother.

Bataille, "Les Mangeurs d'étoiles"[195]

Nature, when she gave birth to man, was a dying mother.

Bataille, *L'Expérience intérieure*[196]

Caesar, then, is initially the name of someone whose mother died bringing him into the world. This deadly delivery will continue to mark all caesarizing (the czar, the kaiser, etc.). Whenever mastery and servility are in complicity. Caesarean power is mastered by that which it dominates. This servitude extends also into science and language. The profound, ineradicable complicity between science and imperialism must be considered in relation to this caesarean birth.

In this caesarean birth what is sacrificed is, perhaps, less the mother as such than the double origin: two parents is one two many. Double origin is the door to the labyrinth. Consequently the pyramid requires that there be only one. Science (imperialism) kills the mother, not to eradicate her, but to replace her, to take her place (and remember the republic's miraculous synthesis: *la mère patrie*, the mother-fatherland). Galileo, no doubt, got rid of the earth as immovable ground, but only to assign to truth this same stable, referential function. The center shifts, it does not vanish. The mother is killed only to save the concept. She rises to the heavens, transposed, idealized, immaculate. Icarian caesarean.

But Dionysus, too, is the fruit of a caesarean operation: Zeus tore him from the belly of his mother, Semele. This second caesarean, the other caesarean (because caesareans also split, divide, and are overcome by scissiparity), this Dionysiac rather than Icarian caesarean, steals from science the very ground it takes for a basis. Instead of being simplified into a unitary pyramid, the double origin disperses into a labyrinth. There is no more ground upon which to inscribe lasting traces. Gone the book—in shreds. Gone with the flow. Monuments are carried away on the river of time. Suddenly, on the Place de la Concorde, there is silence. The name changes: Place de la Terreur. Obelisks and pyramids collapse as the metonymic pollutions of nearby rivers (whether Nile or Seine) reach them. The second caesarean lops off the head of Caesar. The supreme and sovereign operation: heads roll, rattlebrains.

Death, in the person of the dead king, was transformed into solar radiance, transformed into indeterminate being. The pyramid is not only the most lasting monument, it is also the equivalent both of the monument and of the monument's absence, of a passage and of obliterated traces, of being and the absence of being.[197]

Rome, August 1972–January 1973.

Like the Archbishop of Paris who when he walked with a mistress in his gardens had three men with rakes following to erase their footprints, we are obliged to dissolve into silence a sentence scarcely formed.[198]

Notes

All translations of Bataille in this book are by Betsy Wing. The following are the published translations of his work in English.

The Accursed Share. Translated by Robert Hurley. New York: Zone Books, 1988.

The Blue of Noon. Translated by Harry Mathews. New York: Urizen Books, 1978.

Georges Bataille: Writings on Laughter, Sacrifice, Nietzsche, Un-Knowing. Edited and translated by Annette Michelson. Special issue on Bataille, *October* 36 (1986).

Guilty. Translated by Bruce Boone, introduction by Denis Hollier. Venice, Calif.: Lapis Press, 1988.

Inner Experience. Translated by Leslie A. Boldt. Albany: State University of New York Press, 1988.

Story of the Eye. Translated by Joachim Neugroschel. New York: Urizen Books, 1977.

Visions of Excess: Selected Writings, 1927–1939. Translated by Allan Stoekl, Carl R. Lovitt, and Donald M. Leslie, Jr.; edited with an introduction by Allan Stoekl. Minneapolis: University of Minnesota Press, 1985.

Introduction: Bloody Sundays

1. Georges Bataille, "Architecture," in *Oeuvres Complètes*, 12 vols. (Paris: Gallimard, 1971–88), 1: 171–72. This edition of Bataille's writings will be cited as *OC.*

2. Michel Foucault, *Surveiller et punir: Naissance de la prison* (Paris: Gallimard, 1975), p. 174.

3. Jacques Derrida, "Point de folie—Maintenant l'architecture," in Bernard Tschumi, *La case vide: La Villette 1985 (Folio VIII)* (London: Architectural Association, 1986), p. 18.

4. Bernard Tschumi, *Cinegram folie: Le parc de la Villette* (New York: Princeton Architectural Press, 1987), p. vii.

5. Bataille, "Architecture" (*OC*, 1:676).

6. Bataille, "Abattoir," *OC*, 1:205.

7. Bataille, "Musée," *OC*, 1:239.

8. Emile Zola, "Les Squares," in *Contes et nouvelles*, ed. Roger Ripoll (Paris: Gallimard, 1976), pp. 319, 321.

9. T. J. Clark, *The Painting of Modern Life* (New York: Knopf, 1985), p. 194.

10. Ibid., p. 280 note 115.

11. Emile Zola, *Oeuvres complètes*, ed. Henri Mitterand, vol. 13 (Paris: Cercle du Livre Précieux, 1968), p. 194.

12. Ibid., p. 195.

13. Zola, "Celle qui m'aime," in *Contes et nouvelles*, p. 40.

14. Zola, *Travail*, in *Oeuvres complètes*, vol. 8, p. 669.

15. Ibid., p. 908.

16. Zola, *Paris*, in *Oeuvres complètes*, vol. 7, p. 1487.

17. *Travail*, p. 549.

18. François René de Chateaubriand, *Essai sur les révolutions, Génie du Christianisme*, ed. Maurice Regard (Paris: Gallimard, 1978), p. 328 (note added in 1826).

19. Victor Hugo, "En passant dans la Place Louis XV un jour de fête publique," *Les Rayons et les ombres*, in *Oeuvres poétiques*, ed. Pierre Albouy, vol. 1 (Paris: Gallimard, 1964), pp. 1081–82.

20. *The College of Sociology (1937–39)*, ed. Denis Hollier, trans. Betsy Wing (Minneapolis: University of Minnesota Press, 1988), p. 196. He announced the title of one of his lectures as "The Celebration of Mardi Gras," and then spoke on "The Spirit of Democracies."

21. Katerina Clark and Michael Holquist, *Mikhail Bakhtin* (Cambridge, Mass.: Harvard University Press, 1984), p. 303.

The Hegelian Edifice

1. G. W. F. Hegel, "Architecture," in *Aesthetics, Lectures on Fine Art*, trans. T. M. Knox, 2 vols. (Oxford: Clarendon Press, 1975), 2:624. [Whenever possible I have used this translation for quotations from Hegel. The French edition of *La Prise de la Concorde* takes its quotation from the translation of Hegel into French by S. Jankelevitch (Paris: Aubier, 1944). Occasionally the wording of the French version is important to Denis Hollier's text and in those instances I have translated the Hegel quotations from Jankelevitch's translation, and so noted.]

2. Ibid., p. 630.

3. Ibid., 1:89 ("Introduction").

4. Ibid., 1:13.

5. Hegel, Ibid., 2:631 ("Architecture").

6. Ibid.

7. Ibid., p. 632. [This passage, however, is my translation from the French as quoted by Hollier. Where the French reads *origins*, the English of Knox's translation reads *beginning;* other differences are slight.]

8. Ibid., p. 632.

9. Ibid., p. 633.

10. Ibid., p. 638. [Translated here from the French.]

11. Ibid., 1:304.

12. Ibid., p. 305.

13. Ibid., 2:638. [For consistency I have replaced the word "holy" by the word "sacred."]

14. Ibid., p. 637.

15. Ibid., p. 631.

16. Ibid., p. 639.

The Architectural Metaphor

1. Bataille's pamphlet was published in Saint-Flour (Cantal) by the Imprimerie du *Courrier d'Auvergne.*

2. Contrast this with the work of the canon Maurice Landrieux, *La Cathédrale de Reims: un crime allemand* (Paris: H. Laurens, 1919): "When we say just as easily 'the cathedral' as 'Notre-Dame,' we are not confusing the Palace with the Queen. . . . We mean that the Cathedral is her realm, her sanctuary; that to touch the Cathedral is to touch Our Lady and that to insult the Cathedral is to insult Our Lady" (p. 126).
The title page of this work states that Canon Landrieux was priest at the cathedral of Reims from 1912 to 1916. He also published during the war a collection of *Quelques prônes de guerre—Reims, 1914–1915*. Later he, along with Cardinal Luçon, would write a few introductory words to the poem *La Cathédrale de Reims*, published in Limoges by the abbot Charles Chalmette in 1921. Cardinal Luçon, the archbishop of Reims at the beginning of the war, was sent afterward to Aurillac, in Haute-Auvergne. He is the cardinal who said the mass mentioned by Bataille on page 5 of *Notre-Dame de Rheims:* "In the morning there was silence as the cardinal most fervently offered a mass for France"; see also Landrieux, *La Cathédrale,* p. 7: "Every morning up until he left on August 24 for the Conclave, Cardinal Luçon said mass there for the Army."

3. *Le Petit* (*OC,* 3:60).

4. Ibid., p. 61. Bataille's change in attitude on this subject is made clear very specifically in the review he gave for *La Critique sociale* (no. 6, Sept. 1932) of two works by an ecclesiastic, H. Pinard de la Boullaye. "The eloquent Jesuit's Jesus-God, on the scale of the one conceiving him, can only be defined as a lady. . . . As for most devout women, the family framework, for him, is of the greatest importance: whereas the Gospel represented Jesus as scorning not just the family in general but also his own mother" (*OC*, 1:295–96).

5. Landrieux cites a statement by the German general Hummel: "I and my other compatriots were far from thinking that the destruction of the cathedral of Reims would be the object of such unanimous reprobation on the part of the French. As a Lutheran, and actually a freethinker, in my hatred of Catholicism I rejoiced in the destruction of the churches of France that resulted from the law of separation and from religious persecution. What did we do that was different, when we knocked down the cathedral of Reims with cannon fire? And now the French are accusing us of vandalism!" (p.81).

6. He found out by reading an article in an issue of *L'Express* of March 1961 where Madeleine Chapsal put forward the reminiscences of *Histoire de l'oeil* as authentic matters of fact. There followed a letter to the demasked Lord Auch (Bataille's pseudonym for this work), a pained and scandalized letter where it comes out: 1. that Martial never believed his brother capable of having said or written such horrible things about their parents; 2. that moreover these horrible things are absolutely untrue and consequently all the more harmful to their memory; 3. that finally he, Martial, was the only one who had access to the secret of the family drama (a reference to his being the eldest who would have known a thing or two, or possibly an allusion to his presence with his father who was dying, abandoned by the rest of his family?). A letter that would be traumatic as well, or traumatic again, perhaps, for the recipient (this recipient was to die a year later): Bataille responded to Martial: "If I did not answer sooner it is first because I was away over Easter vacation and your letter was forwarded to me ["pursued me," in French: an Orestian term for an Erynnian letter] to Vezelay whereas I had left for the Vendée. Next, this letter really upset me and I am still literally sick over it." What is remarkable about this response (or rather this draft of one; since it was among Bataille's papers, it is also possible that it was never sent or at least not in this form) is that Bataille never defends the truth of his reminiscences; the only phrase taking something of this turn does not go very far ("Your letter drove me to despair. It drove me to despair all the more because there is some foundation to the allegations made in *L'Express*"). He thus does not defend the truth of the reminiscences at issue, but leaves it all up to his desire, at the time he wrote *Histoire de l'oeil*, to pull through illness under the supervision of a psychoanalyst: "For me this is hell. I ask your pardon to the extent that my imprudence resulted in my hurting you. But I can tell you that, first of all, I came out of all of what is at issue, unhinged for life. I cannot hold a grudge against you in the least, however, for being disappointed in me. But I want to tell you this right now, what happened nearly fifty years ago still makes me shudder and I do not find it surprising that one day the only means I could find for getting through it was in expressing myself anonymously." (*OC*, 1:612.)

7. *Le Petit* (*OC*, 3:61).

8. "La 'Vieille taupe' et le préfixe *sur* dans les mots *surhomme* et *surréaliste*" (*OC*, 2:93–109).

9. After Bataille's death, Maurice Blanchot wrote: "Complete works are the thing now. Publishing 'everything,' saying 'everything' is what people want; as if they were only anxious about one thing: that it all be said; as if the "all is said" was supposed to allow us finally to stop words that are dead: to stop the pitiful silence coming from them and firmly contain within a thoroughly circumscribed horizon that which an ambiguous

posthumous expectation still mixes deceptively in with our words of the living." *L'Amitié* (Paris: Gallimard, 1971), p. 327.

10. "Méthode de méditation" (*Somme athéologique*, vol. 1, *L'Expérience intérieure;* Paris: Gallimard, 1954), p. 216 (*OC*, 5:200).

11. *Le Coupable* (*Somme athéologique*, vol. 2; Paris: Gallimard, 1961), p. xiii (*OC*, 5:241).

12. Ibid., p. 59 (*OC*, 5:284).

13. *Sur Nietzsche* (Paris: Gallimard, 1945).

14. He wrote in *Sur Nietzsche:* "I could only write the projected book on Nietzsche *with my life*" (*OC*, 6:17).

15. This text is reprinted in *Brisées* (Paris: Mercure de France, 1966), p. 11.

16. Antonin Artaud, *Oeuvres Complètes*, vol. 1 (Paris: Gallimard, 1970), p. 330.

17. André Breton, *Le Surréalisme et la peinture* (1929; rpt., Paris: Gallimard, 1965), p.10.

18. "Informe," in *Documents*, no. 7, Dec. 1929 (*OC*, 1:217). The association formless/spit is also suggested, in this same period, in Leiris's contribution to the article "Spit" in the *Documents* dictionary. His contribution is called "L'eau à la bouche": "Spit, because it is runny, shapeless, of no precise color, and wet, is finally the very symbol of the *formless*, the unverifiable, the unhierarchical" (p. 43 of *Brisées*, where this text is reprinted). In 1930 Leiris would publish in *Cahiers du sud* a poem entitled "L'amoureux des crachats" (The man who loved spit) that is dedicated to Bataille (collected in *Haut Mal* [Paris: Gallimard, 1943], p. 47).

19. Hubert Damisch spoke of "the specifically structural—one would say today, structuralist—notion formed by Viollet-le-Duc concerning the relationship between the architectural whole and its constituent elements." If only the *Dictionnaire de l'architecture française* were read, he continues, "with attention to the dialectic of the whole to its parts and the parts to the whole which is the avowed motivation for this 'descriptive' dictionary, it will inevitably seem to be the manifesto, or at least the oddly precocious, definite outline of the method and ideology of the sort of structural thought that is famous today in linguistics and anthropology." Introduction to *L'Architecture raisonnée*, extracts from the *Dictionnaire de l'architecture française* of Viollet-le-Duc (Paris: Hermann, 1964), p. 14.

20. Jacques Lacan, "A la mémoire d'Ernest Jones: Sur sa théorie du symbolisme," *Écrits* (Paris: Seuil, 1966), p. 698.

21. André Félibien, *La Vie des architectes*, book I.

22. M. Quatremère de Quincy, *Encyclopédie méthodique: Architecture*, vol. 1 (Paris, 1788), p. 120 (from the article "Architecture").

23. Hippolyte Taine, *Philosophie de l'art*, I, I, VI.

24. Étienne Louis Boullée, *Architecture, Essai sur l'art*, ed. Pérouse de Montclos (Paris: Hermann, 1968).

25. Leon Battista Alberti, *Della tranquillità dell'animo*, quoted in Franco Borsi, *Leon Battista Alberti*, trans. Rudolf G. Carpanini (New York: Harper & Row, 1977).

26. Émile Mâle, *L'Art religieux du XIIIe siècle en France* (Paris: A. Colin, 1902), ch. 2; translated by Dora Nussey as *The Gothic Image: Religious Art in France in the Thirteenth Century* (New York: Harper, 1958).

27. Bataille cites Mâle (*L'Art religieux en France* and *L'Art religieux du XIIe siècle*) in "L'Apocalypse de Saint-Sever," an article studying the illustration of an eleventh-century manuscript (*O.C.*, 1:164–170).

Mâle, for his part, published in 1921 a *Nouvelle étude sur la cathédrale de Reims* that omits none of the nationalist, religious, and aesthetic clichés that seemed to have become obligatory since the ravages of war inflicted on this edifice: "I saw the cathedral of Reims after its final wounds: a ghost church surrounded by a ghost city. In this desert there was nothing that was as it seemed. . . . The scorched cathedral, covered with deep wounds, showing its bare bones, was terrifying at first. . . . But soon a feeling began to grow that made one forget the others: a gentle, profound veneration. The cathedral was like a martyr who had just undergone torture and whom the executioners had been unable to finish off. The cathedral too had undergone her Passion: from then on saintliness was added to her beauty." (Reprinted in *Art et artistes du Moyen Age* [Paris: Flammarion, 1968], p. 166.) However, in this case the saving synthesis, the *Aufhebung* allowing the cathedral to survive its wounds, is not the cathedral of prayers of *Notre-Dame de Rheims* but rather an album of photographs restoring to the cathedral her immaculate splendor from the days preceding the catastrophe.

The quintessential version of these clichés is to be found in the previously mentioned work by Landrieux, *La Cathédrale de Reims: un crime allemand* (Paris: H. Laurens, 1919).

28. "La Mort des cathédrales. Une conséquence du projet Briand sur la séparation." The article was published in *Le Figaro* of August 16, 1904. Proust would include it in 1919 in *Pastiches et mélanges*, the last of the texts making up "En mémoire des églises assassinées." This time he would shorten it: "This is a rather mediocre study; I am only giving a brief excerpt to show how, with several years' remove, words change their meaning," he wrote in the introductory note. The complete version from *Le Figaro* would be reprinted after his death in the posthumous volume *Chroniques*. From 1904 to 1919, the words have changed their meaning. Specifically the expression "death of the cathedrals": "Ten years have gone by, 'the death of the cathedrals' is the destruction of their stones by the German armies, not the destruction of their spirit by an anticlerical legislature that today is united with our patriotic bishops." (*Pastiches et mélanges* in *Contre Sainte-Beuve* [Paris: Gallimard, 1971], p. 142. See also Proust's preface to *Propos de peintre* by J.-É. Blanche, in the same volume, p. 573.)

29. This sentence appears only in the version published in *Le Figaro*, and therefore it predates the war (1904); it is the version reprinted in the posthumous volume *Chroniques*. In 1919 it disappeared from the version provided by *Pastiches et mélanges:* the actual ravages of war made this preference an untenable position.

30. *Du côté de chez Swann* (*A la recherche du temps perdu* [Paris: Gallimard, 1955–56], vol. 1, p. 62).

31. Ibid., p. 58. The pages about the church at Combray make use again of a column that was also published by *Le Figaro* in 1912, entitled "L'Église de village." It would be republished separately in the posthumous *Chroniques*.

32. Cited by André Maurois in his preface to the 1955–56 Pléiade edition of *A la recherche*, p. xvii.

33. See Bataille's review in *Critique* in December 1948: "What makes Proust's lesson privileged is doubtless the rigor with which he reduced the object of his *search* to an

involuntary find" (*OC,* 11:391–393). The find thus is less the result of the search than its contradiction. Proust's research (search) does not take the form of a project. It is authoritative less because of its construction than because of its "destruction," less because of how it is made than because of how it undoes itself.

When did Bataille first read Proust? He never cites him before "Digression sur la poésie et Marcel Proust" in *L'Expérience intérieure.* However, the title of his first important article, "L'Amérique disparue" (1928), is oddly Proustian. And as early as 1929 he mentions a story about rats that today is part of the Proustian legend. ("At night, however, when there is no longer anything to be heard, there are great empty sections of the city where one meets only rats, real *rats* that one can kill by piercing with a hat pin . . ." ["Dali hurle avec Sade," *OC,* 2:115].) If this attribution is the result of a retrospective illusion, it is certainly one maintained by Bataille himself, who in "Histoire de rats" would take up this perverse scenario again, attributing it to a Proust wearing the most transparent of disguises, the mask of the unknown: the letter X (*OC,* 3:122).

34. *Du côté de chez Swann,* p. 61.

35. See Jacqueline Risset, "Théorie et fascination," *L'invenzione e il modello* [Rome: Bulzoni, 1972].

36. The second Nicaean council (787), when it condemned the iconoclasts, clearly formulated the Church's position on this point, recalling that "the composition of religious images is not something left to the inspiration of artists; it is a matter of principles laid down by the Catholic Church and by religious trandition. Art alone belongs to the painter; composition belongs to the Fathers." See J. Gimpel, *Les Bâtisseurs de cathédrales* (Paris: Seuil, 1958), p. 99.

37. Erwin Panofsky, *Gothic Architecture and Scholasticism* (New York: Meridian Books, 1957).

38. Ibid., p. 103.

39. Ibid., p. 93.

40. Ibid., p. 89.

41. *The Summa Theologica of St. Thomas Aquinas,* trans. by Fathers of the English Dominican Province, rev. by Daniel J. Sullivan, 2 vols. (Chicago: Encyclopaedia Brittanica, 1952), 1:6.

42. Ibid., p. 341.

43. Ibid., p. 154.

44. Ibid., p. 91.

45. "Analogy, in general, is a similarity crossed with a dissimilarity of partial similarity. It steers a middle course between total similarity and complete dissimilarity. It is encountered at every step in the area of theology. Theologians endlessly assert that the same *nouns* applied to God and to creatures do not have entirely the same meaning; that *properties* common to both the infinite and the finite exist in each of these in a different proportion; they make use of a multitude of analogies to make the *mysteries* clear. The analogy is therefore one of the most frequent processes of theological knowledge, language, or reasoning." (A. Chollet, "Analogie," in A. Vacant, E. Mangenot, and E. Amann, *Dictionnaire de théologie catholique* [Paris: Letouzey et Ané, 1930], vol. 1.)

46. *L'Expérience intérieure* (quotes from the second edition, *Somme athéologique*, vol. 1 [Paris: Gallimard, 1954], p. 16; *OC*, 5:18).

47. Ibid., p. 64 (*OC*, 5:60).

48. Ibid., p. 80 (*OC*, 5:70).

49. "Marcel Proust," *Critique*, no. 31, Dec. 1948. (*OC*, 11:391).

50. *L'Expérience intérieure*, p. 77 (*OC*, 5:70).

51. "Architecture," *Documents*, no. 2, May 1929 (*OC*, 1:171). Anyone who thinks Bataille jumped to conclusions here might compare this statement by Maurice Druon of the French Academy, when he was France's Minister of Cultural Affairs: "I am deeply convinced that one of the reasons for what we certainly must call urban decadence results from the absence in our cities of temples, palaces, statues, or anything that represents the superior faculties of human beings: faith, thought, and will. An urban civilization's vitality is measured perhaps by the prestigious monuments it is capable of erecting." (May 1973, statement made to the National Academy of Arts, Sciences and Belles-lettres of Bordeaux, reproduced in *Le Monde*.)

52. *La Part maudite* (Paris: Minuit, 1949), p. 59 (*OC*, 7:52).

53. "L'Amérique disparue," in *L'Art précolombien. L'Amérique avant Christophe Colomb* (1928; *OC*, 1:153).

54. Ibid., p. 152. Other examples of stifling architecture for Bataille: the feudal castle—for example, the castle of Gilles de Rais. In the illustrations of *Les Larmes d'Éros* the ruins of de Rais's castle will be side by side with those of Sade's and with the ruins of the castle of the "bloody" countess," Erzsébet Bàthory (*OC*, 10:619–620): "These castles were huge piles of rock, within which there were nooks and crannies that could be inaccessible, or very nearly so, as deeply buried as any tomb" (*La Tragédie de Gilles de Rais* [Montreuil: J.-J. Pauvert, 1965], p. 66; *OC* 10:317). Another example—the tomb of the Revolution, the "mausoleum of Red Square" that holds "like a Pharaoh's" Lenin's mummy. ("Le Fascisme en France," *OC*, 2:209.)

55. See Denis Hollier, "Le Matérialisme dualiste de Georges Bataille," *Tel quel*, no. 25 (1967); Philippe Sollers, "Le Toit" in *Logiques* (Paris: Seuil, 1968); Julia Kristeva, "Word, Dialogue and Novel," in *Desire in Language*, trans. Leon S. Roudiez (New York: Columbia University Press, 1980).

56. "Le Cheval académique," *Documents*, no. 1, April 1929 (*OC*, 1:160).

57. Ibid., p. 161.

58. Ibid., p. 160.

59. Ibid., p. 163.

60. "Architecture" (*OC*, 1:171).

61. "L'Apocalypse de Saint-Sever," *Documents*, no. 2, May 1929 (*OC*, 1:166).

62. Ibid., pp. 167–68.

63. Ibid., p. 166.

64. Ibid., p. 165.

65. "Architecture" (*OC*, 1:171–72).

66. In his letter to Chanteloup dated 20 March 1642 (Poussin, *Lettres et Propos sur l'art*, ed. Anthony Blunt [Paris: Hermann, 1964]).

67. For example: "Nietzsche et les fascistes," *Acéphale*, no. 2, Jan. 1937 (*OC*, 1:463); *Le Coupable* (quote from the second edition, *Somme athéologique*, vol. 2, pp. 28, 30; *OC*, 5:260–61).

68. "Le Problème de l'État," *La Critique sociale*, no. 9, Sept. 1933 (*OC*, 1:334).

69. "Métamorphoses," *Documents*, no. 6, Nov. 1929 (*OC*, 1:209).

70. In speaking of the "weaning complex," Lacan will set side by side, in the series of sublimated returns of the maternal imago, simultaneously the products of architecture (one's dwelling being only the symbolic repetition of the "prenatal habitat") and, more abstract, ideological positions where the homogenizing, assimilating, systematizing, totalitarian impulse can be seen (fusion, harmony, concord): "Even when sublimated, the imago of the maternal breast continues to play an important psychic role for our subject. . . . If one had to define the most abstract form in which this is found we would characterize it in this manner: the perfect assimilation of everything into a being. In this somewhat philosophical-looking formulation will be found humanity's nostalgic longings: the metaphysical mirage of universal harmony, the mystical depths of affective fusion, social utopia under totalitarian tutelage, all outflows from the haunting notion of a paradise lost preceding birth and from the deepest desire for death." ("Les Complexes familiaux," *Encyclopédie française*, vol. 8, *La Vie mentale* [Paris, 1938].)

The Labyrinth, the Pyramid, and the Labyrinth

1. "La Mère-Tragédie," *Le Voyage en Grèce*, no. 7, Summer 1937 (*OC*, 1:493–94). *Le Voyage en Grèce* was published by a tourist interest, the Neptos company; according to a prospectus, it organized "summer trips for artists on board the *Patris II*. Ask for detailed information." In the preceding issue (no. 6, Spring 1937) a text by Roger Caillois appeared: "Jeux d'ombre sur l'Hellade. Styles de vie du monde minoen" (reprinted in *Le Mythe et l'homme* [Paris: Gallimard, 1938]). In it Caillois glorified, by contrast with the play of lights of classical Athenian civilization, the other Greece, the archaic and somber Greece that archeology was in the process of rediscovering in Crete: "There is no possible comparison between the Parthenon and the palace of Minos."
Bataille had thought to make a trip to Greece in 1937 . . . perhaps using the services of the Neptos company. (See a letter from André Masson [the painter], dated May 1937: "I am sorry I won't see you before you leave for Greece.") But he went to Sicily instead with Laure (see *OC*, 5:500–501). During this trip to Italy he composed "L'Obélisque" ("I wrote it during a rather long voyage," he said in a letter from Siena dated August 7, 1937, to Jean Paulhan who was to publish it in *Mesures*). This text brings in all the accumulated mythological stratifications in the Mediterranean basin, from Egypt (with its pyramids and obelisks) to the Greece of Herodotus and Socrates to Rome of the baroque period.
"La Mère-Tragédie" is a text on theater in antiquity, in which Bataille describes in a Dionysiac way a world in which *means* can never be seen as *ends*. A world where the end is the absence of means: "The end is not there to make things easy; it cannot be found in daytime works: it is apprehended in the night of labyrinth."

2. *Le Coupable*, p. 16 (*OC*, 5:251).

3. Following Philippe Sollers's use of the term. See "Le Coupable," *Tel quel*, no. 45, Spring 1971.

4. *Sur Nietzsche*, p. 27 (*OC*, 6:23).

5. *Le Coupable*, pp. 28–30 (*OC*, 5:260–61).

6. There is abundant material concerning the thematics of the labyrinth in Gaston Bachelard's book *La Terre et les rêveries du repos* (Paris: Corti, 1948).

7. Bacon gave his "new" *Organon* the subtitle "filum labyrinti." The image is also important in Descartes; see G. Nador, "Métaphores de labyrinthes et de chemins chez Descartes," *Revue philosophique*, Jan.-March 1962. For Leibnitz, see Michel Serres, *Le Système de Leibniz et ses modèles mathématiques* (Paris: Presses Universitaires de France, 1968), vol. 1, p. 11. "I call thread for thinking a method, easy and sure, that one only needs to follow in order to proceed, with no hesitation, no dispute, no fear of error, as securely as if in the labyrinth with Ariadne's thread at his disposal." (Louis Couturat, *Opuscules et fragments inédits de Leibniz* [Paris: Alcan, 1903], p. 420.)

8. *L'Expérience intérieure*, p. 80 (*OC*, 5:73).

9. "La Planète encombrée," *La Ciguë*, no. 1, Jan. 1958 (*OC* 12:477).

10. On the subject of Janus, consult Georges Dumézil's *La Religion romaine archaïque* (Paris: Payot, 1966), pp. 323–28 and 397–400. See also Arnold Van Gennep, "Janus bifrons," *Revue des traditions populaires* 22 (1907), and *Manuel de folklore français*, vol. 1, book 7 (Paris: Picard, 1958); Pierre Grimal, "Le Dieu Janus et les origines de Rome," *Lettres d'humanité* 4 (1945); Robert Schilling, "Janus, le dieu introducteur et le dieu des passages," *Mélanges d'archéologie et d'histoire de l'École française de Rome*, 1960; L. A. Mackay, *Janus* (Univ. of Calif. Publications in Classical Philology, vol. 15, 1954–61).

11. Previously unpublished manuscript of *Le Coupable* (see *OC*, 5:523).

12. "La Conjuration sacrée," *Acéphale*, no. 1, June 1936 (*OC*, 1:445).

13. Ibid.

14. *L'Expérience intérieure*, p. 38 (*OC*, 5:35).

15. Ibid., p. 37. ("Words, their mazes, the exhausting immensity of what is within their possibility, finally, their treachery, are somehow like shifting sands.") See also ibid., p. 10: "Lost among the garrulous, in a night where we can only hate the seeming light that emanates from chatter."

16. *L'Anus solaire* (*OC*, 1:81).

17. Michel Foucault, *Les Mots et les choses* (Paris: Gallimard, 1966), p. 109.

18. Jacques Derrida, "Le Supplément de copule," in *Marges* (Paris: Minuit, 1972), p. 243.

19. Lecture at the College of Sociology, January 22, 1938 (*OC*, 2:318). Translated in *The College of Sociology (1937–39)* (Minneapolis: University of Minnesota Press, 1988), p. 112.

20. Ibid., final lecture, entitled "The College of Sociology" (*OC*, 2:370). Translated in *The College of Sociology (1937–39)*, p. 338.

21. "La Scissiparité" was the title of a short piece published by Bataille in 1949 in *Les Cahiers de la Pléiade* (see *OC*, 3:255). But scissiparity (schizogenesis), which, insofar as it unites birth and death, reproduction and extinction, would constitute the truth of copulation (specifically refusing to make substantive *the wound uniting bodies* or to hypostasize the copula), is a theme appearing much earlier in Bataille's analyses. For example, in his last lecture at the College of Sociology, where he wrote: "If I take the reproduction of a simple, asexual cell, the birth of a new cell seems to result from an incapacity of the whole to maintain its integrity: a scission, a cut is produced" (*OC*, 2:369). It will also reappear in *La Part maudite* (p. 41; *OC*, 7:39), connected to a form of immortality and to the absence of parents. Then again in *L'Érotisme* (*OC*, 10:20), where it is expressed in this way: "The primitive *one* becomes *two*."

22. *L'Expérience intérieure*, p. 64 (*OC*, 5:59).

23. "Le Labyrinthe" (*OC*, 1:433).

24. *L'Expérience intérieure*, pp. 106–20 (*OC*, 5:97–110).

25. "Le Labyrinthe," *OC*, 1:436.

26. *L'Expérience intérieure*, p. 108 (*OC*, 5:98).

27. "Le Labyrinthe," *OC*, 1:435. A slightly different text is found in *L'Expérience intérieure*, p. 108 (*OC*, 5:98).

28. "Le Labyrinthe," *OC*, 1:433.

29. Ibid., p. 434. The phrase "its own labyrinth" had appeared in Antonin Artaud's "Lettre aux recteurs des universités européennes," which was published in *La Révolution surréaliste*, no. 33, April 1925: "Enough playing with language, syntactical tricks, and phrase-juggling; what must be found now is the great Law of the heart, the Law that is not a law or a prison, but a guide for the mind lost in its own labyrinth." These lines are not by Artaud but rather by Leiris, who wrote the first two paragraphs of the letter (see Artaud's *Oeuvres complètes*, vol. 1, 1970, p. 439).

30. *L'Expérience intérieure*, p. 112 (*OC*, 5:102). This passage does not appear in the first version of "Le Labyrinthe."

The Caesarean

1. "Bouche," *Documents*, 1930, no. 5 (*OC*, 1:237).

2. Bataille writes in praise of the animality of the horse in "L'Amitié de l'homme et de la bête." Twenty years earlier, however, he connected horses morphologically to the birth of humanism. This article appeared in an issue of the review *Formes et couleurs* (1947, no. 1) that was devoted to the horse (*OC*, 11:168–71). Specifically, Bataille contrasts Pegasus, who carries away the (Icarian?) poet on wings of inspiration (and who is thus "not the *real* horse"), with the demands of Dada, which is closer to the real horse because it is less academic.

Although he did not participate in the movement, there is considerable reference to Dada in Bataille. In "Les Pieds nickelés," published in *Documents* (1930, no. 4), he evokes it apropos this "activity of human beings" that, for "the solidity of the edifice upon which our intellectual existence depends," finds it essential that "it cannot be designated by any term" (OC, 1:233). In the "Chronique nietzschéenne," published in Acéphale (nos. 3–4, July 1937), Bataille—joining Dada's liberties to a Nietzschean practice—writes: "What could it mean that, for several years, a number of the most talented men have done their utmost to shatter their intelligence, believing that by so doing they explode intelligence itself. Dada is generally considered as an inconsequential failure, whereas, for others, it becomes liberating laughter—a revelation transfiguring human beings." (OC, 1:490).

Several of those signing Un Cadavre (the reply to the Second manifeste published by André Breton in December 1929 in La Révolution surréaliste) were former dadaists: Ribemont-Dessaignes, Vitrac, Baron. Bataille was also close to Théodore Fraenkel, who actively participated in several demonstrations by the movement. Etc.

Generally speaking, it could be said that, by setting himself against the intellectual ambitions of surrealism, Bataille was brought to valorizing Dada for what must certainly be called here its bêtise.

3. "Oeil," Documents, no. 4, Sept. 1929 (OC, 1:187).

4. "Le Gros orteil," Documents, no. 6, Nov. 1929 (OC, 1:200).

5. Ibid., p. 204.

6. See Karl Abraham in "Restrictions and Transformations of Scopophilia in Psycho-Neurotics" in Selected Papers, trans. Douglas Ryan and Alix Strachey (New York: Hogarth), p. 182: "They never spoke of their eyes but, with a regularity which excluded all chance, only of an eye as though only one eye existed. This is quite intelligible if we keep in view the mechanism of 'displacement upwards.' 'The' eye is a substitute for an organ which exists only in the singular." See also S. Ferenczi, "Le Symbolisme des yeux" (Oeuvres complètes, vol. 2, p. 66): "The eyes, being a pair, represent the testicles."

7. "La Mutilation sacrificielle" (OC, 264).

8. Ibid., p. 267, n. 2. "Neolithic" is the word Bataille uses. He was not yet familiar with the divisions of prehistoric periods.

9. "Bouche" (OC, 1:237).

10. Ibid., p. 238.

11. Noted in the files for "L'Oeil pinéal" (OC, 2:417).

12. L'Érotisme, p. 17. (OC, 10:17).

13. Les Larmes d'Éros, foreword (OC, 10:577).

14. L'Érotisme, p. 117 (OC, 10:106–7).

15. Les Larmes d'Éros, p. 234 (OC, 10:627).

16. H. Claude, A. Borel, and G. Robin, "Une Automutilation révélatrice d'un état schizomaniaque," Annales médico-psychologiques 1 (1924):331–39.

17. See the documents quoted on this subject (OC, 2:444). At the end of his life Bataille made it understood that he would not have written if he had not been psychoanalyzed. See his statements to Madeleine Chapsal during an interview:

—Didn't you try psychoanalysis?

G. B.: Yes, I was psychoanalyzed in what was perhaps not an orthodox manner, because it only lasted a year. It was a bit short, but, in the end, it transformed me from the altogether unhealthy being that I was into someone who was relatively viable.

—Did it interest you?

G. B.: I was fascinated by it and really set free.

—A freeing that you would not have attained by writing your work?

G. B.: I think not. The reason is easily explained: that is—the first book I wrote, the one I was telling you about, I could only have written after psychoanalysis, yes, when I left it. And I think I can say that it is only having been freed in that manner that I was able to write.

(M. Chapsal, *Quinze Écrivains* [Entretiens] [Paris: Julliard, 1963], pp. 14–15.)

A further indication: Bataille never forgot to send Borel a numbered copy of each of his books—if possible no. 1.

And finally we should remember that the "Récit de l'éditeur" with which *L'Abbé C.* begins ends with a "literary treatment": "I thought I was going mad, to the extent that I went to see a doctor. . . . He suggested that I come back regularly. I accepted. I would write my part of the story and would bring the written pages to each session. It was the essential element in a psychotherapy without which I would have had difficulty pulling through." *OC*, 3:250–51.)

18. Notes for *Le Coupable, OC*, 5:517 (see *La Tombe de Louis XXX, OC*, 4:165–66).

19. "Le Toit du temple" in "L'Orestie," which would be reprinted as the third part of *L'Impossible* (*OC*, 3:203).

20. See Hegel, *Aesthetics*, 2:655.

21. "The Earth, as a celestial body, differs from a star by being cold and not shining." "The absence of shining, the cold, abandons the surface of the Earth to an overall movement that seems to be a movement of general *devouring* of which life is the most pronounced form." ("Corps célestes", *Verve*, vol. 1, no. 2, Spring 1938 [*OC*, 1:517, 518].)

22. "La Valeur d'usage de D. A. F. de Sade" (*OC*, 2:60).

23. "Philosophy has always insisted on that: thinking its other," J. Derrida, *Marges*, p. 1.

24. "La Valeur d'usage de D. A. F. de Sade" (*OC*, 2:62).

25. Ibid., p. 63.

26. "Figure humaine," *Documents*, no. 4, Sept. 1929 (*OC*, 1:183, note).

27. *Histoire de l'oeil* (*OC*, 1:34).

28. "La Structure psychologique du fascisme," *La Critique sociale*, no. 10, Nov. 1933 (*OC*, 1:350).

29. *L'Érotisme*, p. 43 (*OC*, 10:40).

30. "L'Absence de mythe," in *Le Surréalisme en 1947* (Paris: Maeght, 1947), p. 65 (*OC*, 11:236).

31. A review of a selection from "Pages mystiques by Nietzsche," *Critique*, Oct. 1946, no. 5, p. 466 (*OC*, 11:128).

32. "L'Apprenti sorcier" (*OC*, 1:525). Translated in *The College of Sociology (1937–39)*, p. 15 (fn).

33. "La Notion de dépense," *La Critique sociale*, no. 7, Jan. 1933 (*OC*, 1:319). In this title "notion" is contrasted with idea or concept. There is neither an idea nor a concept of *dépense*. This usage of the "concept" (?) of notion goes back to Jean Wahl's book on *Le Malheur de la conscience dans la philosophie de Hegel* that Bataille had just cited in a note in *La Critique sociale* (no. 6, Sept. 1932; see *OC*, 1:299). Later, using the concept of notion as if it were synonymous with concept, he will speak of "opening notions up beyond themselves." ("Discussion sur le péché," *Dieu vivant*, no. 4, 1945, p. 123: "Language is lacking because language is made from propositions causing the intervention of identities, and from the moment that, because there are excess sums to spend, one is obliged to spend no longer for gain, but for the sake of spending, one can no longer be confined to the level of identity. One is obliged to open notions up beyond themselves." *OC*, 6:350.) Thus it is extravagant expenditure that opens notions up beyond themselves, refusing them self-identity, precisely because it is a nonlogical difference. The notion of *dépense* as unthinking, extravagant expenditure is the notion opened up beyond itself.

34. This formulation from *Essai sur le don* is quoted by Bataille in "La Notion de dépense" (*OC*, 1:310).

35. "L'Oeil pinéal" (1) (*OC*, 2:22).

36. Notes from the files of "L'Oeil pinéal" (*OC*, 2:416).

37. "L'Oeil pinéal" (1), ibid., p. 23.

38. "Métamorphoses," *Documents*, no. 6, Nov. 1929 (*OC*, 1:208–9).

39. [*Sens* throughout this section is translated as "sense" when certain turns of phrase really require it. Sometimes, however, the more philosophically burdened word "meaning" will be used, and it should always be kept in mind.]

40. *L'Expérience intérieure*, p. 141 (*OC*, 5:129).

41. Contact is always connected with a threat. The body who engages in it always risks not returning intact. On the problems these dangers from contact pose for empiricism, see Alain Grosrichard, "Une expérience de psychologie au xviiie siècle," *Cahiers pour l'analyse*, no. 2, March-April 1966 (2d ed., p. 103): "If, to *know* objectively, one must come in contact with bodies, this contact can be fatal to my body: the requirement of objectivity is at the same time a threat of death."

42. *L'Érotisme*, p. 12 (*OC*, 10:12).

43. "Le Non-savoir," *Botteghe Oscure* 11 (April 1953): 25 (*OC*, 12:284).

44. "L'Apprenti sorcier" (*OC*, 1:526). Translated in *The College of Sociology 1937–39*, p. 15, n. 5. Science is simultaneously true and meaningless, the articulation of these two attributes is by no means accidental: it serves here, in particular, to oppose science to fiction, which, although it has meaning for man, cannot pretend to be true. In this denunciation we can read the very beginnings of a redistribution of the roles our culture has traditionally assigned to knowledge and art.

45. "Sommes-nous là pour jouer ou pour être sérieux?" (II), *Critique*, nos. 51–52, Aug.– Sept. 1951, p. 735 (*OC*, 12:111).

46. *L'Expérience intérieure*, p. 129 (*OC*, 5:119).

47. "De l'existentialisme au primat de l'économie" (II), *Critique* no. 21 (Feb. 1948), p. 136 (*OC*, 11:300).

48. "Sommes-nous là pour jouer ou pour être sérieux?" (II), p. 741 (*OC*, 12:118).

49. "Plan," *OC*, 2:388.

50. "L'Oeil pinéal" (1) (*OC*, 2:23).

51. The first of these epigraphs is a note from "La Valeur d'usage de D. A. F. de Sade" (1) (*OC*, 2:61), of which the second is an earlier formulation (ibid., p. 424, n. 12).

52. Plato, *Parmenides*, 130c, from R. E. Allen, *Plato's Parmenides, Translation and Analysis* (Minneapolis: University of Minnesota Press, 1983). [Allen's translation reads "character" for "form" in these two instances, whereas the French translates εἶδος as *forme*.]

53. The category *aeidès* can, in fact, indicate simultaneously that one has gone beyond the world of the senses (by attaining the world of ideas), and that, while remaining within the world of the senses, one has entered into contact with something that is no longer dependent on vision. The invisible can be read equally as intelligible and as tangible.

54. Plato, *Philebus*, trans. Robin A. H. Waterfield (New York: Penguin Books, 1982), p. 147 (66a).

55. Plato, *Gorgias*, trans. Donald J. Zeyl (Indianapolis: Hackett Publishing Co., 1987), p. 38 (473c).

56. "La Valeur d'usage de D. A. F. de Sade" (*OC*, 2:64).

57. *Sur Nietzsche*, p. 104 (*OC*, 6:85).

58. Ibid., p. 111 (*OC*, 6:90).

59. Ibid., p. 150 (*OC*, 6:124).

60. *Le Coupable*, p. 151 (*OC*, 5:355).

61. The common measure of comparison is never anything but metaphor. Bataille, in "Figure humaine," attempts in the same gesture to *denounce* this metaphor and to *enunciate* (with no transposition) "the absence of a common measure," producing through a "concrete expression" the "absence of relationship" that different "human entities" have between them. Denouncing "the so-called continuity of *our* nature" from one individual to another, from one generation to another. Denouncing also the anthropocentrism requiring that man have "his" place in the universe. "It is understood," writes Bataille, "that a presence as irreducible as that of *self* has no place of its own in an intelligible universe and that, reciprocally, this external universe only has a place in a *self* with the help of metaphors." (*OC*, 1:182–83.) If metaphors allow comparison through a common measure, it is also true that the only common measures are metaphoric. A little earlier, Bataille evoked the system of architectural metaphor with his spiritual cathedral, the *Summa theologica:* the idea that there is some common measure between man and his surroundings is only the product of "this vulgar intellectual voracity for which we are indebted to both Thomism and present-day science" (p. 182).

62. "La 'Vieille taupe' et le préfixe *sur*" (*OC*, 2:108).

63. Quoted by Bataille in "Les Propositions contenues ici" (*OC*, 2:74). It had been published by Maurice Heine in the fifth issue (May 1933) of *Le Surréalisme au service de la révolution* (reprinted in the collection *Le Marquis de Sade* [Paris: Gallimard, 1950], p. 95).

64. Sic: these phrases are from Gilbert Lély's book *Sade, études sur sa vie et sur son oeuvre* (Paris: Gallimard, 1967), pp. 218–19. The whole passage from which they are taken should be quoted in its entirety:
"But if, in *Les 120 journées de Sodome*, this natural history of paresthesias, Sade provided evidence of his genius as a precursor, if a number of his psychosexual observations, independent of their high literary value, have to be considered as masterpieces of the genre, one must nonetheless remark that there is a prevailing error compromising in many places the didactic value of such a work: we mean the monstrously exaggerated place reserved in it by the author for coprolagnic aberration carried to its farthest extremes. Of the six hundred abnormal cases narrated by the women, in fact, not counting the strictly fictional examples, in which this repugnant practice abounds, more than half offer an image of ingestion of excrements, either as an independent image or one connected to another passion. Now whereas visual, olfactory, or tactile coprolagnia (which must stem simultaneously from fetishism and sadomasochism) is a relatively frequent anomaly, its fanatical sister, coprophagia, can only be classed among the number of sexual perversions that are least widespread. Mentioned only once in the nine hundred pages (in quarto) of Krafft-Ebing's collection, it is the result above all of mental alienation, a separate domain from that which the Marquis de Sade proposes to examine here. Thus, in *Les 120 journées de Sodome*, verisimilitude is often jarred because it is gratuitously dominated by an aberration of the most disgusting sort, one that other subtler points, essentially erotological, might have replaced to advantage. Besides the monotony and disgust resulting from such an abuse, certain of the most striking cases, like the one of the necrophiliac president who is only interested in 'women who are going to be executed,' are somehow stripped of their universality, because of the coprophagic element that Sade felt he had to join to the principal perversion."
Also the note at the bottom of the page referring to this paragraph: "If the ghost of the Marquis de Sade, through the medium of séance tables, deigned to inquire how we felt about *Les 120 journées de Sodome*, and, in one word, what we thought about this work, we would dare reply to him, like Captain Bordure to Père Ubu's question about whether his guest had dined well: 'Fine sir, except for the shit' (*Ubu roi*, act 1, scene 4)." Curiously, in the *Second manifeste*, Breton had already evoked the same passage from *Ubu*: "When the 'unmentionable brush' Jarry spoke of fell into his plate, Bataille," he writes, "declared he was enchanted." This is the remark referred to by the note on the bottom of the page on "excrement-philosophers" that is cited farther on.
It is rather remarkable that, in a text of this sort, there is not one word belonging to Sade's vocabulary. The scientific terminology here has a function that is quite precisely antiscatological. Nowhere is translation more obviously a betrayal: scatological words are not transposable. But this lexicological sublimation of Sade's text is perhaps already implied in the project of reading him on the basis of Freud, and in making him a precursor. The first sentence of Lacan's "Kant with Sade": "That Sade's work anticipates Freud's, even with regard to the catalogue of perversions, is one of the most frequently repeated belletristic stupidities . . ." (*Écrits*, p. 765).

65. Breton, *Second manifeste du surréalisme*, p. 218.

66. "Arrivé ici" (*OC*, 2:85).

67. S. Ferenczi, "On Obscene Words" (1911), in *First Contributions to Psychoanalysis*, trans. Ernest Jones (London: Hogarth, 1952), p. 137.

68. J. Lacan, "D'une question préliminaire à tout traitement possible de la psychose," *Écrits*, p. 535. See also ibid., p. 391.

69. X. Gauthier, *Surréalisme et sexualité* (Paris: Gallimard, 1971), p. 216.

70. "Le Surréalisme au jour le jour" (*OC*, 8:179): "I understand Breton's horror of me. Was that not what I wanted? Was I not truly obsessed?"

71. "Dali hurle avec Sade" (*OC*, 2:113).

72. These make up the portion of the book entitled "Les Possessions." This is preceded by a sort of foreword in which Breton and Éluard say they wanted to show that it is within the power of the poetically trained mind "to conquer at will the principal delirious ideas without being permanently troubled."

73. See *Second manifeste*, pp. 217–19.

74. "Le Gros orteil" (*OC*, 1:204).

75. "Dali hurle avec Sade" (*OC*, 2: 113).

76. Note on"Conformismes freudiens, d'Emmanuel Berl," *Documents*, 1930, no. 5 (*OC*, 1:241).

77. Ibid., p. 242.

78. "L'Esprit moderne et le jeu des transpositions," *Documents*, 1930, no. 8 (*OC*, 1:273). See Leiris's article on Giacometti that appeared in *Documents*, no. 4 (Sept. 1929): "In the realm of works of art one finds scarcely more than a very few objects (paintings or sculptures) that are capable of corresponding more or less to the requirements of this real fetishism." See also my "The Painter without His Model," *Raritan*, Summer 1989.

79. Notes to "L'Esprit moderne et le jeu des transpositions" (*OC*, 1: 623–24, n. 4).

80. Crime must be spoken. Unconfessed crime is not a crime. But it must be spoken *in spite of everything*, that is, while intensifying itself through this confession. The confession does not diminish it; on the contrary it emphasizes it. See Theodor Reik's *The Compulsion to Confess; On the Psychoanalysis of Crime and Punishment* (New York: Grove Press, 1961).

81. Notes from "L'Esprit moderne" (*OC*, 1:624, n. 5).

82. Review of Krafft-Ebing's *Psychopathia sexualis* in *La Critique sociale*, Oct. 1931, no. 3 (*OC*, 1:275). Krafft-Ebing figured as a "do not read" in the surrealist index (in contrast to Freud). Bataille read Krafft-Ebing and borrowed several cases of perversion from it. For example the case of "The fifty-year-old man" that he quotes in the text "Je ne crois pas pouvoir" (*OC*, 2:129).

83. "L'Oeil pinéal" (1) (*OC*, 2:22).

84. "La Valeur d'usage de D.A.F. de Sade" (2) (*OC*, 2:72).

85. "Le Langage des fleurs," *Documents*, no. 3, Jan. 1929 (*OC*, 1:176).

86. Gaspar and Thomas Bartholin, *Anatomia* (Lyons, 1631), p. 356.

87. "Le Jésuve" (OC, 2:14).

88. In any case this is the opinion of Michel Leiris: "Of this novel one episode survived, the story of 'Dirty'" ("De Bataille l'impossible à l'impossible Documents," Brisées, p. 258).

89. Hegel: "The positive realization, in the strict sense of the word, of the beginning, is at the same time a negative performance regarding this beginning, that is regarding its unilateral form according to which it is only immediately, or is end. The realization can therefore be considered as the refutation of that which constitutes the foundation of the system." (Phénoménologie de l'esprit, trad. Hyppolite, vol. 1, p. 22.) This seems closely related to paragraph 22 of the preface to Phenomenology of Spirit: "The result is the same as the beginning, only because the beginning is the purpose; in other words, the actual is the same as its Notion only because the immediate, as purpose, contains the self or pure actuality within itself. The realized purpose, or the existent actuality, is movement and unfolded becoming." (Phenomenology of Spirit, tr. A. V. Miller [Oxford: Clarendon Press, 1977], p. 12.) But the notion of refutation that constitutes the foundation, etc., is not present in the English version here.

90. Not classical but mystical Latin, that being the title of Rémy de Gourmont's book that served Bataille as pillow-book during the time he was writing Notre-Dame de Rheims and then at l'Ecole des Chartes (cf. OC, notes, 1:611): "The Latin condescendingly known as Church Latin is, it seems to us, rather more appealing than that of Horace, and the soul of these ascetics richer in ideality than that of the gouty, sneaky old egoist. Whether one is a believer or not, only mystical literature is appropriate for our immense fatigue" (Gourmont, Le Latin mystique [Paris: Crès, 1913], p. 5). According to Bataille, it was in this church Latin that "the voices of homosexual angels" sang that so shook the sensibility of Gilles de Rais, "mad with music and church hymns" (Bataille, La Tragédie de Gilles de Rais [Montreuil: J. J. Pauvert, 1965], pp. 43, 74).

91. Bataille, Manet (New York: Skira, 1955), p. 71 (OC, 9:145). "This world," of which the Olympia is the negation, is the world of religion.

92. Lacan, "Remarque sur le rapport de Daniel Lagache," Écrits, p. 665.

93. "Bouche" (OC, 1:237).

94. See G. Deleuze, Logique du sens (Paris: Minuit, 1969), especially pp. 292–98. See also P. Klossowski's article, "Le Simulacre dans la communication de Georges Bataille," Critique, no. 195–96, Aug.–Sept. 1963.

95. "L'Art primitif," Documents, 1930, no. 7 (OC, 1: 252). This memory will reappear in "Méthode de méditation" (Somme athéologique vol. 1, p. 228): "I have very little to do with laziness (I have rather, I think, an excess of vitality). At thirteen (?), however, I asked a friend who was the laziest in the study hall: me; but who in the entire school? me, again. In those days I made my life difficult, because of not writing under dictation. The first words the teacher said used to form themselves docilely under my pen. I can still see my notebook as a child: soon all I did was scribble (I had to look like I was writing)" (OC, 5:203).

96. "Méthode de méditation," in Somme athéologique vol. 1, p. 219 (OC, 5:203).

97. "L'Oeil pinéal" (4) (OC, 2:41).

98. "Le 'Jeu lugubre,'" Documents, no. 7, Dec. 1929 (OC, 1:211).

99. See Hegel's remarks in Logic (in the note at the end of the first chapter of the first

section of Book I): "One might find it surprising that a language come to use a single word to designate two opposite determinations. Speculative thought can only rejoice at finding in language words that have in themselves a speculative meaning. . . . One can only eliminate something by seeing to it that this thing forms a unity with its opposite" (Jankélevitch translation, 1:102).

100. Lacan, "The Signification of the Phallus," in *Écrits: A Selection*, trans. Alan Sheridan (New York: Norton, 1977) p. 288.

101. J.-J. Goux, "Numismatiques," in *Freud, Marx: Économie et symbolique* (Paris: Seuil, 1973), p. 68.

102. "La Structure psychologique du fascisme," *La Critique sociale*, no. 10, Nov. 1933 (*OC*, 1:355).

103. Ibid. (*OC*, 1:363).

104. "L'Oeil pinéal" (4) (*OC*, 2:43).

105. "L'Oeil pinéal" (3) (ibid., p. 39).

106. "L'Oeil pinéal" (4) (ibid., p. 46).

107. *L'Anus solaire* (*OC*, 1:81).

108. "Qu'est-ce que le sexe?", *Critique*, no. 11, April 1947, p. 372 (*OC*, 11:233). See Lacan: "It can be said that this signifier [the phallus] is chosen because it is the most tangible element in the real of sexual copulation and also the most symbolic in the literal [typographical] sense of the term, since it is equivalent there to the (logical) copula." ("The Signification of the Phallus," *Écrits: A Selection*, p. 287.)

109. Karl Abraham, "Limitations et modifications du voyeurisme chez les névrosés," in his *Oeuvres complètes*, vol. 2, p. 18.

110. "La Valeur d'usage de D.A.F. de Sade" (*OC*, 2:55–56).

111. *OC*, 2:419 (notes).

112. "L'Oeil pinéal" (1), ibid., p. 35.

113. The first expression ("nonlogical difference") appears in "La Notion de dépense" (*OC*, 1:319). The second ("nonexplainable difference") in "La Structure psychologique du fascisme" (ibid., p. 345).

114. *Sur Nietzsche*, p. 75 (*OC*, 6:60).

115. "De l'existentialisme au primat de l'économie" (II), *Critique*, no. 21, Feb. 1948, p. 136. (*OC*, 11:300).

116. "Le Bleu du ciel," in *L'Expérience intérieure* (*Somme athéologique*, 1:101; *OC*, 5:92).

117. *OC*, 3:560 (notes).

118. *Le Bleu du ciel* (*OC*, 3:395). In the version in *L'Expérience intérieure* this aphorism is found on page 104 (*OC*, 5:95). See my "Bataille's Tomb: A Halloween Story," trans. Richard Miller, *October* 33 (Summer 1985): 73–102.

119. *Sur Nietzsche*, p. 155 (*OC*, 6:127).

120. *L'Expérience intérieure*, p. 101 (*OC*, 5:92).

121. See Freud, "The Antithetical Sense of Primal Words," trans. M. N. Seal, in *Character and Culture* (New York: Collier, 1963). Contemporary linguistics has not retained Abel's thesis. See Emile Benveniste, "Remarks on the Function of Language in Freudian Theory," in *Problems in General Linguistics*, trans. M. E. Meek (Coral Gables, Florida: University of Miami Press, 1971): "The double meaning of the Latin *sacer*, 'sacred' and 'damned,' would be of this sort. Here the ambivalence of the notion should no longer come as a surprise, since so many studies on the phenomenology of the sacred have banalized its fundamental duality: in the Middle Ages, a king and a leper were both literally 'untouchables,' but it does not follow that *sacer* encompasses two contradictory senses; it is the conditions of culture that have determined vis-a-vis the 'sacred' object two opposite attitudes." (See also Benveniste, "Profanus et profanare," *Collection Latomus* [*Hommages à Georges Dumézil*], no. 45, 1960.)

Bataille, no doubt, had read Freud's essay. The following note found among his papers (7 Aa fo 39) would be evidence: "On the ambivalence of words see a review by S. Fr. in *Jahrbuch für psychoa- und psychopath. Forschungen*, vol. 1, 1910, concerning Abel's work *Gegensinn der Urworte*."

122. Freud, *Essais de psychanalyse appliquée*, p. 65.

123. "Le Bleu du ciel," in *L'Expérience intérieure*, p. 102 (*OC*, 5:93). This phrase appears in the third aphorism of *Le Bleu du ciel*.

124. "Les Mangeurs d'étoiles," in *André Masson*, a collective volume published in 1940 (*OC*, 1:567).

125. *Histoire de l'oeil* (*OC*, 1:44).

126. "Les Présages" (*OC*, 2:270).

127. The invitation to this show is reproduced in the notes of vol. 1 of the *Oeuvres complètes* (p. 613).

128. Quoted in *OC*, 2:443 (notes).

129. "Les Présages" (ibid., p. 267).

130. Ibid., p. 269

131. For this see Alexandre Koyré, *Études galiléennes* (1935–39; rpt., Paris: Hermann, 1966).

132. Koyré, *Études galiléennes*, p. 178.

133. "Le Bas matérialisme et la gnose," *Documents*, 1930, no. 1 (*OC*, 1:225). Derrida, in comments that are closely connected to Bataille, writes thus: "The signifier 'matter' only seems problematic to me at the moment that its reinscription would not avoid making it into a new fundamental principle, where, through theoretical regression, it would be reconstituted as a 'transcendental signified.'"

134. "Le Bas matérialisme et la gnose" (*OC*, 1:225).

135. G. Genette, "Une poétique structurale," *Tel quel*, 7.

136. G. Genette, "L'Univers réversible," in *Figures* (Paris: Seuil, 1966), p. 20.

137. *L'Expérience intérieure*, p. 67 (*OC*, 5:62).

138. Ibid., p. 102. (This sentence is found in one of the aphorisms of "Le Bleu du ciel"; *OC*, 5:93.)

139. "L'Obélisque," *Mesures*, April 15, 1938 (*OC*, 1:502). An excerpt from Nietzsche's *The Gay Science*, tr. Walter Kaufmann (New York: Vintage Books, 1974), p. 181 (#125). Bataille will frequently refer to this text of the Madman announcing, to those who don't believe, that they have killed God.

140. [*Genre* in French includes both genre in a literary sense and genus in a philosophical or scientific sense; it also means gender.]

141. Hegel, *Encyclopédie des sciences philosophiques*, tr. Gandillac (Paris: Gallimard, 1970), pp. 241–42, #250. Bataille cites it in the article written with Raymond Queneau, "La Critique des fondements de la dialectique hégélienne," *La Critique sociale*, no. 5, March 1932 (cf. *OC*, 1:279), to point out that Hegel himself was careful "to indicate that it was precisely nature that 'through its powerlessness to realize notions set limits on philosophy.'" The general theme of this paragraph is the exteriority of the idea to itself, which constitutes the definition of nature. This exteriority is manifested in the contingency that is the earmark of natural products. Among other examples of this sort of contingency, which make up a kind of system of "heterology," Hegel brings up, along with monsters, the subject of writing (through the intermediary of the ingenuous Mr. Krug who asked philosophy to deduce "the pen with which he writes").

142. "Les Écarts de la nature," *Documents*, 1930, no. 2 (*OC*, 1:229).

143. "Le Paradoxe de l'érotisme," *Nouvelle NRF*, no. 29, May 1955, p. 836 (*OC*, 12:322). This article is devoted to the *Histoire d'O* by Pauline Réage.

144. "L'Inculpation d'Henry Miller," *Critique*, nos. 3–4, Aug.–Sept. 1946, p. 380 (*OC*, 11:107–108).

145. Quoted by Jacques Roger, *Les Sciences de la vie dans la pensée française du XVIIe siècle*, 2d ed. (Paris: Armand Colin, 1971), p. 362.

146. See J. Roger, p. 382.

147. Quoted by J. Roger, p. 295.

148. Quoted by J. Roger, p. 304, no. 329.

149. Quoted by J. Roger, p. 181.

150. Quoted by J. Roger, p. 317.

151. Quoted by J. Roger, p. 318.

152. La Mettrie, *L'Homme machine* (Paris: J. J. Pauvert, 1966), p. 90.

153. Hume, quoted by G. Deleuze and A. Cresson, *Hume* (Paris: Presses universitaires de France, 1952), p. 63.

154. Georges Canguilhem, "Le Concept et la vie," in *Études d'histoire et de philosophie des sciences*, p. 336.

155. An abbot at Sisteron was supposed to have been victim of such a misadventure. See J. Roger, pp. 188–89.

156. Quoted by J. Roger, p. 188.

157. Karl Abraham, "Restrictions and Transformations of Scopophilia in Psycho-Neurotics," in *Selected Papers*, trans. Douglas Bryan and Alix Strachey (New York: Brunner/Mazel, 1927), p. 210.

158. See K. Abraham, "Ejaculatio Praecox" (1917), in *Selected Papers*, trans. Douglas Bryan and Alix Strachey (London: Hogarth, 1927) p. 248. Also S. Ferenczi, "The Effect on Women of Premature Ejaculation in Men" (1908), in *Final Contributions to the Problems and Methods of Psycho-Analysis*, trans. Eric Mosbacher and others (London: Hogarth, 1955).

159. *Histoire de l'oeil* (*OC*, 1:45).

160. *Madame Edwarda* (*OC*, 3:13).

161. Quoted in the notes to *Madame Edwarda* (*OC*, 3:491).

162. *OC*, 2:392.

163. "Declaration of the College of Sociology on the International Crisis," in *The College of Sociology (1937–39)* (Minneapolis: University of Minnesota Press, 1988), p. 45.

164. *L'Expérience intérieure*, p. 10 (*OC*, 5:9).

165. *Le Coupable*, p. 7. See also "A Tale of Unsatisfied Desire," my introduction to *Guilty*, Bruce Boone's translation of *Le Coupable* (Venice, Calif: Lapis Press, 1988).

166. "Méthode de méditation" (*Somme athéologique* 1:219).

167. Melanie Klein, "A Contribution to the Theory of Intellectual Inhibition," in *Love, Guilt and Reparation and Other Works* (New York: Dell, 1977), p. 241.

168. See Serge Leclaire, *Psychanalyser*, ch. 2 (Paris: Seuil, 1968).

169. Alexandre Kojève, *Introduction à la lecture de Hegel* (Paris: Gallimard), pp. 387–88. These lines are quoted by Bataille in "Hegel, l'homme et l'histoire," *Monde nouveau Paru*, no. 97, Feb. 1956, p. 5 (*OC*, 12:362).

170. Hegel, *Phenomenology of Spirit*, tr. A. V. Miller (Oxford: Clarendon Press, 1977), pp. 197ff.

171. *La Tombe de Louis XXX* (*OC*, 4:159).

172. Following J. Wahl, *Le Malheur de la conscience dans la philosophie de Hegel* (1929; rpt., Paris: Presses Universitaires de France, 1951), p. 17.

173. "De l'existentialisme au primat de l'économie" (1), *Critique*, no. 19, Dec. 1947, p. 523 (*OC*, 11:286).

174. Ibid., p. 518 (*OC*, 11:282). The exclusion of the subject by science is one of the points Bataille thought to develop in "Paradoxe sur l'érotisme," which was to be the

final piece in *Divinus deus*. In particular, we read in the notes that he left for this: "Science is attention, complete attention, accorded the object. There is not, nor can there be, a science of the subject." Putting the subject of a discourse at stake is the very definition of the act of writing (as a signifying production as opposed to a scientific communication): "Writing, I am conscious of what, because I am writing, takes place within me: this account puts me personally at stake, all my life has its outcome at that moment. It is not an objective view, independent of the subject I am. What I now write is my life, it is the subject himself, and nothing else." Bataille denies there is an alternative between one or the other of these two discourses. To put the subject at stake again in the discourse that excludes it. "In principle there is nothing more foreign to philosophy than the work of art. . . . At least in principle. Because there is also the need I feel to unite with a hoped-for, complete philosophical framework another work that equally well reflects the incoherence of everything." (*OC*, 4:396–97, notes.)

175. *Madame Edwarda* (*OC*, 3:15).

176. *Madame Edwarda* (*OC*, 3:31). (In separate editions of the narrative this note is alone on the final page.)

177. "Le Supplice," in *L'Expérience intérieure*, p. 71 (*OC*, 5:65).

178. Given in a note (*OC*, 1:653).

179. *Ma mère* (*OC*, 4:183). The frequency and dramatic violence of the word "know" and words with similar meaning in the dialogues of *Ma mère* should be noted: p. 184: "'You are too young,' she said, 'and I should not be talking to you, but in the end you must *wonder* if your mother . . .'"; p. 186: "You will never *know* the horrible things I am capable of. I would like you to *know*. I like the mire I'm in"; p. 191: "'I'm not sick,' I told her. 'I *knew* it,' she said"; p. 192: "'I *guess* what you're thinking,' she told me again"; p. 197: "Since the other day you have *known* the extent of my weakness. You *know* now, perhaps, that desire reduces us to weakness. But you still don't *know* that I *know*"; p. 208: "It's not as if you didn't *know* that your answer . . ."; p. 211: "I want Pierre to *know* this. . . . Réa, I want to take away his innocence. . . . I want you to *know* once and for all . . . I am happy. I want you to *know* that: I am the worst of mothers"; p. 213: "'I *know* what I want,' she said maliciously. . . . 'I *know* what I want,' she said again. Distraught, I said 'Mother, I want to *know* what you want. I want to *know* and I want to love it.'" The same sexual intensification of the verb *to know* can be found in Marguerite Duras's *L'Amant*.

180. Ibid., p. 213.

181. *L'Abbé C.* (*OC*, 3:353).

182. *Ma mère* (*OC*, 4:185).

183. Ibid, pp. 235–36.

184. Ibid., p. 222.

185. Ibid., p. 236.

186. *OC*, 4:399 (notes).

187. *La Part maudite*, p. 41.

188. "A propos de *Pour qui sonne le glas?* d'Ernest Hemingway," in *L'Espagne libre* (Paris: Calmann-Levy, 1945), p. 120 (*OC*, 9:26).

189. "Discussion sur le péché," *OC*, 6:358.

190. *La Littérature et le mal* ("Sade"), p. 119 (*OC*, 9:244).

191. Ibid. ("Kafka"), p. 161 (*OC*, 9:270).

192. *Le Coupable*, introduction, p. xiv (*OC*, 5:242).

193. This quotation is from the first edition of *Le Coupable* (1944, p. 174). It was slightly changed in the second edition (p. 164).

194. *L'Érotisme*, p. 292 (*OC*, 10:258).

195. "Les Mangeurs d'étoiles" (*OC*, 1:565). This quotation is from the manuscript. The published version gives only "killing" without saying specifically "killing the mother."

196. *L'Expérience intérieure* ("Le Bleu du ciel"), p.102 (*OC*, 5:93).

197. "Le Paradoxe de la mort et la pyramide," *Critique*, no. 74, July 1953, p. 639 (*OC*, 8:518).

198. [1989] This book is almost twenty years old. More than once, on rereading it, I wondered to what extent it was possible for me to claim that I wrote it, without feeling that I was taking its author's place, a place, in fact, I often felt (as a reader) it was not for me to take. It was written at a rather feverish pace after I had explored with an excitement—that still comes through, I think—the manuscripts that Bataille left behind at his death. It was in one of these stacks of paper that I found the sentence "Like the Archbishop . . . ," written without quotation marks on a separate piece of paper in that rather broad handwriting that, if my memory as an editor is correct, is found in Bataille's earliest manuscripts. I do not remember its being in quotes but to my ear it did not sound like Bataille's (the unpunctuated crescendo of the first part of the sentence, until the break and the brisk ending in a principle clause; not to mention the absence of any contextual reference: who is this Archbishop? and who is his lover?). Later I found the anecdote to which it refers, in one of the chapters of *Du sang, de la volupté et de la mort* where Barrès says he is borrowing it from Saint-Simon, the chronicler of the end of Louis XIV's reign. When the Archbishop of Paris received "his good friend," the Dutchess of Lesdiguières in his garden at Conflans, "as the two of them walked along, gardeners followed behind at a distance to erase their footprints with rakes" (Paris: Plon, 1921, p. 101). But the sentence itself is not to be found either in Saint-Simon or in Barrès. Maybe, in the end, it is from Bataille's hand?

Index

Index

Against Architecture

OCTOBER Books

Joan Copjec, Douglas Crimp, Rosalind Krauss, and Annette Michelson, editors

Broodthaers, edited by Benjamin H. D. Buchloh

Aids: Cultural Analysis/Cultural Activism, edited by Douglas Crimp

Aberrations, by Jurgis Baltrušaitis

Against Architecture: The Writings of Georges Bataille, by Denis Hollier